Order this book online at www.trafford.com
or email orders@trafford.com

Most Trafford titles are also available at major online book retailers.

Printed in Victoria, BC, Canada.

ISBN: 978-1-4269-2589-4 (sc)

*Our mission is to efficiently provide the world's finest, most comprehensive book publishing
service, enabling every author to experience success. To find out how to publish your book, your
way, and have it available worldwide, visit us online at www.trafford.com*

Trafford rev. 2/9/10

 www.trafford.com

North America & international
toll-free: 1 888 232 4444 (USA & Canada)
phone: 250 383 6864 ♦ fax: 812 355 4082

Abstract

This research looks into executive education and learning, as portrayed in interviews with 14 business leaders in Canada; and as provided by nine world-renowned universities that specialize in executive education; and as experienced by this researcher during a long career in business.

The methodology used is that of a collective case study featuring three separate categories as units of analysis: Namely, the 14 executive interviews, the nine universities and the personal experience. Executive interviews and university program descriptions are presented, appreciated and analyzed both as individual entities, and all together as two separate collectives.

The theoretical framework that has inspired my point of view about learning is the educational philosophy of Alfred North Whitehead - philosopher, mathematician, and physicist. Chapter Three is devoted to an in-depth look at Dr. Whitehead's work in this respect.

This research should be of interest and of use for firms and universities wanting to consider or reconsider their plans for executive education and learning.

Acknowledgements

I would like to thank my supervisory committee at the University of Calgary for their support through the candidacy and dissertation preparation phases of my doctoral studies: Dr. Ian Winchester and Dr. Peggy Patterson from the Graduate Division of Educational Research (GDER), and Dr. P. Michael Maher from the Haskayne School of Business at the University of Calgary. Especially, I would like to respectfully honour the warmth and subtle advice of Dr. Winchester, my supervisor. It seems to me, from all my reading about Dr. Alfred North Whitehead, who is a major inspiration for my research, that Ian Winchester is remarkably similar in his scientific background, his educational philosophy and in his excellence as a teacher. Thanks as well to the GDER staff, and particularly to Sylvia Parks who has been so helpful in managing and explaining the technical details of the doctoral journey.

I want also to express thanks to the wonderful, tireless, and downright dog headed work of librarians at the University of Calgary, and also at other universities including Harvard and Claremont Graduate University's Center for Process Studies.

Finally, I am most grateful for the work done by my sister, Diana Fowler LeBlanc, in proof reading this entire dissertation as well as my candidacy paper: What started out as a joke about her correcting our childhood letters when we were all teenagers, has evolved into an excellent and meticulous expertise and understanding of grammar, flow and meaning that have been of immense help to me during this endeavour. In addition, Diana is the person who has steadfastly supported my current learning efforts, and who has insisted that I never consider the possibility of not finishing what has been a particularly arduous and yet rewarding learning process.

Author's Note

With the completion of course work, written and oral candidacy exams, a written dissertation and its oral defence on December 7, 2009, and delivery of an approved copy to the Faculty of Graduate Studies on December 8, I satisfied all the requirements for the degree of Doctor of Education (Higher Education Leadership) from the University of Calgary. I will graduate officially at a convocation in June 2010.

Except for some minor changes (the exclusion of the appendices, the addition of this author's note, and the changing of format, font and pagination to be more book-like), this content is close to being a replica of my doctoral dissertation. I have published the research in this format in order to share it with those executives who participated in the interviews, and with each of the nine institutions I have featured in this work. I will also be sending copies to a few additional institutions, firms, consultants and individuals whom I feel might be interested in this topic. This is done with a view to encouraging conversation about excellence in executive education and learning, and promoting the idea of a tighter connection between theory and practice, and a fruitful relationship between academic and applied pursuits.

Because this is a dissertation, included are some academically required sections that may be of little interest to the business reader (for example: aspects of the methodology, ethical considerations and approvals, researcher bias, and study limitations). Scrutiny of the detailed Table of Contents will provide information as to which sections might attract different readers. There may be practising executives or others who are themselves considering doing post graduate learning and research, and this book will serve as a sample in format, style, content and rigour for those endeavours.

Chapter One introduces the research, including its purpose, significance, the research questions, and ethical considerations. Chapter Four describes the specifics of the collective case study research design that I have used for this work.

Chapters Two, Three and Eight will be of the most interest to many readers: The Literature Review (Chapter Two) provides good reading about the topics of executive learning featured in the data gathering efforts as well as in the resulting conclusions and recommendations. Chapter Three outlines the valuable educational philosophy of Dr. Alfred North Whitehead. As my chosen theoretical framework, it represents the principal influence, inspiration and guide in dealing with all aspects of my research on executive education. Chapter Eight contains the conclusions and recommendations based on the gathered data.

For readers and researchers seeking more depth and wishing either to arrive at their own conclusions or to better understand how I arrived at mine: they will want to look at all the data findings and analysis in Chapters Five, Six and Seven.

Should anyone wish to contact me, that can be done by e-mail at: bgrfowle@ucalgary.ca

Table of Contents

CHAPTER SIX – PRESENTATION OF FINDINGS AND ANALYSIS (PART 2)

List of Tables

Chapter One - Introduction

Description

This multi-case study will look into the opinions about, and experiences of, executive learning according to 14 senior executives at ten mid to large sized corporations in Canada. It will also compare those opinions with descriptive material about executive educational programs at nine universities in North America and Europe. These data will be embellished with my own experience of executive education, based on my attendance at such programs while an executive for a major Canadian pulp and paper company.

The theoretical framework underlying this research is Dr. Alfred North Whitehead's straightforward prescriptions about education, which to a large extent evolved from his study of physics, and his experience as an academic administrator and teacher. Chapter Three is devoted to an in-depth look at his educational thought. The Whitehead framework is an inspirational model for what good education should resemble from a teaching as well as a learning perspective. At the beginning of Chapter Six, I will draw some connections between this guiding framework and my research findings. Whitehead's admiration for the Harvard Business School and his statement in 1928 that it deserved an honourable place among academic programs at a university, rather than being relegated to the status of a mere trade school, makes the opinions of this philosopher/mathematician all the more appropriate as a foundation for this dissertation.

The Problem, the Challenge, and the Opportunity

As research about university executive education programs presented here will show, there are some stellar programs, which certainly merit the attention of firms seeking learning opportunities for their senior people. These excellent programs are ones like Henry Mintzberg's International Masters in Practicing Management (IMPM) described in Chapter Five, which provides an executive education experience marrying practical experience with reflective learning.

Some large Canadian corporations visited in the interviews have in place carefully orchestrated plans concerning executive education, and these are exemplary in their foresight, flexibility and relevance. Many of those programs are solidly grounded in sound educational principles and learning philosophies or models. Some firms already have such meticulously planned learning programs for *all* levels of their organizations; not just for their executive ranks. These are the kinds of firms that talk about, and actually become over the long haul, "learning organizations". They implement systems to make positive changes in the field of education for all of their employees. Often, they will have a senior vice president or a director-level executive in charge of learning, or may be operating a corporate university with an academic president in charge. These corporate universities often award academically recognized degrees to their successful students.

However, there is too vast and confusing an array of learning opportunities available for corporations regarding the education of their senior managers. External providers, including universities and consultants, plus internal training departments, or even corporate universities, all vie with each other to create programs. Those are often more in sync with the latest management fad than connected to what an institution wants to or can deliver, or indeed to what clients require or desire. The resulting educational offerings can therefore be helter-skelter, to say the least. Most likely, they will have a short shelf-life, probably not unlike that of the standard MBA programs, so criticized by Henry Mintzberg (2004a), as being merely memorable to students for about six months. There is often little effort made by providers or by their client sponsors to gather feedback about these learning events after they have taken place, other than possibly to discover whether participants enjoyed themselves, by having been afforded time away from the office. In such cases, there is rarely any measurement of the connection between potential benefits of the learning and business objectives, or improvement in performance; corporate clients may not be receiving learning benefits they are paying for.

Some corporations may have a shotgun approach, or no approach at all, to providing their executives with learning opportunities. In those firms, learning can be a piecemeal affair, with curricula that lack cohesion and continuity. Telltale signs of this *laissez-faire* approach include the already mentioned startling lack of participant or provider accountability, as well as a seemingly incredible dearth of analysis regarding the cost-effectiveness of learning programs. This is a veritable anomaly for private sector enterprises, in which all expenditures from large expansion projects or acquisitions right down to use of paper clips and pencils are so regularly scrutinized.

To give an idea of the magnitude of these training costs, Doh and Stumpf (2007) stated that more than $50 billion was spent on training in the United States. Of that amount, fully $500 million went to the top ten providers of custom and open enrolment management programs. Clearly, a great deal of money is being spent on executive education, but is it being well spent in providing clients with the learning they require and want?

Purpose

The discerning corporation that cares about executive learning will properly research the instances of available, excellent open enrolment programs, or they will create customized programs specifically tailored to their needs. The purpose of this research study is to look into current executive learning practices, as described by top level managers within some large corporations in Canada, and as offered by some respected business schools. The objective is to find out the opinions of the executives within those firms about their own first hand experiences with education and learning. A secondary objective is to look at some of the best open enrolment and custom programs available from universities, with a view to seeing whether what the executives say they want is what they can in fact obtain from those providers. A third objective is to report on my own experience as a participant in executive learning events.

Specifically, the study will deal with executive education and learning with respect to topics of relevance, scope, style, design, curriculum content, technology, delivery, and faculty. As Winchester (1986) stated, "the business of educational research is to make a difference in practice" (p. 3). That is also an underlying purpose of this study: to attempt to make a difference at least in the perception of the practice, if not the actual practice of executive education.

Significance

The Environics Research Group's Report on Executive Education in Canada (2006) surveyed the attitudes and opinions of 400 senior executives in Canada. They found that "when it comes to continuing business training and education for managers and executives, the majority of respondents (60%) admit their own organization has 'room for improvement'" (p. 2).

The potential significance of this research was firstly to engender, through 14 interviews, a conversation about the importance, relevance and nature of executive learning with leaders of influential corporations in Canada. In some small way, those conversations will likely have some play throughout the private sector community in Canada, and possibly even farther afield. Beyond that, ideas for curriculum improvement, and how to conceivably tighten the connection between the learning and business objectives may have begun to be forged during this research process. The fact that every executive interviewed has requested that a copy of this dissertation be sent to them upon completion is a positive indication of their interest.

The research findings, which comprise a comparison of interview content with the availability of executive education programs from selected universities, may encourage further studies along these same lines. The combining of a high level of practicality, with the kind of academic discipline inherent in some excellent institutional programs featured in Chapter Six, is clearly desired by the senior people interviewed. Such combinations, or ones very similar, might serve as best-practice models for improving the quality of executive education and learning in Canada and beyond. It is reasonable to expect that this study could also spark work by other researchers about executive learning in the public sector, in non-profits, and in NGOs (Non governmental organizations) within Canada and elsewhere.

Researcher's Professional Background

Even as a management trainee in 1971, who started work with a large forest industry company based in western Canada, I had a keen interest in management training and development. My 31 year career in this business saw me working in the sales and marketing departments for essentially the same business unit throughout its many organizational guises of ownership and product mix.

The paper mill business unit in which I worked experienced internal change at an alarming but exciting rate while I was there. During those 31 years, output tripled, and product mix evolved from producing, marketing and selling uncoated commodity paper (the type used in copy machines) to doing the same thing for an utterly changed product mix of 100 percent coated printing paper (the type used in coffee table books and in full-colour advertising brochures).

Starting out as a marketing research trainee and then order desk supervisor, I graduated to outside sales into positions of increasing regional responsibility. Following that, as was quite typical with such on-the-job training progressions, I did time on the "inside" as marketing director in charge of all sales support, logistics and market planning. Finally, during the last 12 years of my career, I was Vice President Sales and Marketing, responsible for managing a group of 65 people, and for selling $300 million of printing paper in North America.

Recognition of Professional Bias

As far as bias is concerned, my business career experience has helped my research much more than it has hindered it. My practical familiarity in the field of business has fostered an *à priori* understanding that was of great assistance in properly setting up my research design, and in subsequently enhancing my ability to get closer to the participants – fellow executives all. The danger lay in the possibility of second guessing or anticipating results before the evidence presented itself. I needed vigilance and discipline to rein in ideas that tended to make that dangerous quantum leap from reasonableness based on experience, to unwarranted bias based on habit and intellectual stubbornness. In retrospect, I believe I acted properly and conservatively. Indeed, given the strength of convictions inherent in the executive psyche, I likely could have been a little more forceful in the interviews, such that even stronger opinions might have been elicited; But then, I am not Charlie Rose!

Multi case Study Units of Analysis

1. 14 executives from 10 corporations in Canada who volunteered to participate in this research from among Canada's largest corporations.

2. Nine universities: including five from Canada, two from the United States and two from Europe.

3. A review of my own experience as a participant in several types of executive education programs.

The Research Questions

1. In the opinion of key leaders at some corporations in Canada, what are the learning practices and programs that they consider the most valuable in executive development?

2. What are the ingredients of some of the stellar executive open enrolment and custom programs available from universities? How are these designed, facilitated and delivered?

3. What were my own experiences in management education programs; and which of these stood out and why did they stand out as being particularly useful and exemplary?

The Sub Questions

- How do leaders view executive education: its importance, its providers, its unfolding?

- Is there a preference for open enrolment or customized programs in developing learning plans for executives?

- What should an executive program look like in terms of design, curriculum and delivery?

Limitations of this Research

Generalizability of the research findings from participating executives to those at other large Canadian corporations could likely be safely made. However generalizability beyond that to other executive groups in other countries, or to executive members of organizations outside the private sector cannot be safely made. Even so, this research may point the way for future similar case studies about executive learning to be conducted on units of analysis beyond the limits of this one.

This is not a longitudinal study. It is one which glimpses executive learning at corporations in Canada during a specific period of time, in which the interviews were conducted between April 21 and June 16, 2009: a period of worldwide economic upheaval. However, there is no evidence that this timing and the related external economic factors could have substantively altered what was said in the interviews.

My research does not look into the kind of executive programs that might be crafted and delivered by corporate universities, as that was beyond the designed scope of this study. For some other study, however, it might be useful to look at such programs, as they would likely be most relevant in their alignment with corporate goals.

Some of the pre-fieldwork assumptions that I made about executive education, particularly apparent in the statement of the problem, are based on my own business experience over many years. That experience ended seven years ago when I took early retirement, and I had been concerned that perhaps things had changed since then. Perhaps corporate life had since become a kinder gentler way of being! As it has turned out, the executives I interviewed from various sectors of the economy appear indeed to be a little gentler, and are far less hierarchical in their modus operandi, than what I had experienced in my industry.

Related to my being "out of the loop" in corporate affairs was the possibility that I might experience some difficulty in reconnecting with corporate executives, and in persuading them to participate in my study. Reconnecting with them turned out to be nothing but a great pleasure, and could almost be termed as a return to the motherland, if not to the fray. None of the participants was at all sceptical about my having morphed into an academic skin, or indeed that I had become someone who was critically checking out the quality and efficiency of their executive training programs. However, it was extremely difficult, in these awfully challenging times of worldwide financial upheaval, to get some of them to agree to the interviews, and this difficulty is underscored in Chapter Five.

Finally, it should be admitted that participants who agreed to be interviewed were likely already positively predisposed to the importance of executive education in their own lives and in the lives of their corporations.

Ethical Considerations

Approvals

Dr. Kathleen Oberle, the Acting Chair of the Conjoint Faculties Research Ethics Board (CFRB) at the University of Calgary issued an initial approval for my research in a letter dated December 22, 2008.

A first set of revisions was approved on March 30, 2009 by the CFRB Chair, Dr. Janice Dickin, and included my requests to (1) expand the protocol to include retired executives known to me through previous business relationships; (2) no longer include observations of executive learning events as part of my data collection methodology, due to a growing realization that a majority of potential participating corporations would not permit me to do so; and (3) conduct semi-structured interviews guided, but not limited to, the set of questions that would be provided to participants in advance of the initiation of such interviews.

The same Chair approved a final revision concerning the use of a revised consent sheet (not requiring signatures), and indicating that interviews might be audio taped was approved on April 14, 2009 – just prior to conducting the first interview on April 21, 2009.

The interviews were an instance where signed consent was not necessary for the protection of either participant or researcher. The participant was provided with a sheet, which initially spelled out the project information that was subsequently included in the consent form. It was pointed out by the Ethics Chair that signed consent would not be necessary in my original protocol, because participants would remain anonymous. The two revisions to that protocol did not alter that anonymity.

Bridging the gap between Academia and Business

Despite my long business career, because I have spent the last seven years in graduate studies as an avid member of the academic community, it was necessary for me to instil confidence in potential participants about the positive, uncritical intentions of this study: to attempt to help and improve executive learning practices, and not to pointedly criticize the ones in existence.

Protection of human participants

My study fell into the "low-risk-to-participants" category, because it involved interviews with executives who are confident about their roles within their respective organizations, and who did not feel threatened by an academic study about their learning practices. Difficult in a single case study, concerns about personal anonymity as well as confidentiality were assuaged by the multi-case approach, in which the identity of corporate entities and their attendant personalities is diluted – safety in numbers.

Confidentiality

Another ethical consideration concerned the protection of organizations themselves. Because this dissertation will eventually find its way into the public domain, there might have been some reticence on the part of participating executives to divulge what they could consider to be strategic information about their executive education programs. While ensuring anonymity, I still had to be sensitive to these confidentiality concerns. Where there may have been any vulnerability in protecting such data, I had to create ways for it to remain confidential. One year following publication of this dissertation, all records about the interviews (notes, and audio recordings) will be destroyed.

Chapter Two –
The Literature Review

Introduction

The research and its analysis have entirely driven the selection of literature topics reviewed in this chapter. Therefore, included here are the same executive education issues which came up in conversation with business leaders, in the data gathering about the nine universities described, and in my own experience of management learning: namely, topics such as relevancy, curriculum content, diversity, knowledge and practice of electronic communications including social platforms, and scepticism about the latest management fads in organizational learning, teaching methods preferred by executives and used in university programs. These are subjects the reader will therefore recognize later in the description of findings and their analysis in Chapters Five, Six and Seven.

I would like to invite the reader to consider Chapter Three as a continuation of the Literature Review. That chapter, which is entirely devoted to the theoretical framework concerning teaching and learning which inspired this research, features the educational philosophy of Dr. Alfred North Whitehead. It also includes other frameworks that were considered but not used: the work of Pierre Bourdieu (concepts of *habitus* and *field*), and Peter Senge (five learning disciplines), as well as Royal Dutch Shell's concept of Scenario Planning, and the concept of Communities of Practice originally introduced in the work of Etienne Wenger.

A nagging assumption, based on my long experience in the pulp and paper industry had crept into my thinking about executive education. It is that, although most large private sector corporations know how usefully to develop or enhance their employees' technical, on-the-job skills in short bursts of training, many of them do not have much of an idea of how to 'educate' their people about how to learn, reflect and think critically – even though they might have an inkling that to do so would improve their competitive position. A recurring theme in this research is that executive education is inextricably linked to an organization's overall learning plan, and cannot be reasonably segregated into its own private compartment. All employee levels must take part in a cohesive educational process in order for all to play a part in the successful management of the firm. As stated by Heifetz et al (2009), "An organization that depends solely on its senior managers to deal with challenges risks failure" (p. 64).

Relevance

In explaining how business schools have lost their way, Bennis and O'Toole (2005) described how they were "too focused on scientific research, [and were] hiring professors with limited real-world experience and graduating students who are ill equipped to wrangle with complex, unquantifiable issues – in other words, the stuff of management" (p. 96). They stated that those schools were in fact "failing to impart useful skills, failing to prepare leaders, failing to install norms of ethical behavior". They maintained that this criticism came not only from students, employers and the media, but also internally from the business schools themselves. In these authors' opinions, the bedrock reason for this shortfall was an inappropriate and self-defeating model of academic excellence: namely, the scientific model, wherein business schools having been chastised in the early 1960s for their lack of academic rigour have let their guiding pendulum swing away from practicality towards theory. This scientific model has also motivated an internal demand by business faculty for research, more palatable to their academic peers, – an approach Bennis and O'Toole characterized as "sometimes waggishly referred to as *physics envy*" (p. 98).

The Deans and other leaders of those business schools, although their words sound promising, seem to be somewhat confused about how properly to balance their academic with their practical mandates; how to stay true to the Academy while also serving their various stakeholders. Therefore, authors such as these have reasonably called for a balance between scientific rigour and practical relevance for business school curricula and for teaching emphases. Bennis and O'Toole (2005) implied that if this disconnection between theory and practice persists, then businesses will simply look elsewhere for educational guidance (for instance, from corporate universities, consultants, or simply through learning-on-the-job).

Jeffrey Pfeffer is professor of organizational behaviour at the Graduate School of Business, Stanford University, and Christina Fong was a PhD candidate at Stanford Business School. Pfeffer and Fong (2002) have suggested that business schools are not very effective in their formal goals "to impart knowledge [to their students] and influence the practice of management [in organizations]" (p. 80). In other words, this article calls into question the professional relevance of management scholarship. There are many rising competitors (consultants, in-house training, even corporate universities, as well as new forms of online program delivery) all vying for a piece of the action in business education. According to these authors, this means "that business schools may soon confront some substantial challenges" (p. 79). Pfeffer and Fong maintained that business schools do not have to be in this condition, and supported this idea by saying that medical and other professional schools provide interesting models of success. What is taught in those professional schools is closer to what is practiced in their corresponding fields, and they implied that it could also be so for business schools. Their article provides a good historical overview of the evolution of the North American business schools from quasi trade school status (practical but lacking a scientific foundation) in the 1950s, to progressive attempts to achieve academic legitimacy ever since by imitating the traditions and ways of mainstream academia. This resulted in curricula that became too focused on analysis and problem solving, rather than on synthesis and problem setting.

However, as Usher, Bryant and Johnston (1997) stated in defence of the academic and theoretical aspects of adult education, "Feeling threatened by theory and dismissing it as remote and 'airy-fairy' allows practitioners to cocoon themselves in 'experience', [and in] their craft knowledge and customary ways of doing things. Hence, a private world that is safe and unchallenged can be created" (p. 124).

Henry Mintzberg is the outspoken Cleghorn Professor of the Desautels Faculty of Management at McGill University. He is famous for his scathing attack in his book entitled *Managers Not MBAs* about the uselessness of MBA programs in preparing managers for the job market. Many of the criticisms in that book are equally applicable as warnings about executive programs. For instance, Mintzberg (2004a) criticized the emphasis on analysis rather than on synthesis, which is the very essence of management. In a Conference Board interview (2004b), Mintzberg clarified this issue when he said that "while business schools have been successful in *analyzing* things, in separating all these specialized functions, they have not been successful in putting them together, in synthesizing them into a coherent vision or integrated system" (p. 20).

Dr. Mintzberg's thesis is basically that you cannot learn to lead an organization from a classroom, and he has put this thesis into practical play by co-founding his now world-renowned *impm*® International Masters in Practicing Management. The banner heading on that program's website is a Mintzberg quote: "This is the next generation of management education – managers learning from their own experience" (retrieved July 20, 2008 from http://www. impm.org/). In Mintzberg's own words, headlined on the website, "it is a program to make better managers of people who already are managers".

Essentially Mintzberg, and others like him, would have us make the management curriculum relevant by keeping it inextricably connected to the real world. He would accomplish this by having operating managers develop their own learning in their places of business, with professors acting only as facilitators. That is surely a worthy, reasonable and modest proposal. Too often the criticisms in these journals were plentiful without offering alternatives, let alone suggesting solutions. The great thing about Henry Mintzberg is that we manage to swallow his stinging criticism because he offers a plan to improve the situation. He has done this through at least two successful management programs at McGill. However, a certain uneasy feeling tends to creep into the stories when one realizes, for example, that Henry Mintzberg will not be around forever. Although his theories may be, other professors at McGill need to be featured as well as this superstar.

Accountability

Return on Investment (ROI) and Alignment of Executive Education with Business Goals

In 2006, *Business Week* estimated that $50 billion was spent on training in the United States, with approximately $500 million of that going to the providers of custom and open enrolment programs in Executive Education. Dulworth and Bordonaro (2005) at $51 billion are close to the overall figure, but they estimate the proportion for executive training at 14% of that number, or at $7.1 billion. However, that lofty figure includes just over $6 billion for salaries paid while executives are attending those programs, ergo, not doing their jobs. The implication, of course, is that if their training could somehow be combined with, or be included in the performance of their jobs, then there would be a hugely beneficial impact on the training return on investment (ROI). This implication is made even more compelling and astonishing by Scott Saslow in Dulworth and Bordonaro (2005), when they stated that "although 90 percent of learning happens on the job and 10 percent happens in informal training programs, yet 75 percent of executive education resources are spent on formal programs and [only] 25 percent on on the job training" (p. 26). Interestingly, one corporate university (Caterpillar) has begun to refer to "Return on Learning" (ROL) rather than the more standard ROI.

There is a paradox inherent in the controversial issue concerning measurement of return given the huge resources spent every year by corporations on management development programs and executive education. The paradox is simply that everyone seems to think that it must absolutely be measured, but so very few actually measure it. Firms spend great care and attention analyzing and accounting for all their expenses, right down to the amount spent on paper clips. Therefore, it follows that there should be at least as much scrutiny and financial accountability for the big-ticket items such as training and management development programs, but very often there is not. If indeed it is such a burning issue, why are so few firms attempting it? Bleak and Fulmer (2009) cited a study that looked specifically at European based multi-nationals, in which 63 percent reported never measuring return on investment in learning and development (p. 4). From my own interviews, for instance, I know that in two specific cases, senior people who attended one of the long executive programs at Harvard Business School were under no obligation whatsoever to report back to their respective firms about these very expensive learning experiences. Was it perhaps because other benefits of that learning experience were recognized by those firms as being something beyond financial ROI: time for reflection, a new learning experience, a change of pace?

Charlton and Osterweil's (2005) research findings supported a recognition of a greater good coming out of executive training than can be measured financially: They received 270 responses from a questionnaire, comprising 156 from Human Resources professionals and 114 from sponsors, mostly CEOs, managing directors and general managers. These authors did a good job in uncovering some of the toxic assumptions about ROI in executive education: for instance, the rather glaring if basic one that financial ROI about learning initiatives was an important issue in most organizations, and implied that this concern often scuttled or minimized educational program development. One of the main findings, and one of great relevance, was that often the impetus for doing a financially oriented ROI on executive education programs emanated from the Human Resources Departments. It was suggested that this was because HR departments might want to emulate the respected and expected business-like behaviour of the operating departments, where all the rubber was hitting the road. It was found that this impetus was not really coming from on high: from the CEO or the senior executives who seemed to have a more flexible and generalized view of education.

Essentially, it was found that while nobody was willing to give up the quest for doing an ROI analysis on executive education programs, ROI itself meant different things to the HR professionals compared to the sponsors. Somewhat ironically, many of the CEOs and other senior sponsors felt that there were important qualitative as well as quantitative aspects that needed to be appreciated concerning return on investment. There was a groundswell of belief from on high that executive education should be viewed "as an activity that delivers results through individuals and [to] regard proof of individual benefit as evidence of positive ROI – seeing the appropriate focus for evaluation as the individual themselves" (Charlton and Osterweil, 2005, p. 11). It turned out that few sponsors had an interest in calculating *financial* ROI. In fact, the majority of sponsors were more interested in understanding "how they [could] influence, through organizational climate, how effectively participants [could] transfer and apply their learning" (p. 13).

Some other authors, such as Robert Terry (2005), were a great deal more pragmatic about how executive programs must "lend themselves to comprehensive evaluation and measurement in order that ROI can be clearly demonstrated in the boardroom" (p. 232). Terry went on to say that "training and development must accept new disciplines that identify and deliver business rather than learning outcomes" (ibid). In other words, it is not 'good old school days', it is learning and development that places the organization and its goals before the individuals and their goals. Like it or not, providers of executive education need to realize this. It is a realization that often flies in the face of the more altruistic and perfectly admirable learning objectives of academic institutions.

In direct contrast to what Charlton and Osterweil (2005) said about there being more to ROI in executive education than the mere numbers, Terry (2005) stated that we need a new paradigm that "embraces all that is best in learning, is couched in the language of commercial accountability and defines success in terms that would be applauded by the finance director" (p. 233). Terry's model, The 6 Ds™, incorporates the stages of an executive program comprising Define (outcomes), Design (complete experience), Deliver (for [specific] application), Drive (follow-through), Deploy (active support), and Document (results).

The Internet, The Worldwide Web, Electronic Communication and Social Networks

For a long time now, many organizations have failed to understand and utilize properly the internet and intranet for more than merely diffusing information. The evolution of the worldwide web has taught younger generations and innovative organizations to recognize and welcome the internet as a powerful and helpful partner in sharing knowledge and expertise, in a way that fosters transparency, and in fact penalizes secrecy. It is an atmosphere in which employees can interact truthfully among themselves and with customers.

The Levine, Locke, Searls and Weinberger (2000) classic *Cluetrain Manifesto* was hailed by the Harvard Business Review on the book's back cover with the words, "While others work on turning the internet into the perfect medium for reaching traditional business goals, these four net-philes hope cyberspace will give commerce a *human voice*". One of Christopher Locke's chapters described the phenomenon this way:

> A strange and oddly playful attitude is in evidence nearly everywhere online, an ironic shared intelligence that subverts the core assumptions of traditional institutions. There's fun afoot on the internet, and business had better take it seriously. When paradox becomes paradigm, it's already too late to look for a magic-bullet cure for Corporate Linguistic Deficit Disorder. It's time to imagine entirely new roles, new reasons, new worlds. (p. vii)

Tapscott and Williams (2008) in a similar vein, but fully eight years later, were still warning that the immense kind of online force, into which N-Geners were self-organizing, was increasingly providing its own goods and services and that firms were risking becoming irrelevant spectators: "Only the smartest and most sincere companies stand a chance of becoming meaningful participants in the networks these N-Geners are forging" (p. 50). Like Levine et al. (2000), Tapscott and Williams (2008) highlighted the playfulness of online communications, and the new roles and expectations inherent in it, when they explained that the N-Gen norms of "speed, freedom, openness, innovation, mobility, authenticity and playfulness – can form the basis of a revitalized and innovative work culture, but they also raise tough challenges for employees seeking to adapt to new expectations" (p. 54). Judy Rosenblum (2009), advisor to the CEO and board member at Duke Corporate Education, stated that "Generation X and Y together will shape the norms of professionalism for the next 30 years" and that "they take for granted the interconnectedness of the world" (p. 2).

Goldsmith (2009), in an article entitled "CEOs stay old-school; most shun social media", reported on research done by the blog UberCEO.com. That research looked at Fortune's 2009 list of the top 100 CEOs regarding their use of Facebook, Twitter, LinkedIn, Wikipedia, and it found that they were, for the most part, missing from those forums. For instance, the study found that only two of those CEOs had twitter accounts, only 19 of them had a personal Facebook page, and only 13 had profiles on the professional networking site called LinkedIn; not even one had a blog. Goldsmith quoted the editor of UberCEO.com, Sharon Barclay, as having said:

> It's shocking that the top CEOs can appear to be so disconnected from the way their own customers are communicating. They're giving the impression that they're disconnected, disengaged, and disinterested....They're missing a fabulous opportunity to connect with their target audience and raise their company's visibility. (p. L2)

As readers will witness in Chapter Five, I asked a very similar question of the executives I interviewed, although they seemed a little more connected to social media than is criticized in this article. Despite the validity at least of the flavour of this criticism, it could be argued that the kind of job occupied by a Chief Executive Officer is one that does not require a personalized presence on Facebook. It might even be inadvisable to have a twitter account, but it would be hard to argue against at least a presence on LinkedIn. The point is that although CEOs should have a good knowledge and understanding of these social communication platforms, they do not need personally to expose themselves there. A new study, which broke 2000 Twitter posts into six categories, showed that 40.55% of Twitter posts were "pointless babble" (*The Globe and Mail, August 18, 2009, pp L1 and L3)*. There is no way that any self-respecting CEO, given those statistics, would want to be anywhere near Twitter.

On Wednesday, May 13, 2009, FT.com (*The Financial Times*) conducted an online forum entitled "Ask the Experts: Executive Education Online Q&A" available via the following link:

http://www.ft.com/cms/s/2/1d45db9a-3af3-11de-ba91-00144feabdc0,dwp_uuid=87c504f8-2b20-11dc-85f9-000b5df10621.html?ftcamp=rss

The panel of experts comprised two senior academics and the business editor at *The Financial Times*. Rory Simpson, Associate Dean of Executive Education at the London Business School stated that business schools "need to move from their *once bitten twice shy* attitude to e-learning and completely grasp all aspects of new media. Millions were spent over the past ten years on e-learning but it is still miles away from its potential. Nobody has cracked it, and certainly not the so-called online universities" (p. 2).

This criticism is key, and for the most part valid, but I disagree with Simpson's comment that nobody has cracked it. Universities that deliver graduate programs partly online, such as Royal Roads, Athabasca and the Fielding Institute, all of whose programs I am familiar with, are conversant in all aspects of online, highly collaborative learning. I am particularly aware of Royal Roads University's capabilities in that respect, having graduated in 2005 from a two-year MA program in leadership from that university.

Because there is no professor physically in front of the class, online learning needs to contain a significant element of collaboration and shared facilitation among the learners. Palloff and Pratt (1999) stated that "the instructor must control the urge to lead and become more like a follower, thus engaging in the type of collaborative work we have been discussing" (p. 123). Such a scenario might appear threatening to some teachers whose whole teaching persona is based on being visibly in front of the class. In addition, some of the reticence about online learning may come from the amount of time it takes to deliver instruction in this format; Palloff and Pratt have indicated that instructors will find that it is in fact two to three times greater than delivering a face-to-face class (p. 49).

Even a decade ago, the technology for online learning was relatively advanced, and yet its effective use has managed to elude so many universities. Indeed, those institutions have a long way to go in understanding the must-have flexibility of online learning, as well as the power potential of the kind of collaborative and creative work that can be done both synchronously and asynchronously through online formats; not to mention the surprising hidden benefits of giving voice to students otherwise marginalized for a whole host of reasons, including that of simply being so introverted that face-to-face formats work much less well for them. For instance, Palloff and Pratt (1999) found that students "who are shy in social settings learn something about social skills by interacting in an electronic course" (p. 34). They quoted some of their students who favoured online over face-to-face learning formats because "Cyberspace lets you squirm in peace. You are able to rethink without having people questioning you" (p. 136); and "We have become so dependent on the ability to do this at our time and our own rate of thinking that the creative thinking is beginning to develop" (p. 139).

Program Design

Several authors (among them, Das Narayandas, 2007; and Charleton and Osterweil, 2005) have reported a significantly higher growth in custom compared to open enrolment programs for executives, and this data is explained in Chapter Six.

"Open enrolment programs are by definition built around organizational imperatives" (IMD's Peter Lorange in Doh and Stumpf, 2007, p. 394). However, to be widely popular, they have to be built around general organizational imperatives, and not around the narrow and specific ones, which could be more effectively addressed through custom tailored programs and courses.

Bleak and Fulmer (2009) stated that "alignment with business strategy and priorities was seen to win out over a hodgepodge of benchmark programs" (p. 3). Because such alignment can really only be effectively engineered into custom programs, this implies a preference for that type of program over the open enrolment format. It should perhaps be noted that Jared Bleak is an executive director of Duke Corporate Education, which is an institution that only provides custom programs. Robert Fulmer is a professor at Pepperdine University in California. According to Bleak and Fulmer, company executives should help in designing leadership development programs and that those programs should use "executive faculty" who can bring a strategic perspective to participants (p. 6).

Tushman, O'Reilly, Fenollosa, Kleinbaum and McGrath (2007) gathered together one Stanford and three Harvard professors and the vice president of corporate strategy at IBM, to study individual and organizational outcomes of action learning in executive open enrolment, compared to custom programs. They looked at this through various lenses including: for education-oriented, compared to action oriented, programs; for senior, compared to more junior, executives; and for individuals compared to teams. They found that action learning programs significantly enhance both individual and organizational outcomes, compared to traditional executive education formats, and that action-learning programs also enhance teaching and research efforts for the universities providing these programs. They found that "the most effective form of action learning, where senior teams came to campus to work on their strategic issues with professional group facilitation..., had the most significant impacts across all individual and organizational outcomes" (p. 352). Especially germane to my research, they found that "If rigor and relevance are important criteria for business school research, then executive education, with its more experienced students, becomes a useful crucible within which business school faculty can test the relevance of their research" (p. 348). They also discovered that the most successful Leading Change and Organizational Renewal (LCOR) workshops involved teams that made substantial investment in "problem definition, data gathering, and fact finding prior to their arrival on campus" (p. 353), and they equally found that the most successful LCOR designs had a set of common actions both immediately after the workshop and then at regular intervals after that. Tushman et al. (2007) concluded their report on this research by saying that "the relations between business schools and thoughtful firms have the potential to create virtuous cycles of knowing and doing" (p. 357).

Doh and Stumpf (2007) asked interviewees about a common criticism often levelled at Executive Education, namely, "that it emphasizes entertainment over learning" (p. 393). Indeed, in my own experience it seemed that, too often, written feedback at the end of a session sought to find out whether participants had enjoyed a program, more than it asked about whether anyone thought they had learned anything. These same authors stated that "EE [executive education] clients are increasingly interested in additional comprehensive and meaningful systems for evaluation – beyond the standard participant assessment that occurs after a program" (p. 394).

Business Schools – Their Future and Their Commercialization

Starkey and Tempest (2008) pointed out that Business tends to see business schools as providers of services – research, consultancy or teaching, but that academics in those schools see themselves "as disinterested students of business, producing knowledge of business rather than for business" (p. 379). They spoke of the tendency of business schools "to have inexorably moved along a vector which tends to emphasise business – and one model of business – at the expense of school" (p. 379). One of this article's section headings is foreboding in the extreme: "The condition of the business school – rigorous irrelevance, icy hearts, shrunken souls, market shakeout" (p. 381). In that section, they warned that the business school is implicated in the excessive commercialization in every part of the university – implying rather surprisingly that such corporatization is contagious, and cannot be resisted by other impressionable faculties.

Starkey and Tempest stated that "Universities, once places of public purpose have become merely agencies of personal advantage" and that this is the fault of the business school philosophy.

According to these authors, the likely outcome will be that whereas the elite business schools will probably survive and dominate the market, there will be a shakeout of the other players. In business circles, we might call such an outcome natural attrition or even a beneficial evolution, but such a businesslike attitude is obviously at the crux of this argument. Does the Academy really expect, or even want, survival of its un-fittest players? In their predicted survival, are the Harvards, Yales, INSEADs, McGills and Westerns of the world not capable of carrying the torch of academic excellence that those which fall by the wayside were unable to do? Will those surviving schools not be able to keep their balance on that fine path between commercialization and the Quixotic mandate of universities?

Stanford Emeritus professor Jim March, delivered a convocation address to Business School graduates, in which he beautifully dealt with this argument about the pragmatic outcomes versus the altruistic aims of business education: March (2003), took a middle road in proposing a balance for business schools between academic rigour and relevancy (remarks which he originally made at a faculty seminar at the Stanford Graduate School of Business in 1996). In fact, at Stanford the goal of this balancing act is enthroned as part of the mission statement as "balanced excellence" and "relevance with rigor". While March bewailed the lack of distinction between business school metaphors and those of the marketplace, he still thought that such a market conception could yield useful insights. Nevertheless, he stated that the market characterization "fails to capture the fundamental nature of the educational soul" (p. 206). For him, a university is only incidentally a market, and he argued that it is more essentially a temple. With this attitude in play, it is unlikely that a lasting marriage will happen between what universities have to offer and the urgent, relevant, just-in-time educational programs that organizations seem to want. March further stated that, "higher education is a vision, not a calculation. It is a commitment, not a choice. Students are not customers; they are acolytes. Teaching is not a job; it is a sacrament; Research is not an investment; it is a testament" (p. 206).

March realized that many might think of these statements as romantic nonsense, but he still insisted on their value, however Quixotic they might appear. It is indeed a balancing trick to remember his spine-tingling words as a vision of business school excellence in the face of all the insistence on effectiveness, measurable outcomes and bottom-line results. As the Stanford slogan suggests, what is required is "relevance with rigor".

A few months ago, March (2009) was once again addressing a graduating class; this time at the University of Alberta School of Business, where he said:

> As you leave this University,...
> I hope you will do whatever you do,
> not because of its consequences, but
> because it is appropriate for the human
> being you aspire to be. But most of
> all, I wish you a life in which you are
> able to say honestly to yourself and
> to others: "I know who I am." "Yo sé
> quien soy" [Cervantes, Don Quixote]

Winchester (1988) talked about six features of universities that are continuous with their medieval counterparts – ones that "have always been present, whenever the university amounted to anything worth having" (p. 181). These included: its independence, its neutrality and impartiality, its bookishness, its concern for the passing on of knowledge critically, its interest in the advancement of knowledge, and, its role as a cultural centre. He said that "if you deny or remove any one of these things, while you may have an institution, you will not have a university-like one" (p. 181). Perhaps business schools that are trying to maintain relevance with the world of commerce, while also wanting to occupy an honoured place within university institutions, should remember these six aspects Winchester has described. Business schools need not fear adopting some of these arms-length, academic behaviours as an integral part of their operational guidelines; they must walk the thin line between where they are and who they are. This might land them somewhere between the idealism James March spoke about and the worldliness expected by their commerce students, and their executive learners.

The Curricula – Opinions from the Leaders

Fully 13 years ago, Fulmer and Vicere (1996) talked about three major trends shaping a transformation in executive development:

1. More customized, strategic programs: "corporations are demanding programs that support their specific strategic objectives, reflect their vision and values, and involve a critical mass of key players" (p. 35). They specify that, in 1996, 75 percent of all executive education dollars went toward customized programs, rather than to open enrolment programs.

2. Shorter, more focused, large-scale, cascaded programs: a trend brought about because of cost cutting measures to minimize executives' time away from the office, and to provide large numbers of senior managers with high impact learning regarding shifts in strategic direction, or changes in corporate culture.

3. More action-learning projects with measurable results: providers stated that "the majority of their new initiatives were relying less on classroom time led by a professor and more on facilitated, small-group, action learning applications" (p. 36).

These descriptions of major trends in 1996 appear to be remarkably similar to the same ones we are seeing today, in the literature cited here, and in the interviews and university program research of this dissertation. Sadly, the obvious conclusion to be drawn from this evidence is that change and progress are slow in the realm of executive education.

Büchel and Antunes (2007) remarked on an underlying assumption about executive education: that it can improve managerial decision making. They stated that the programs "that combine the cognitive and behavioural aspects are particularly likely to produce higher quality results" (p. 401). In this article, Bettina

Büchel, a professor of strategy at IMD (Switzerland), and Don Antunes, associate fellow at Warwick Business School, interviewed three high-level international executives. In the opinion of one of those executives from Europe's largest insurance company came the haunting statement: "I have worked for a number of companies that didn't invest in executive education – and I would argue that their leaders were just as successful, without investing in executive education"(p. 402). However, that leader went on to explain that those companies took different approaches to developing new capabilities in their executives, such as more international assignments, on-the-job coaching, training and mentoring. I would argue that if those approaches are formalized and recognized in some way, and are not merely ad hoc or helter-skelter in their unfolding, then they *are* part of a firm's executive education plan, whether or not an official provider of executive education is involved. In other words, these firms have in fact invested in executive education.

The second executive, from Hitachi, made a useful comment aptly applicable to the delivery of executive learning curriculum: "People will not have a balanced executive education when they study by themselves" (Büchel and Antunes, 2007, p. 402). This underlines the importance of group work and working in teams, which is an aspect of learning, on which providers and clients all seem to agree. The third executive, the CEO from Tetra Pak, Lausanne, made the comment that the main reason for executive education was to drive major change initiatives (p. 403). This same person described that the items he required in curriculum design from providers of executive education were: "pragmatism and customization to our needs - somebody that will take the trouble to sit down with us, understand what we want, and then run a pilot before deciding to roll out the program to a large group over multiple sessions" (p. 403).

Nevertheless, the possibility that there might be no appreciable difference in the success of those companies that invest in executive education, compared to the ones that do not, is surprising and would certainly be disconcerting to the providers of such programs. It would be tempting to dig into this more deeply to find out what successful business people have to say about what part, if any, academic education, and other forms of learning, have played in their climb to the top of their fields. Warren Buffet of Berkshire Hathaway, Don Keough of Coca Cola, Jack Welch of General Electric, and Steve Jobs of Apple come screaming to mind here, as exemplars of brilliant business acumen. There is no question about the degree of their success and philanthropy, and the significance of their contribution to the world. However, all of those good things may have little to do with executive or management education. All seem to be staunch supporters of higher education, at least in principle, but several have nonetheless stated that it did nothing for their careers.

All of these above-mentioned corporate luminaries regularly tour business schools, giving talks featuring their colourful and straightforward war stories – much appreciated by adoring audiences. The loudest applause seems to honour those stories, which demonstrate how success has come from the use of common sense (for example Warren Buffet's 88 minute talk, in 2006, to MBA students at the University of Florida (http://video.google.com/videoplay?docid=-6231308980849895261). During Steve Job's Commencement address at Stanford University in 2005, the moment of truth seemed to come when he proudly admitted quitting his university program after only one semester, because it was so irrelevant to what he wanted to do in life. You might think that the graduates would be offended by such a comment, but they loved it!

My view is a little jaundiced regarding the content of books written by terribly successful business people and the interviews they give: there we so often see extremely successful, extraordinarily wealthy individuals with huge egos who obtained riches in a steely-eyed, focused, albeit creative manner, which was initially self-serving, and later partly served the public good. They are generally good storytellers, and they appear friendly and approachable on national television - for example in conversation "around the oak table" with Charlie Rose. The generally facile nature of the manner in which these successful people portray their accomplishments may be entertaining, but it does not appear to be all that meaningful or useful.

Much of the conversation of these great ones sounds to me like the same kind of business babble I have heard for so many years during my career. In my view, that conversation mostly contains platitudes or pithy one-liners and quotable quotes about hard work, swimming against the stream, taking advantage of opportunities, and using common sense. There appears to me to be precious little from those practising corporate leaders about reflection, personal mastery, worldliness, inner peace, spirituality, education, good manners, sportsmanship, elegant behaviour, sophistication and dialogue. I know there are some notable exceptions to this diatribe, and I would like to mention ex-Microsoft CEO, Bill Gates, in that respect. After scoring 1590 out of 1600 in the SAT, he went to Harvard, but left after only two years. Despite this, Gates stated in his book, *The Road Ahead*:

> More than ever, an education that emphasizes general problem-solving skills will be important. In a changing world, education is the best preparation for being able to adapt. As the economy shifts, people and societies who are appropriately educated will tend to do best. The premium that society pays for skills is going to climb, so my advice is to get a good formal education and then keep on learning. Acquire new interests and skills throughout your life. (Gates, Myhrvold and Rinearson, 1995, p. 25)

"Soft" and "Hard" Aspects of Program Design and Curricula

This question of "soft" and "hard" programs in executive education not only refers to the specifics of course content, but also to the general approach to those programs. For instance, it refers to teaching participants how to think and reflect, rather than teaching them about generic solutions to specific types of problems. Kingwell (2000) reminded us of what Socrates repeatedly insisted on in his encounters with fellow citizens: "that we must examine our beliefs, not merely hold them" (p. 43). The "soft/hard" issue deals with appreciation of the long view, as well as respect for the urgency of just-in-time. It addresses tolerance of ambiguity alongside pragmatic analysis; it fosters the idea that senior executives should spend as much time relating to people as leading them. A good example of this is seen in the behaviour of Jack Welch, the former CEO of General Electric who was reputed to have spent half of his time on people development, and to have visited GE's Corporate University campus at Crotonville every two weeks.

Rosenblum (2009) promoted the idea that for people to advance as professionals, they should be immersed in problems – in other words, in action learning. She stated that "Well-designed education brings the student as close as possible to practicing [sic] in context through experiential learning and simulations" (p. 3). She further made the prominent and innovative comment that we need to recognize that "those skills we have termed soft skills actually determine whether our hard skills can be successfully applied and differentiate us in the marketplace" (p. 5). Rosenblum stated that we should, therefore, be looking for every opportunity to build the "soft" skills at work. She went on to say that we need to shift from a teaching mindset to a learning mindset and that "only content can be codified into bullets. Thinking, reflection and interaction cannot" (p. 6).

Bennis and O'Toole (2005) recommended a return to the way things were when business schools were designed to be bastions of interdisciplinary study – intellectually stimulating and exciting places to be. They also denigrated the current trend to specialization, favouring instead the need for generalization. They promoted the requirement to teach ethics, and the "softer" side of business management and leadership, such as prudence, practical wisdom and interpersonal skills. They cited philosopher and mathematician Alfred North Whitehead and his comments about the importance of engaging imagination to illuminate facts. They challenged and chided us when they commented that "the dirty little secret at most of today's best business schools is that they chiefly serve the faculty's research interests and career goals, with too little regard for the needs of other stakeholders" (p. 103). Authors, like Bennis and O'Toole constantly underlined that most issues facing business leaders are questions of judgments, and they maintained that business schools do not deal with those in their curricula, likely because such intangibles cannot be properly measured. Alsop (2002) stated that "The major business schools produce graduates with analytical horsepower and solid command of the basics – finance, marketing and strategy. But soft skills such as communication, leadership and team mentality sometimes receive cursory treatment" (p. R12).

De Geus (1997) suggested that "the essence of learning is the ability to manage change by changing yourself" (p. 20). Related to the creation of the Scenario Planning process at Royal Dutch Shell, De Geus (1997) and Schwartz (1991) promoted the need for executives to gain a wider perspective of forces outside the limited worlds of individual companies; to read widely far outside immediate business interests; to look at the fringes; and to talk to people with whom one disagrees. The two activities of decision making and learning became separated, likely due to some of the "soft/hard" differences created between the divergent thinking, assumptions and expectations of academics and managers. De Geus described his realization that decision making was indeed a learning process" that it was in fact "a social process, simple, unheroic, and unscientific" (p. 57).

Burns and Stalker (1961) showed us that "all managers some of the time, and many managers all of the time, yearn for more definition and structure" (p. 200). And this *modus operandi* is not necessarily incompatible with a looser, democratic style. A case in point is the resounding efficiency and phenomenal success rate that the Navy Seals, an elite commando unit, has experienced in their military missions. They operate under the contingency theory in organizational dynamics: in the preparation phase for those missions, teams work in a "soft", completely non-hierarchical and democratic way, sometimes in even an ad hoc manner, planning their strategy with the equal participation from each person's realm of expertise. Then, when this unit moves into the operational phase, the "hard", line-of-command, hierarchical rules apply as the disciplined group goes into action. Peters and Waterman (1982) referred to something very similar when they described firms with simultaneous loose-tight properties – a type of hybrid. These authors commented: "Organizations that live by the loose-tight principle are on the one hand rigidly controlled, yet at the same time allow (indeed, insist upon) autonomy, entrepreneurship, and innovation from the rank and file" (p. 436). The authors pointed out that in such a firm "rules can reinforce positive traits as well as discourage negative ones" and that these companies "are simultaneously externally focused and internally focused" (p. 438). Such organizations are worthy of careful scrutiny as being those that have perhaps wisely and deftly managed to take the middle road in this debate about emergent and flat, versus linear and hierarchical structures.

Goleman and Boyatzis (2008) researched the "soft" issue of social intelligence as the relationship-based construct for assessing leadership. They found that followers literally mirror their leaders in an effort to navigate their social world more fluently, and to create an instant sense of shared experience. These authors postulated that if leaders want to get the best out of their people, they should "continue to be demanding but in ways that foster a positive mood in their teams. The old carrot and stick approach alone doesn't make neural sense" (p. 77). In other words, "being in a good mood, other research finds, helps people take in information effectively and respond nimbly and creatively" (p. 77). Thus, the finely tuned leader possesses what this article described as a social guidance system, in which ultrarapid connections of emotions, beliefs, and judgments are created. This happens through *spindle* cells which, for instance, also help to gauge whether someone is trustworthy. The article reported that follow-up metrics revealed that such "thin slice" judgments can be very accurate. Although there are no clear-cut methods to strengthen mirror neurons, one of the case studies in the article talked of a Fortune 500 company that used personal coaching, the repeated practice of the desired behaviour, and developing a personal vision for change as the means of improving a senior executive's social intelligence. This was similar to Olympic athletes putting hundreds of hours into mental review of their moves (p. 79).

Kotter (1999) explained that the differences between management and leadership, are enormously important, and are sources of great confusion. He described leadership as dealing with development of vision and strategies and the alignment of relevant people behind them, and the empowerment of individuals to make the vision happen; he described management as keeping the system operating through planning, budgeting, organizing, staffing, controlling and problem solving: "Leadership works through people and culture. It's soft and hot. Management works through hierarchy and systems. It's harder and cooler" (p. 10). Therefore, in its design and content, executive education needs to concentrate more on the softer aspects of leadership than on the harder aspects of management. Thus Kotter has given guidance here as to what such curricula should contain.

Curricula Content

Benchmarking programs involve the study of best practices, but these seem to have become outdated in the current fast paced business environment of constant change. In explaining the dual requirements of executing tasks to meet urgent challenges and adapting in order to thrive in tomorrow's world, Heifitz, Grashow and Linsky (2009) talked about needing to develop "*next practices* while excelling at today's best practices" (p. 65). They suggested some crucial abilities to accomplish this, which included improving adaptability; embracing disequilibrium; generating leadership deeply within the organization through a distributed model, in which everyone generates solutions, and in which everyone acts "like they own the place" (p. 68). They suggested taking care of oneself, by managing one's own thinking and emotions – similar to personal mastery, one of Peter Senge's (1990) five disciplines that is required in a learning organization. Charlton and Osterweil (2005) mentioned their current curricular priorities at the Ashridge Consulting firm as being around globalization, culture change, post merger integrations and organizational repositioning.

Doh and Stumpf (2007) wrote an article which views executive education from the perspective of the heads of five leading providers. General curricular trends mentioned included a clear tendency toward more leadership and entrepreneurship; a tendency away from how-to-do-it programs toward more integrated suites of programs; emergence of issues of sustainability and sustainable growth; a focus on the emerging geographies, namely China and India; a greater focus on working across boundaries, adaptability, collaboration and change management; the classics of: leadership and strategy, understanding and executing strategy, and building leadership at various levels within the organization (p. 391). The five corporate leaders interviewed felt that the attributes which defined the top providers of executive education included: offerings that encompassed not just programs and courses, but also seminars, projects, conferences -offerings that were considered educational services rather than skill training; staffing mainly with faculty members who were operating business experts in the areas of most interest to clients; the programs offered should be generally for cohort groups or cells rather than individuals, including online elements that are integral to the learning experience, but this online component was only mentioned as useful for pre and post program orientations; and finally that programs should be distinctive without being odd (pp.394-396).

From Scott Saslow's Chapter Two contribution to Dulworth and Bordonaro (2005, p. 25), some statistics have been reported about curriculum from a study comparing the 20 top performing firms out of a general pool of 240 candidate firms (in each case the higher and first number represents the practices of the top performing group of 20, followed by the same practices of the general pool):

- internal leadership training - 89 percent/39 percent

- developmental assignments – 79 percent/32 percent

- rotational assignments – 48 percent/17 percent

- external coaching – 47 percent/10 percent

A further comparison among the same firms was then made regarding CEOs active involvement in these training initiatives (p. 32):

- CEOs developing leadership talent – 92 percent/65 percent

- CEOs committing necessary resources – 92 percent/55 percent

- CEOs holding senior management accountable for developing leaders – 92 percent/45 percent

In summary, the 20 top performing firms used internal leadership training, developmental assignments, rotational assignments and external coaching as mainstays in their developmental programs significantly more than did the less well performing firms. Furthermore, CEOs of the 20 high performing firms were significantly more actively involved than the CEOs of the less well performing firms in developing talent, in committing necessary funds for that to happen, and in holding senior management accountable for developing that talent.

Harlan Cleveland is someone who knew a great deal about leadership and the formation of executives. Following the Second World War, he played a senior role in the Marshall Plan. In 1960, Dean Rusk asked him to coordinate actions taken among the 53 international organizations in which the United States was involved. This required him to coordinate, "from below", a trio of strong players that included Adlai Stevenson, Dean Rusk and President Kennedy. Cleveland was a Rhodes Scholar, US Ambassador to NATO, and dean of the Maxwell School of Citizenship. He was president of the University of Hawaii, director of International Affairs at the Aspen Institute, and founding dean of the University of Minnesota's Institute of Public Affairs. He was awarded an astounding 22 honourary degrees, and countless other awards, including a prestigious international one for "accomplished generalists" called the Prix de Talloires. He died last year, aged 90 years and was very active to the end. Cleveland (2002) stated that "Those of us who presume to take the lead in a democracy, where nobody is supposed to be in charge, seem to need an arsenal of eight attitudes indispensable to the management of complexity" (p. 7). Those attitudes are precisely the same ones that must be fostered, and then mastered, by senior executives in corporations - people who can also be considered as leaders in a democracy. As described by Cleveland, the eight pithy attitudes around which, in my view, an excellent executive learning curricula could be crafted are (pp. 7-8):

1. A lively intellectual curiosity, an interest in everything – because everything really is related to everything else, and therefore to what you're trying to do, whatever it is.

2. A genuine interest in what other people think, and why they think that way – which means you have to be at peace with yourself for a start.

3. A feeling of special responsibility for envisioning the future that's different from a straight-line projection of the present. Trends are not destiny.

4. A hunch that most risks are there not to be avoided but to be taken.

5. A mindset that crises are normal, tensions can be promising, and complexity is fun.

6. A realization that paranoia and self-pity are reserved for people who *don't* want to be leaders.

7. A sense of *personal* responsibility for the *general* outcome of your efforts.

8. A quality I call "unwarranted optimism" – the conviction that there must be some more upbeat outcome than would result from adding up all the available expert advice.

Some of Mintzberg's acerbic criticisms that follow from his article, "Leader to Leader" (1999) serve to continue this consideration about the kind of curricula to be included or excluded from executive learning programs:

- Shareholder Value: "This mercenary model of management is so antisocial that it will doom us if we don't doom it first" (p. 2).

- Empowerment: "Maybe the really healthy organizations empower their leaders, who in turn listen to what is going on and so look good" (p. 2).

- Leadership: "The white knight will ride in on his white horse and fix it all. Except that these knights mostly ride into territory they have never seen. (That's why they hire consultants)" (p. 3).

Dye, Kletter and McFarland (2006-2008, p. 3) talked about seven predominant types of what they referred to as "organizational DNA". The three that they described as basically working were the Just-in-Time, Military Precision, and Resilient DNAs. The four that did not work were the Fits-and-Starts, Over managed, Outgrown and Passive-Aggressive DNAs. Those responsible for executive curriculum would do well to consider these DNAs, and to consider building *how-to* and *how-not-to* curricula around them. There could, for instance, be all sorts of active group learning around simulations and role plays in this regard. One of the DNA types which deserves more scrutiny is the Passive-Aggressive behaviour prevalent in some firms, which Dye et al described as one that appears "so congenial as to seem conflict free, [and a] workplace where everyone agrees to change. But no one ever actually does. Building consensus to take action is easy at these companies; actually taking action, however, is next to impossible" (p. 2). One can easily see the potential here for a course or short executive program on Taking Action, or on Decision Making and Consensus that would be built around this idea of the dangers of a culture in which Passive-Aggressive DNA was festering.

Globalization and Internationalism

Just as Cleveland (2002) stated seven years ago, but which is ringing even truer now: "In today's disordered world, the collision of cultures with global trends is in evidence everywhere" (p. 77). The collision is happening among ethnicities, faiths, businesses, and professional groups with all their inward loyalties, in a world where populations have become much more mobile. People are coming together in new settings and are looking for cohesion, similarity and like-mindedness, but until that evolves, and as the global perspective increases, "acceptance of variety, the protection of diversity, and doctrines of tolerance [will be] more essential to security and survival" (p. 85).

As we will see in Chapter Six, many universities talk of being international or global, when what they really mean is that they have sales offices or satellite operations for learning in foreign countries. Whereas many have done excellent pioneering work in placing facilities and operating programs at various locations around the world, that is but one aspect of being international or having a global reach. Equally important is instilling the diversity that comes from having participants attend programs from all over the world, having curricula that reflects and digs into current global issues, and having an international faculty to facilitate or teach the courses. The combination of these factors is what makes for a collaborative and worldly learning atmosphere, in which one culture and narrow points of view cannot dominate.

Leonard-Barton (1995) spoke of globalization in terms of the drive of some innovative companies regarding "the quest to harness the skills of the world, wherever they may be found" (p. 216), and how new information technologies are making this increasingly possible. However, Kumar and Usunier (2004) stated that "Educators, consultants and trainers are grappling with identifying a set of critical skills that global managers need to possess" (p. 292); but that "it might very well be the case that on the content side the American business schools are not all that well globalized" (p. 296).

Mintzberg (1999) stated that, "Global coverage does not mean a global mind-set" (p.2), and went on to say that the closest thing to a global company he knew about was perhaps Royal Dutch Shell, most of whose senior management come from two countries – twice as many as almost any other company he could think of (but still a long way from the Red Cross Federation). Mintzberg's *impm*® (International Masters in Practicing Management) was created in 1996 and is offered jointly by McGill University, England's Lancaster University, Hitotsubashi University in Japan, the Indian Institute of Management, and INSEAD in France. Each class comprises around 40 participants from around the world, and each class spends time learning in those five countries. Now that is an international program!

Diversity

Winters (2009) interviewed 20 titans of business who together commanded revenues of $1 trillion and employed three million people. Each one of these leaders recognized diversity as a key driver of business success. She reported that these leaders "consistently define diversity as leveraging all talent in pursuit of business success" and quoted one of them as having said, "A group of diverse people with different backgrounds, experiences and leadership styles will out-think, out-innovate and out-execute a homogeneous group of people anytime" (p. 2). This might give us pause concerning the wisdom of some recruiting initiatives still often used to ensure the homogeneity of senior management teams as to their way of thinking, of doing things and generally of being, as they say "on the same page". It should also underscore the importance of including topics about diversity (its worth and its power) in executive program curricula.

It is important to note the obvious about diversity: although it comprises the expected issues such as inclusiveness where any marginalization of minorities might be occurring, it also comprises cognitive diversity regarding the ways in which people think, innovate or create, or the way they approach problem solving. This is highlighted nicely by George Halvorson, Kaiser Permanente's CEO, whom Winters (2009) interviewed for this study: That leader made radical changes in the demographic makeup of his senior team very quickly after assuming the top job, because it was not sufficiently diverse. Winters concluded her article with the statement that the magic of the CEOs who really understand and properly engage in these principles lies in their ability "to lead mammoth global enterprises while at the same time being prodigious stewards of diversity not only because it is the right thing to do but because they understand that diversity is a key driver of business success" (p. 4). Wheatley (1996) stated that "systems become healthier as they open to include greater variety" (p. 101).

Female/Male Diversity – a Case in Point

In the specific example of maintaining the female/male diversity in the workplace, Whitney and Packer (2000) suggested that things can go better for business when women work alongside men, and they imply that some of these "softer", female qualities can rub off on men in a positive way: "When women work alongside men in the marketplace, the chemistry changes. It's healthier, it's more alive, it makes more demands on us" (p. 129). Later these authors added that "Having women in the workforce makes a difference in the way business gets done; the power struggles are more complicated; dress codes loosen up; conversations have more variety; feelings have been known to be discussed" (p. 130). Harris (1993) talked about the differences between the networks created by upwardly mobile men and women when he stated that "men develop network relationships as a means to an end, whereas women see the relationship as an important end in itself" (p. 8). Harris concluded that what works for women in networking is different from what works for men, and he said that "Networking may take [a] woman to the top, but not if she copies the style of the guy in the office next door" (p. 9).

However, these positive benefits of men learning from women through osmosis are eclipsed whenever women suppress their natural tendencies. Senge (1999) talked about a case of a Shell executive who reported that "As a woman in a highly technical culture, I had been used to avoiding emotional situations, because I wanted to deflect any stereotype that I was 'soft' or 'flaky'" (p. 178). But after her transformation, this executive concluded: "But now, it felt very liberating to realize that I did not have to be tough to be effective" (p. 179).

Ferguson (1984) stated that in the experience of women, there is "a way of conceiving of the relation between the self and others that is neither purely self-interested nor purely altruistic and self-sacrificing. Rather, self and other are seen to be attached to and continuous with one another in important ways" (p. 25). She went on to state that women "pass judgments that are based more on contextual rather than on abstract criteria and that focus more on process than on outcome" (ibid.). However, Ferguson warned that "Women's acknowledgement of their need for others, while more honest than men's repressed affiliation, results in a great, sometimes too great, vulnerability" (ibid). But Ferguson also added the crucial point that the "dialectic between connectedness and vulnerability is an essential part of what it means to be a human being" (ibid).

Teaching and Learning

Clinebell and Clinebell (2008) have recommended that one of the new ways to help executives is to teach them how "to structure their thinking and, instead of training based on past decisions, [they are] educating students by providing a conceptual foundation that can be used to analyze a wide variety of future business problems" (p. 100). For instance, De Geus (1997) stated that "There is a considerable difference between companies that stared blindly at threat and opportunity and those that reacted and changed" (p. 25).

Gareth Morgan (2006) described effective managers and problem solvers as being "born rather than made and [having] a kind of magical power to understand and transform the situations they encounter" (p. 3). He described them as having "a capacity to remain open and flexible, suspending immediate judgments whenever possible, until a more comprehensive view of the situation emerges" (p. 4). This serves as a lesson or caution about curriculum development for executive level managers: There needs to be respect for that magical, innate knowledge that most of them likely already possess for their art. It is something to be recognized, honoured and promoted - possibly by enthusiastically aligning it to some of their own stories about doing their jobs, and to perhaps more grandiose descriptions of some of the more heroic and charismatic actions of leaders in history.

From Morgan's (2006) influence comes an understanding of the powerful tool of metaphor as a flexible instrument for reflection about modeling managerial behaviour – that is, the understanding of one element of experience in terms of another. Thus, a 'must-have' in executive curriculum would certainly be Morgan's idea of "becoming skilled in the art of using metaphor: to find fresh ways of seeing, understanding, and shaping the situations that we want to organize and manage" (p. 3).

In a similar vein, there is the possibility of tying leadership concepts to the beauty and poignancy of poetry or literature: For instance, some Shakespeare plays lend themselves very well to lessons about management and leadership. Henry V's speech to his troops prior to the Battle of Agincourt is one that has been often used. In fact, Lawrence Olivier's son has made the rounds in corporate America inspiring executives with Shakespearian prose. This golden connection between literature and organizational theory is also one promoted successfully by Irish poet and lecturer David Whyte, whose recordings and books are readily available, and whom I have witnessed in person delivering inspired lectures. Whyte has made quite a name for himself as a keynote speaker at corporate retreats and training events where he reads his own poetry and that of other famous writers, and where he talks about literature in relation to preservation of the soul in corporate America. Whyte (1994) stated "The corporation needs the poet's insight and powers of attention to weave the inner world of soul and creativity with the outer world of form and matter" (p. 9).

Tichy and Cardwell (2002) referred to the teaching organization as one in which "everyone is a teacher, everyone is a learner, and reciprocal teaching and learning are built into the fabric of everyday activities" (p. 7). They indicated that in such an organization the CEO must assume the role of head teacher, and must "set the direction, shape the culture and share the valuable insights in his or her head" (p. 7). This model of reciprocal teaching is the one that is recognizable in the best executive programs, where professors rejoice in an exchange with senior managers with whom they have a mutual respect and desire to learn; "where the teacher is also a learner and becomes smarter through interaction with the students" (p. 11). It is a model that Tichy put into practice with three executive levels at General Electric's Crontonville Corporate University. There, he helped lead the effort to transform that institution from a traditional one-way teaching infrastructure to his action-learning model, which he described as a "Virtuous Teaching Cycle". This same learning scenario was also envisioned by Wood (1995) who said: "We might see an educational workplace in which every one is a learner and teacher; where students are involved in developing their own curriculum" (p. 415).

Coaching and Mentoring

Coaching and mentoring are activities that are concerned with the transfer of knowledge about best practices, in a personalized learning framework. Leonard-Barton (1995) stated that, "Good coaching requires an appreciation of how knowledge is conveyed: that knowledge is often tacit – held in the head – " (p. 251), and generally cannot be transferred easily. Vicere and Fulmer (1996) reported that researchers found that few bosses were actually good teachers, but that "exposure to a variety of bosses could have a powerful, positive impact on individual leader's development" (p. 108). The authors mentioned that some organizations have inaugurated formal mentoring programs, implying that many had not; but that is was quite common for organizations to use "external mentors, often consultants or well-known university professors, to provide advice and support for senior leaders facing critical issues or challenges" (p. 108). Megginson (2003) has suggested that one of the drivers of mentoring as a development tool was the conflict that managers with coercive management styles found between the dictates of command and control: "Mentors were suggested as an alternative, and in many organizations they are proving a useful adjunct in the development process, but they are often too peripheral to take the central role" (p.93). Megginson added the important point that responsibility for development has moved inexorably to individuals themselves.

Jack Welch arrived late into an understanding of the power and multi-faceted uses of the internet. In a reversal of the standard mentoring model, in which experienced people coach the less experienced, Welch "asked" the top 500 leaders at General Electric to get Internet mentors, preferably under the age of 30, with whom they would work three to four hours per week. By early 2000, the program had been expanded to the top 3,000 managers in the company. "We even recruited a mentor for the board [the CEO of Sun Microsystems]", stated Welch (2001).

In research done about mentoring, Shepard (2003) found that "Eighty percent of the women surveyed view the role of mentors as protectors, rather than as agents of advancement [whereas] the majority of successful men...state that they make increasing use of their mentors to obtain plum assignments and further their careers" (p. 24).

"Until recently working with a coach was seen as a sign of weakness and as something being wrong with the executive" (p 379, Kets de Vries, 2007). Perhaps that misunderstanding relates to some interesting research and personal experience from Murphy (1995): He promoted the need in organizations to move from *managing* people to *coaching* them, but specifically stated that he did not mean coaching in the way organizations usually use that word, but rather in a manner that he referred to as "generative coaching" – a process that is both self-generating and self-correcting, along the lines of what Murphy correctly attributes to the double-loop and continuous learning process described in Chris Argyris' (1990) book *Overcoming*

Organizational Defenses. The principles of Generative Coaching include the relational qualities of mutual commitment, trust, respect and freedom of expression; a pragmatism about outcomes; a belief that both the coach and the coached are there for the learning; a recognition that individuals view the world from many different perspectives and that they are motivated differently; and that so-called techniques for dealing with people are manipulative and ineffective because they produce resistance.

Playing Games

War games are almost standard learning procedure in the military. Model "toys" are built at Royal Dutch Shell to simulate eventual oil platforms years before they are actually built. They may be toys and are referred to as such, but they are ones that have a very serious reason for being. "We know extremely well in business that play is the best method of learning" (de Geus, 1997, p. 65). Frank (1999) reported that, according to Dr. Mintzberg, we should all just relax a little, try new things, not worry about messy desks, get our hands dirty, and learn as we go. She quotes him as saying, "It is the playful who will inherit the earth" (p. 3). Margaret Wheatley in Wheatley and Kellner-Rogers (1996) devoted a whole chapter to "Organizing as Play". Wheatley stated that "Playful and creative enterprises are messy and redundant. Human thinking is accomplished by processes that are messy and redundant" (p. 23); and that "Playful enterprises are alert. They are open to information, always seeking more, yearning for surprises" (p. 25). Such playfulness in learning, in addition to being fun and being a catalyst to creativity, can often make us notice things that we otherwise might have missed through a more traditional educational approach.

Contrarian Views and Barriers to Executive Learning

The Profit Motive

De Geus (1997) said that "The twin policies of managing for profit and maximizing shareholder value, at the expense of all other goals, are vestigial management traditions" (p. 15). However, in the introduction to his famous book (and documentary), *The*

Corporation, Bakan (2004) stated "The corporation's legally defined mandate is to pursue, relentlessly and without exception, its own self-interest, regardless of the often harmful consequences it might cause to others" (p. 2). The opposite view of course is that "the basic principle of total ethical management is that organizations exist fundamentally to serve people – if not all of humanity – and not the other way around" (Mitroff, Mason and Pearson, 1994, p. 130).

Mainstream media often portray senior executives as being heartless, hard-nosed autocrats, for instance in such prime time television programs as *The Apprentice*, in which the highlight of each episode is usually when Donald Trump himself intones his "You're Fired!" sentencing. Even in Canada we now "enjoy" the *Dragon's Den*, in which viewers can witness ego-centric entrepreneurs aggressively competing with each other to get pieces of other people's good ideas, or delightedly to pulverize minions whose ideas are useless. (One has to wonder why the useless ideas ever make it into prime time). The point here is that executives are consistently portrayed at least as charlatans, but usually as much worse. It is an understandable portrayal given the horrendous criminal behaviour from a few business leaders who have cheated organizations and individuals out of billions of dollars, but it is an inaccurate portrayal when generalized. The executives I have met and interviewed all possessed healthy egos and were terribly busy to the point of being run off their feet, but they were intelligent and caring individuals who looked at far more than their own or their firm's bottom lines.

Even so, we need to be mindful of Kelly's (2001) warnings about what pressures are really at play in the minds of CEOs. She pointed out that whereas corporate boards may take aim against sweat shops, or even executive salaries that are too high, and business schools may teach ethical decision making, that is not the main influence in leaders' lives. Rather, "the prime force is *systemic pressure*" (p. 57). She added, for instance, that "Stockholder governance may be perfunctory. But make no mistake; stockholder power is very, very real" (p. 57). She stated that CEOs faced a clear choice: to pledge allegiance to shareholder value and become fabulously wealthy, or be fired.

The university executive programs that I have researched cannot be blamed for creating some of the monsters that have plagued investors lately, and have come close to ruining the worldwide financial system, although they could perhaps have offered more courses and short programs on ethics and pursuit of the common good. One has to ask however, just how offensive such courses might appear to ultra sensitive business communities that are reeling from concern and embarrassment about their tarnished reputations. Perhaps nobody cares about that sensitivity, but those courses simply will not be offered if they only serve to offend participants, and therefore do not attract sufficient enrolment.

Corporate Power

De Geus (1997) asked the question: "Should a CEO try to guide and steer a company as if it were at war?" (p. 190). To do so would be inappropriate for the operation of a living company: "It reduces the learning capacity of an organization"

Mintzberg (1983) said that, "to understand the behavior of the organization, it is necessary to understand which influences are present, what needs each seeks to fulfill in the organization, and how each is able to exercise power to fulfill them" (p. 334). In a book entitled *Who Really Matters*, Kleiner (2003) put forward the concept that every organization is continually acting to fulfill the perceived needs of its core group. That group usually comprises the CEO and his/her natural reporting team, along with a small number of linchpin thought and action leaders throughout the organization. Kleiner stated that "The influence of these key people trumps all other concerns, not because of some mystical resonance, but simply because of the cumulative effect of the decisions made throughout the organization" (p. 16). These supremely influential individuals are not just at the top of the bureaucracy, they dominate the company's culture. The author maintained that manoeuvring around and dealing with the power of core groups is something that we learn about all our lives: at school, socially, at work and at play. Kliner pointed out the paradox that the Core Group actually wields more influence in less hierarchical and more fluid organizations, in which, because *everyone* makes decisions, the core group becomes critically important to direct all this decision traffic. It stands to reason that if any major executive education initiatives are going to succeed, then they must have the enthusiastic buy-in from this core group. Consultants certainly realize this, probably a good deal more than do the universities, and they are experts at forging close relationships with an organization's core group. It is ironic that, in such a relationship, the consulting firm actually becomes a developer of core group talent, and in so doing actually becomes an insider, and perhaps a veritable member of the organization's "cabal".

One surprising exception to this theory, as pointed out by Kleiner (2003), happens in organizations where the CEO is often not even a member of the core group: He gives the University as the prime example of where such an aberration often can take place. This may explain why universities may not be quite as good as consultants in understanding the core group dynamics in the successful forging of relationships with major corporations.

Fads and Fashions

Micklethwait and Wooldridge (1996) have provided a scathing critique about what they consider to be the nonsense provided by so-called management gurus, in the form of the latest fads or fashions in management education. That critique portrayed management education as being in a high state of confusion and disarray, which has been fertile ground for charlatans to flourish, as they pepper surprisingly gullible corporations with a dizzying array of useless solutions to business challenges. The following quote describes a lack of direction, or lack of theoretical base in the structure of management programs:

> Management theory, according to the case against it, has four defects: it is constitutionally incapable of self-criticism; its terminology usually confuses rather than educates; it rarely rises above basic common sense; and it is faddish and bedeviled [sic] by contradictions that would not be allowed in more rigorous disciplines.

The implication is that management gurus are con artists, the witch doctors of our age, playing on business people's anxieties in order to sell snake oil. The gurus, many of whom have sprung suspiciously from "the great university of life" rather than any orthodox academic discipline, exist largely because people let them get away with it. Modern management theory is no more reliable than tribal medicine. Witch doctors, after all, often got it right – by luck, by instinct, or by trial and error. (p. 12)

Dr Henry Mintzberg of McGill University, arguably a management guru himself, has warned: "Beware of management gurus. While they seem to offer answers, the techniques they push are really just straws at which insecure managers can grasp" (Tema Frank, Frank Communications, 1999, http://temafrank.tripod.com/id31.htm).

Conclusion: A Summary Model of an Excellent Executive Learning Program

There are several model programs that one could look at as being exemplary, and worthy of emulating in setting up executive education programs. There are, for example, the well-known corporate Universities of large enterprises like Microsoft, McDonald's, Walt Disney, Boeing, and Motorola. There are some well-organized internal corporate learning programs, not considered corporate universities, but still very viable. At the end of Chapter Seven, in the personal unit of analysis which is my own experience at Domtar, I have described an example of such an internal program.

In concluding this literature review, I wish to outline some programs created by General Electric's Development Centre (university) at Crotonville, which stand out as a wonderful example of organizational learning. Learning at Crotonville epitomizes many of the principles of excellence that are outlined here in the review of literature, that are evidenced in the data gathered and analyzed in Chapters Five, Six, and Seven and that eventually found their way into the conclusions and recommendations in the final chapter of this dissertation. What follows is a synopsis of Chapter 12 in Jack Welch's book, *Straight from the gut* (2001):

At a very difficult time economically and just before being named chairman-elect in 1981, Jack Welch decided that the corporation's 52-acre development campus at Crotonville needed to be upgraded in order to act as a major catalyst in radically changing the company – a change which would require an undiluted connection with managers deep into the organization. The facilities were ancient, and so was the learning methodology with its old-fashioned principles of Plan-Organize-Integrate-Measure (POIM). Everything was renewed: the curricula evolved from using case studies about other organizations to action-learning projects on current GE issues. Indeed, curricula became so action-oriented that, as Welch (2001) himself stated, "they turned students into in-house consultants to top management..., [but they also] built cross-business friendships that could last a lifetime" (p. 174).

There were three programs – called courses - created for what we could call executive levels that focused on leadership: the EDC (executive development course) which ran once per year for 35 to 50 of the highest potential managers; the BMC (business management course) which ran three times per year for 60 mid-level managers per class; and the MDC (management development course) which ran eight times per year for a total of 500 fast-trackers early in their careers. Borrowing from the Pepsi model, which Welch admired, he decided that every member of his leadership team should teach a session, and twenty years later, 85 percent of the faculty were GE leaders. Fairly early on in this transformation, Welch enthusiastically reported that Crotonville had become "an energy centre, powering the exchange of ideas" (p. 176).

Welch spent an extraordinary amount of his precious time there – once or twice a month for a couple of hours: "When all is said and done, teaching is what I do for a living.... I never lectured. I loved the wide-open exchanges. The students taught me as much as

I taught them" (p. 176). Prior to the MDC class, Welch would send out a hand-written note to participants about issues he would like them to consider before his session with them. These were generally about the competition, local business unit frustrations that he might help them with, what they did not like about their career that they would like to see changed, and how to accelerate the quality initiative in their particular areas. Welch also received feedback from participants in every class a few days after completion, and he read every one of them. The participants had been asked to respond to three questions:

- What did you find about the presentation that was constructive and clarifying?

- What did you find confusing and troublesome?

- What do you regard as your most important take-away?

Welch tried to respond personally to any feedback sheets that were signed. All constructive feedback was used to improve upon the quality of the courses.

The challenge then became how to get all the good exchanges and ideas and enthusiasm generated during the courses at Crotonville back into the workplace, and past the human roadblocks of nay-sayers that were hidden deep in the organization. Welch's answer to this was what he referred to as "a GE game-changer called Work-Out" (p. 182). It was usually a two or a three-day session for groups of 40 to 100 employees, which was patterned after the New England town meeting, and it literally meant "taking work out of the system". During these sessions managers had to make on the spot decisions that were brought forward by participants, or agree to deal with them in a specifically timely fashion – much like what is described in Chapter Seven about how Domtar used the Kaïzen.

By mid 1992, more than 200,000 GE employees had been involved in Work-Outs which, as Welch proudly explained, was an idea that had been hatched at Crotonville, and one that had "helped us create a culture where everyone began playing a part, where everyone's ideas began to count, and where leaders led rather than controlled. They coached - rather than preached – and they got better results" (p. 184). Employees at all levels including the senior group reporting directly to Welch had to espouse the action-learning principles at Crotonville and personified by Work-Out, or they were invited to leave the company.

As the discerning reader has realized from the major sections of this literature review, and as she/he will discover in subsequent chapters of this dissertation, the principles espoused in this General Electric learning model case are exactly the ones required to make executive learning and overall organizational learning a success.

Chapter Three –
Theoretical Framework(S)

Introduction

My decision to devote a whole chapter of the dissertation to the theoretical framework is an invitation to the reader to consider this both as a continuation of the literature review, and as an integral part of the research findings themselves. The wisdom of Alfred North Whitehead (ANW) – educator, philosopher, scientist – is a model for us to follow when we consider and discuss how to inspire people in their learning, and how to encourage them to take responsibility for their own education.

This chapter will focus on outlining Alfred North Whitehead's liberal and startlingly current philosophy of education, hailing from the early 1900s. It is one that is most appropriate to inspire a flexible mindset for my research into executive learning. Executive education is growing in importance as reflected by the huge funds spent on it annually, as reported in the previous two chapters. Yet, as described in the literature review, it is in a constant state of flux, and has not settled down to anything resembling what some refer to as the more mature subjects taught at universities. The pragmatism, mixed with the reasonableness and lack of rigidity of Whitehead's educational ideas still have the clout to nudge learning and teaching in the right direction.

Four other theoretical frameworks or models were considered but not chosen for this research, and they will be briefly described at the end of the chapter.

Theoretical Frameworks

Bailey (1997) underscored the responsibility and discipline required for good research when she stated that no study "can be conducted without an underlying theory or model" (p. 135). Bettis and Mills (2006) warned that such frameworks are not, however, supposed to be straightjackets into which data is stuffed and bound (p. 68). This play between being grounded in theory, while at the same time maintaining flexibility to make discoveries, was a principal consideration in choosing Whitehead as my theoretical guide.

The more rigid frameworks, which will be briefly overviewed later, such as Bourdieu's *habitus and field* theories, Royal Dutch Shell's *Scenario Planning* model, Senge's *Five Disciplines*, and the concept of *Communities of Practice* were all tempting alternatives considered for this research. Each one of those theories had a close relationship to executive learning and education programs, but each one would have led me as researcher and the 14 executives whom I interviewed down too narrow a path of discovery. Indeed, Whitehead would have surely agreed that those theories were too precise for my audience, which comprised very experienced senior practitioners who operate best at the general level; or, to use the business expression, at the 35,000 foot level.

Kearney and Hyle (2006) said that theoretical frameworks should be chosen late in the research process; that "the qualitative purists believe that notions flow only from the data and analysis is done with a completely open mind" (p. 125). However, I chose Whitehead early on, following a serious flirtation with some of French sociologist Pierre Bourdieu's ideas. I steeped myself in reading about Whitehead and his theories, and my candidacy paper, on which I was examined orally, was entitled "Alfred North Whitehead's Concept of *The Rhythm of Education* and its Application in Executive Learning".

Dr. Alfred North Whitehead

Introduction

Dr. Alfred North Whitehead's philosophy of education is closely aligned with his process philosophy: an organic worldview of holistic connectivity between humankind and Nature. One of the main elements of that educational philosophy is the cyclical teaching and learning model he named the *rhythm of education*, which contains three specific stages: romance, precision and generalization. Whitehead was a staunch promoter of including vocational and professional education within the hallowed halls of traditional universities. He was especially keen on Harvard Business School being an integral part of Harvard University, where he taught in the philosophy department. Whitehead had a favourable opinion about business education, and about the leadership role that entrepreneurialism could and should play in the world. This friendliness towards business, combined with the excellence of his educational views - seemingly even more appropriate today than they were a century ago – are the theoretical catalysts for this research into executive education and learning. Some general connections between Whitehead's educational philosophy and executive education will be presented in this chapter. Just how the executive learning portrayed in the executive interviews, in the review of nine universities and in my own experience can be made to jibe with the principal tenets of Dr. Whitehead's educational thought will be approached at the beginning of Chapter Eight.

Relationship of Whitehead's Educational Philosophy to this Research

The educational philosophy Alfred North Whitehead (ANW) mostly addresses learning from childhood through adolescent and young adult years. Dr. Whitehead was writing about this learning spectrum when it typically spanned, in one continuous flow, the formal educational settings from elementary schooling through graduate work at university. At that time, there were usually no breaks between secondary and post secondary, or between undergraduate and postgraduate learning. The freshness, insight and relevancy of Whitehead's educational philosophy are, however, timeless and they apply equally well to any age group. That philosophy therefore fits within the modern contexts of adult education and lifelong learning. I am proposing that it is also pertinent to organizational learning, and would be especially helpful in enhancing executive education.

Dr. Whitehead, in a third career starting at the age of 63, taught at Harvard University, in the Philosophy department. Russell (1956) mentioned that "In England, Whitehead was regarded only as a mathematician, and it was left to America to discover him as a philosopher" (p. 93). Whitehead had an affinity and an affection for the good work and relevancy of Harvard Business School to the activities going on outside it. He once referred to that School as being founded "on a scale amounting to magnificence" (1932/1959, p. 137). He respected and understood commerce, economics and entrepreneurialism as powerful drivers in society, and implied that there should and could be a symbiotic relationship between universities and businesses.

The obsession of modern business firms with relevancy in their educational and training programs is in lock-step with an important part of Whitehead's educational philosophy: namely, that in the curriculum there must be a continuous intermingling of theory with practice. Whitehead complained that the tendency to segregate universities from the real world of practical affairs is a recent development, and commented that the great medieval universities did not make that mistake.

Personal and Professional Contexts of Whitehead's Educational Philosophy

Winchester (2005) referred to Whitehead as "one of the most comprehensive and original of 20th century thinkers on education" (p. 1). Woodhouse (1995) stated, "For too long, philosophers and educationalists alike have undervalued the work of Alfred North Whitehead" (p. 341). Griffen (1995) went so far as to state that "we should aim at nothing less than getting Whiteheadian process thought accepted as the basis for the general worldview of the 21st century" (p. 3), and that it would have a far greater chance of being accepted by the scientific community in the coming decades, than it had in the past (p. 4). University of Exeter professor, Jack Priestly (2000), stated: "Whitehead is a supreme example of that rarity in academic life, an intellectual who does not over-value the intellect but, nevertheless, regards its optimum development as a duty if not necessarily a privilege" (p. 130).

Given these accolades and the obvious impressiveness of ANW's writing about education, it may be difficult to understand why he was not more appreciated in his own time, as well as why his work has not been adopted in a specific way for any learning curriculum. According to Dunkel (1965), Whitehead never set himself up as a philosopher of education. Dunkel referred to Whitehead's writings on education as scattered essays, and said, "he never presented his educational ideas in one organized, coherent statement" (p. 9). Griffen (1995) pointed out that Whitehead's unabashedly metaphysical philosophy, and the kind of speculation that it entails, came on stream just as a strongly anti-metaphysical atmosphere was about to settle on the Western academic landscape. As a result of that, he stated that Whitehead "was less embraced or rejected than simply ignored" (p. 1).

Whitehead was a scientist and a physicist, but also enjoyed a classical education that saw him specializing in Latin, Greek, and mathematics – a type of education typical of his era. He co-wrote *Principia Mathematica* with his famous student, Bertrand Russell, and Whitehead once offered a serious alternative to Einstein's Theory of Relativity. Hendley (1986) spoke of Russell's own characterization of Whitehead as being more tolerant, patient, accurate, and careful than he was, but also more complicated. According to Hartshorne (1954), Whitehead once said of Russell: "Bertie says that I am muddle-headed; but I say that he is simple minded" (p. 60). This exchange, often considered mere banter between these intellectual giants, was actually grounded in their philosophical attitudes: Russell being of the minimalistic or positivist mindset, and Whitehead being of the maximalistic, speculative or metaphysical point of view. The one type insisted on trying to dispel confusion and illusion, while the other espoused ambiguity and made room for all interpretations. Hartshorne explained that to men of the Russell type, the Whiteheads always appear muddle-headed, just as to men of the Whitehead type the Russells appear simple-minded. It is amazing that these two men ever managed to write a major book together, being of such different philosophical persuasions.

Professor Whitehead taught at his alma mater, Trinity College Cambridge, the University of London, and at Harvard. In addition to Russell, Whitehead credits his wife, Evelyn Wade, with having had a profound effect on the development of his outlook on the world, and of being an essential factor in his philosophical output. As reported by Hendley (1986), Whitehead said of his wife that "her vivid life has taught me that beauty, moral and aesthetic, is the aim of existence; and that kindness, and love, and artistic satisfaction are among its modes of attainment" (p. 77). Hendley repeated the charming personal story that "Russell, although often faced with financial problems of his own, surreptitiously lent Evelyn Whitehead money from time to time to help pay for bills that Whitehead would run up but not be able to settle" (ibid).

Whitehead's organic worldview, surely born of his dual philosophical/scientific background, explains how his process philosophy seems so inextricably linked to his educational philosophy. As a philosopher/scientist, he seems to have had no trouble seeing a strong and necessary connection between, for example, sub-atomic particles (or "actual entities", as ANW preferred to call them) having "intentions" or relationships about other particles, and the human species whose members harbour emotional or romantic feelings for each other. Whitehead believed that relationship and interconnectedness are internal properties of actual entities; not external behaviours of them. This applies to people as well: They *are* their relationships with the universe, and they are not separate from them.

This appreciation of the human condition, and its connection and similarity with the rest of the universe translates into an equally holistic philosophy of education. This philosophy insists that we maintain a sense of being a part of a very real natural world. In that respect, Brumbaugh (1982) considered that Whitehead's most important contribution to educational theory was his insistence that any sound educational method include a dimension of concreteness (p. 80). Whitehead's philosophy of education thus follows quite naturally from his process theory in science. In that theory, according to Doll's (2003) conference paper: reality, for Whitehead, "is not made up of material stuff but is… an interactive process between mind and nature" (p. 4).

At this conference, Doll described Whitehead's criticism of our exaggerated emphasis in education on the factual, which has had devastating effects on educational, social and political arenas. Whitehead believed that this overemphasis on things factual overlooks "our human ability to deal with brute facts in a contextualized, imaginative, playful manner" (Doll, 2003, p. 5) – an oversight, which Whitehead referred to as "one-eyed reason".

Most people, children as well as adults, are capable of such contextualizing in imaginative and playful ways. In refuting the idea that childhood learning was merely an embryonic form of adult learning, Egan (2002), who often supported and cited Whitehead's educational ideas, stated in a similar vein: "In terms of simple intellectual energy and imaginative productivity, the average five-year-old leaves the average adult limp with exhaustion" (p. 93). Whitehead believed, as did Egan much later, that postponement of difficulty in childhood education (e.g. basic algebra) is not the answer to navigating the maze of educational practice. The implication here, in my appreciation of it, is for similar imaginative practices from fruitful moments of childhood learning to be brought, later in life, into play (literally), as foils against mere fact-based learning – learning, which Whitehead often described as being "inert".

Highlights of Whitehead's Philosophy in Education

Whitehead's expectations about good educational practice assume a learning process that will incorporate the joy of discovery, the practice of active and fresh thought, and through which learners will become much more than merely well informed. An educational process of the excellent standard of ANW's *rhythm of education* is such a process, and it will permit learners to acquire the art of using knowledge. One of Whitehead's recurring themes is that "education is not a process of packing articles into a trunk" (1932/1959, p. 51). Good educational behaviour means utilizing active thought rather than inert thought. Active thought comprises, for example, the evoking of curiosity, judgment, and the ability to master a complicated tangle of circumstances. Surely this type of expertise in complexity is precisely what is needed as part of an executive education program.

The required cohesive thread running through the various elements that make up an effective learning (and teaching) package is relatedness or connectivity between the individual and the world, or in more Whiteheadian terms, between the individual and Nature. This holistic view is also well known in Eastern sacred writings and teaching. For example, J. Krishnamurti talked about this view repeatedly, in his contention that *you are the world, and the world is you; If you want to change the world, you must first change yourself.* David Bohm, the famous physicist, as well as friend and frequent dialogue partner of Krishnamurti, was yet another great thinker to have addressed this fact of relatedness. He also addressed its antithesis: a certain false way of thinking, of "breaking things up, which are not really separate" (Bohm, 1996, p. 49). He discussed these issues in his writings about the art of dialogue, in recordings of his actual dialogues with Krishnamurti and others, and in his work as a physicist.

Whitehead's Rhythm of Education

A Cyclical and Continual Process

Hendley (1986) referred to Whitehead's *Rhythm of Education* as his most famous contribution to educational thought: namely, "the idea that learning [and teaching] is best accomplished if it proceeds through a rhythmic cycle of stages of romance, precision, and generalization" (p. 95). He added that this is exactly what unfolds in the things we learn naturally. The implication is for this natural learning cycle to be harnessed into a process that parallels human growth. The stages of this rhythmic process comprise **romance** that keeps learning from becoming inert; **precision** that permits the gathering and ordering of facts and knowledge; and **generalization** that synthesizes and generates a balance between opposites, which is similar to wisdom. Woodhouse (1999) was quoting Whitehead when he explained that the aim in this process is to achieve a "balance between the abstract and the concrete, the general and the particular, the theoretical and the practical, the formal and the romantic that keeps knowledge alive" (p. 193) – in short, "a balanced and inclusive understanding of reality" (p. 196).

Midst all these accolades about ANW's magnificent philosophy, a contrarian view deserves to be mentioned: Allan (2005) wrote a chapter about how Whitehead's three rhythmic stages of education are related to his overall metaphysics. Allan criticized Whitehead's famous work about the *rhythm of education* for merely comprising two essays contained in *Aims of Education* (chapters two and three), and running only a total of 26 pages. Allan then proceeded to write 30 pages about one aspect of it. He implies that too much fuss has been made over such a short piece:

> Romance, precision and generaliz-
> ation. They are Whiteheadian notions
> that have taken on a significance all
> out of proportion to the few oracular
> pages in which they are discussed. I
> suspect that this disproportionate in-
> terest is a function of their vagueness,
> their utility as a way to name a wide
> variety of views about the dynamics
> of learning, especially for those who
> rightly reject the excessively modular
> and non-holistic ways in which con-
> temporary lesson plans, courses, and
> curricula are designed. (p. 60)

To me, this is like illogically saying that the "oracle of Omaha", Warren Buffet, is not worth too much attention because, despite his obvious and remarkable success in business, he has written very little about it, and therefore the little he has written is somehow of less consequence.

It is true that, compared to the vast amount of written work Whitehead has completed in other realms (including process philosophy, science and mathematics), the body of his work that deals with education is relatively small. However, my belief is that Whitehead's contribution to education is ultimately of immense value for its freshness, and its potential to be applied to every learning process; and hence, indeed, my choice of it as the theoretical framework for this research into executive learning. Whitehead surely needed to get on with other issues and work of great importance to his own interests and scientific research. In my view, he seems to want us to take his ideas about education, and to use them as the basis or foundation for developing our own ideas around them – the very thing a theoretical framework is supposed to do. He wants us to do some of this development work ourselves, so that we actually learn something in the process. There is certainly enough about education in ANW's writings (and a great deal more material by others about those writings) to provide us, as Whitehead himself might have said, with a lure to engage us into continuing on our own.

Hendley (1976) provided a good rendition of the rhythmic pattern in education, when he described Whitehead as having held that we learn best, and most naturally, "when we start out with an exciting awareness of possibilities that leads to our eagerly seeking greater precision, to be used to attain a fuller understanding that in turn reveals still more exciting possibilities" (p. 310). Essentially this process is one, as Hendley said, of taking the pieces apart, examining and testing each, rejecting some and accepting others, and then returning to the task of putting them back together into some kind of comprehensive whole (p. 312). It is in putting the pieces back together that we face the greatest challenge. Good teachers and energetic pupils can acquire the romance excitement necessary to start the journey, and they can fairly easily understand and even enjoy acquiring the specific skills and learning the details, rules and strategies of the game. However, synthesizing all this detail into the broader view usually only comes with experience, and therein lies the challenge for the lay practitioner.

Whitehead's *rhythm of education* applies to both teaching and learning. He applied this rhythm to understanding the unfolding of a young person's learning through school and university. Although one stage is individually emphasized in each educational period, they are also all experienced as a trio in each stage. They tend to overlap in an organic, rather than in a distinct or linear fashion. Thus students, having already been lured into learning during the romance stage, and practised in managing facts during the precision stage, can then learn to apply the particular to the general in the third stage.

In my view, these cycles are forever with us, throughout our lifelong learning, and not only during the relatively brief period of formal educational. Each stage builds upon the others in a synergetic way, and there are constant overlaps. The learning benefits inherent in each specific stage can surely be harnessed into correcting, improving, embellishing and generally making all learning experiences more useful for all curricula (even for personal enhancement), at any period in one's life. Even though Whitehead seemed to be corralling his rhythms into the schooling years, he did refer to one's whole life as periodic, and therefore invites an interpretation of his rhythms as applicable to the whole of one's learning life. The manner in which these rhythms are recognized and are acted upon, will surely depend on individual, personal factors to do with experience, personality, age and the acquiring of wisdom. It will also require teachers, who can encourage, guide, understand, and facilitate students' learning progress through these stages.

The need for an improvement in the learning process is particularly crucial in the current era, in which people have large gaps of time among the different phases of formal bouts of learning, and in the face of so much information being available at our fingertips. We need to maintain a romantic stance of wonderment about what we learn: to be precise in deciphering all that is being thrown at us, in order to separate the wheat from the chaff, and the sublime from the ridiculous; and then to be able to consolidate and apply the material we have learned to the life we are living.

The Stage of Romance

According to Brumbaugh (1982): "When Whitehead argued that learning must begin with a stage of romance, he was agreeing with Plato that education is pointless without initial motivation" (p. 108). Like Whitehead, Brumbaugh was describing motivation as a feeling of romance that flares up when one learns something, resulting in "a kind of satisfaction, of completeness, to the experience" (p. 76). This stage is an uncluttered one, full of freedom and excitement to explore. It is one of romantic emotion, which according to Whitehead (1932/1959), is essentially the excitement that happens during the "transition from the bare facts to the first realisations of the import of their unexplored relationships" (p. 28). Nunn (1945) stated similarly, and before Whitehead did, that the first step in teaching any subject should be "to lay the firm foundations of a love, by so presenting it as to tempt the pupil to a joyous pursuit" (p. 185).

Instilling, encouraging, refreshing, and rejuvenating the zest or passion for a subject - in other words, effectively leading and managing the romance stage of learning - requires excellence in teaching. This calls for teachers-as-performers: those who lead by example in generously displaying their own passion for a subject; who guide students just enough to make them want to take the next step, and to begin to discover a solution on their own. Such excellent teachers are those who help students recover from their mistakes; who point rather than show the way; and who appear to leave the work of discovery up to the learners, but who join them on their journey, even if that journey seems to be going in the wrong direction for a while.

In my experience, teachers of this ilk stand out like heroes. In some instances, they have been guides of mythical proportions, whose work I have read, and who have inspired me in a secondary way. Whitehead was apparently such a teacher, according to talented former students. His famous pupil, Bertrand Russell (1956) referred to him as "extraordinarily perfect as a teacher" (p. 97). Woodhouse (1999) cited F. H. Page's paper, *A. N. Whitehead: A Pupil's Tribute*, about ANW's cheerfulness, good humour, almost child-like simplicity that seemed at odds with his towering intellect. Students felt glad to attend his lectures, because he himself was glad to be there. Page is also said to have commented on Whitehead's great abilities to inspire, and to show students how it was possible to unify their otherwise fragmented lives. In being an excellent, respectful and respected teacher (and university administrator), Whitehead proved that he was not just interested in the concept of marrying theory with practice, but also in demonstrating it.

Another of Whitehead's students, Paul Weiss (1980) stated in an interview that "Whitehead more or less lectured, not in a coherent fashion, sometimes losing his place. After many hesitations, all would suddenly come together. He would often say exceptionally brilliant things". Later in that same interview, Weiss added that Whitehead "would be set off by your questions in a direction that was not very clear, but eventually by a process of trial and error would come to answers that were, I thought, exceptionally profound and revealing and would throw the whole discussion in a new light". Weiss referred to Whitehead's non traditional approach as one that came at questions with a kind of "sophisticated innocence", and that there was therefore a novel freshness to his illustrations.

The Stage of Precision

Hendley (1976) stated that the precision stage is one of organizing and interpreting, of analyzing and using rules, and that "precision should equip us to master details in order to shed them in favor of general principles" (p. 311). He warned, like Plato, that during this period the young would be tempted to treat argument as a form of sport, solely for the purpose of contradiction. Whitehead (1932/1959) said that this was "the stage of grammar, the grammar of language and the grammar of science" (p. 29).

During the period of precision, we learn what to do with facts and other learning material: gathering it, acquiring it, ordering it, shuffling it and dealing it out; poking at it, saving it; personalizing it, making it active, and interesting. Perhaps we keep a secret diary or journal, and lists of things. Dunkel (1965) mentioned the importance of using the correct sequence among the rhythmic stages: having the precision stage occur in proper sequence, after the stage of romance and before the generalization stage. Whitehead believed that when discipline is not preceded by romance, the result is generally "inert knowledge without initiative"; and that if precision is not succeeded by the generalization stage, then "the knowledge remains inert and unutilized" (Dunkel, p. 111).

The Stage of Generalization

Whitehead referred to this as a final stage similar to Hegel's synthesis (preceded, in Hegel, by thesis and anti-thesis). It has also been variously referred to as the stage of knowing or of satisfaction. Brumbaugh (1982) put it this way: "The outcome of successful teaching is the student's seeing as an interesting single whole the qualitative and structural details he or she has examined one by one" (p. 117). In this stage of synthesis, we have thrown away the rulebook, and the notebooks of our labours, and we reflect on what we have learned so far. Occasionally, we become almost magically able to synthesize to the point of alchemy. We make discoveries and breakthroughs that spur us on to starting the process all over again. This third stage is one in which we are finally able to see patterns, connections and relationships – the stuff of Systems Thinking. It is from this stage of generalization that one can view the whole process and enhance one's understanding of it.

Summary Thoughts About The Rhythm of Education

Use of this learning model should teach us to be able to refresh our own zest for certain subjects, ideas, or pursuits. Being able to recharge the batteries of passion and interest in learning is the key to a real educational skill, and one that, once acquired, will remain forever. It is this skill of the passionate that can stave off boredom, learn a new career, love life and even to prepare for death. The greatest learners are surely the ones who can do this. They are quite noticeable: They are the ones with broad interests. They are intelligent, wise, visibly optimistic, appear childish at times; and one wants to be around them.

There may be an hierarchical stigma about the three stages in the process, despite the recognition that they are cyclical and overlapping. This results from our natural stage-like thinking, but also from Whitehead's own wording. He talked, for example, about generalization being "the fruition which has been the goal of the precise training.... the final success" (1932/1959, p. 30). It might therefore appear that the ultimate aim of this rhythmic learning is to achieve the overall view of generalization in stage three, so often referred to as the "final" stage, even by Whitehead himself; that the romance of stage one is child's play by comparison, and that the precision of stage two is merely the boot camp one must attend in order to graduate. That is simply not the case, in my view. Surely the proper unfolding of the three stages is more valuable in the process it provides, than in the destination that can be reached. The whole process represents a total learning package that needs to be appreciated by both teachers and learners. Furthermore, students consistently and continuously find themselves at different stages in this rhythmic process. One can therefore theorize that this diversity, if properly used within the student body, could be a boon to learning in lending helping hands to fellow learners, as they move at their own pace among the stages of their individual adventures.

These stages, as well as an appreciation of them, can be taught by good teachers and can be learned by motivated students, who put them into practice on a continuous basis – not only in their formal schooling or at their places of work, but throughout their entire lives. This will result in people living more vibrant lives, not just in improving their "performance".

Whitehead's Views on Professional and Vocational Training

Introduction

The business friendliness of Whitehead's educational philosophy, and his *rhythm of education* process includes Whitehead's understanding of the influence of commerce on society; his respect for the excellence of some business Schools, especially Harvard; his obsession with the need to marry knowledge with experience, and theory with practice; his preoccupation with freshness, zest, innovation, and imagination as partners in learning; and his general appreciation of the dichotomies of discipline/freedom, the concrete/the abstract, and focus/playfulness: In my experience, these understandings would all be considered jewels of current and future thinking in management learning.

Whitehead stated in his essay on *Universities and their Function* that the novelty of business schools must not be exaggerated, and he disagreed with a commonly held view when he said that "at no time have universities been restricted to pure abstract learning" (1932/1959, p. 137). This characterization of professional education fits well with Whitehead's general philosophy of education, and with his *rhythm of education* as a tool to implement it.

In this same essay, Whitehead (1932/1959) stated that the way in which a university should operate "in the preparation for an intellectual career, such as modern business or one of the older professions, is by promoting the imaginative consideration of the various general principles underlying that career" (p. 144). In

Whitehead's (1947/1968) essay on *Memories*, he described a small group of advisors to Queen Victoria, who dealt with some difficult situations. He stated that this ability belongs "to the art of preventing minor difficulties from growing into great crises" (p. 19). Learning this ability would indeed be a worthy addition to any executive learning curriculum.

The Harvard Business School Address and The Gifford Lectures

On Foresight, was Whitehead's famous address to the Harvard Business School (c. 1928). It was included as chapter six in ANW's *Adventures of Ideas* (1933/1956), and it was also used by the Dean of that school, Brett Donham, in the introduction to his own book, *Business Adrift* (1931). In this commencement address, Whitehead said: "We must not fall into the fallacy of thinking of the business world in abstraction from the rest of the community", of which it is one main part (Donham, p. xxvii). ANW also implied a warning about narrow-mindedness regarding "our conception of the reliable business man [sic], who has mastered a technique and never looks beyond his contracted horizon" (p. xix).

In this same address (Donham, 1931) Whitehead featured certain characteristics of the modern business mentality including "the habit of transforming observation of qualitative changes into quantitative estimates" and "an unspecialized aptitude for eliciting generalizations from particulars and for seeing the divergent illustration of generalities in diverse circumstances" (p. xxvi). Whitehead praised these aspects of the business mentality, but also thought that they needed to be fostered and learned in close proximity to the real world.

Nevertheless, there are some warning lights in attempting to bring together an educational philosophy that is principally academically or theoretically driven, with one that is principally practice or practically driven. In this respect, we should take note of the contention in Whitehead's Gifford lectures (1929/1978), delivered at the University of Edinburgh, that "the paradox which wrecks so many promising theories of education is that the training which produces skill is so very apt to stifle imaginative zest" (p. 338). Perhaps even more pertinent and controversial is his statement made in 1929 that still may hold true even today, that business school curriculum compared to most other mainstream university curricula, is still in the experimental stage. Possibly slightly less experimental now, it is still considered by some to be on the outskirts of traditional academia.

Whitehead's respect for business schools, and their importance to society, in no way meant those universities should be run like businesses or as businesses. He clearly stated that they each had distinctive characteristics, and those distinctive characteristics are the ones we must remember when applying Whitehead's philosophy about education to management learning. Even so, we must not be too cautious in using the basic principles of his educational philosophy, including those of his *rhythm of education*, in creating a novel, useful and engaging curriculum for executives, which will enhance their learning, their practice and their lives.

The Great Whitehead/Hutchins Debate

Whitehead (1947/1968) continued to view professional and vocational training in a favourable light in his essay *Harvard: The Future*, originally published in *The Atlantic* in September 1936. This essay is especially compelling in its favourable view about vocational and professional training being included in a university setting, thanks to the opposite view having been provided so energetically, two months later in that same journal, by Robert Hutchins, then president of the University of Chicago. The battle emphasized the academically hated and feared corporatization of universities, due to the incursion of entities such as Business Schools.

The controversy was further elucidated by Woodhouse (2000) in his excellent essay *The Seduction of the Market: Whitehead, Hutchins, and the Harvard Business School*, in which Woodhouse mostly took the Hutchins side. He did this partly because, like so many academics, he seemed truly to believe that the corporate interest often could behave like a Trojan horse within the walls of academia. He also criticized Whitehead's apparent contradiction in having said, on the one hand, that Harvard Business School was a boon to the University in providing a closer connection with the outside world than universities normally had (but in fact always used to have in ancient times); and having said, on the other hand, that such incursions were a clear and serious danger to the independent operation of a university. In my view, both of these factors need to be plainly present in dealing with this issue, and it is a strength of Whitehead's argument to have recognized both of them; not a weakness. It is typical of Whitehead to hold two such opposing views, and the simple appreciation of Whitehead's dialectic style of presenting opposite views in logical argumentation is surely all that is needed to explain any apparent contradiction in this respect.

My own take on this controversial issue of academic corporatization is that there is little wrong, and a great deal right, about having a closer contact established between a university and the outside world. Whitehead staunchly and consistently talked in his process philosophy, and in his educational philosophy, about the need for relevancy and connectivity: between the individual and nature, between the institution and the world, between theory and practice. His admonition about keeping knowledge alive, and preventing it from becoming inert (the central problem in education according to ANW), about maintaining a zest for learning, about the fatal dangers of a "disconnection of subjects" within the curriculum – all of these go to this issue of connection with the rest of the world. In *The Study of the Past – Its Uses and its Dangers*, Whitehead (1947/1968) stated that "the sharp distinction between institutions devoted to abstract knowledge [such as universities] and those devoted to application [such as business corporations]… is a mistake" (p. 164).

In the essay *Harvard: The Future*, Whitehead (1947/1968) specifically promoted the relevancy that could occur when reason and learned orthodoxy team up with real life. He described this beneficial alliance as one that is gained "by the absorption into the university of those schools of vocational training for which systemized understanding has importance. These are the professional schools which should fuse closely with the more theoretical side of university work" (p. 220).

The Lowell Lectures

Whitehead's eight Lowell Lectures, from which the following series of quotations come, were delivered in February 1925, and were then published in his book, *Science and the Modern World* (1925/1967).

Chapter 13, "Requisites for Social Progress" (pp.193-208), contains many of the author's ideas about vocational and professional training, in which the objective is "immediate apprehension with the minimum of eviscerating analysis". The thrust of this lecture is that effective knowledge is specialized, professionalized knowledge, which is supported by a limited acquaintance with other, somewhat related subjects. Whitehead pointed out that the danger here is that this produces "minds in a groove", and that "there is no groove of abstractions which is adequate for the comprehension of human life". This, likely music to corporate ears, demonstrates his commitment to (professional) learning as one that, although specialized, needs to be connected to the real world, and must not become "too bookish".

Perhaps less business friendly is Whitehead's veiled criticism that professionals and vocational trainees tend to see this or that set of circumstances, but not both sets together. Therefore, "the generalised direction lacks vision", and/or that "the whole is lost in one of its aspects", such that directive wisdom is lacking. Whitehead beautifully stated that:

> There is something between the gross specialised values of the mere practical man, and the thin specialised values of the mere scholar. Both types have missed something; and if you add together the two sets of values, you do not obtain the missing elements. What is wanted is an appreciation of the infinite variety of vivid values achieved by an organism [including corporations and business in general] in its proper environment. (p. 199)

Regarding seeing this or that circumstance separately, but not both sets of circumstances together, it will be fascinating to revisit this same idea, which Whitehead enunciated in 1925, reincarnated in the form of something remarkably similar to Dean Roger Martin's invention of Integrative Thinking ™ at the Rotman School of Business at the University of Toronto, featured among the nine universities profiled in Chapter Five.

Conclusion

One might consider Whitehead's philosophy of education, and its subset *rhythm of education*, simple common sense: a process in which one moves logically and progressively through the stages of romance, precision and generalization. But it is more than that: Whitehead's educational philosophy not only encompasses a discipline that does not leave things out, or gets them in the wrong order, but it also contains attitudinal components: a positive attitude that promotes a zest for learning, and an insistence that teaching/learning should be fresh and imaginative, rather than dealing with inert knowledge; that it should be consistently related to the real world, and to each individual participant's place in it; and that there be a workable marriage between theory and practice.

Connecting executive education to the Whitehead educational philosophy, and particularly to its rhythmic model, would ground it in the kind of theoretical base, discipline, logic and progressiveness that would yield effective results. This is urgently required to assuage the apparent feelings of malaise about management education, which seems to be crying out for greater relevancy to the actual practice of management; better tools to deal with complexity; and getting beyond a mindset of analysis to one of synthesis.

A robust and logical model of this type should resonate well with the private sector, principally because it is similar to its existing mindset. Whitehead's obvious support of entrepreneurialism, of business schools and of business in general, will not go unnoticed by corporations, which could become quite interested in his learning model. Application of this model in the private sector would likely improve corporate executive learning from what is often a hit or miss, a non-existent, or a helter-skelter affair, favouring management fads.

There is, I believe, a need for a cyclical process that pertains to executive education, but that also has connections to the whole life of the individual and the firm. Whitehead's *rhythm of education* seems to be such a process – one that could be both initially and then continually useful, effective and attractive. It can be applied in the teaching of actual skills and practices; it respects the experience and existing knowledge of the participants; it encourages a blossoming of understanding in a natural manner, in which it can ultimately generalize learning, resulting in better performance on the job, and a better personal life as well.

Through the use of Whitehead's process, executive learning could become recognizably successful, and an integral part of executive life, in which the individual, the corporation, and the world would all benefit. The process might even be an enjoyable one for all concerned. It might improve the sagging reputation of business generally, and bridge the gulf of alienation that sometimes exists between business and academia.

Other Theoretical Frameworks or Models Considered but not Used

There follows a very brief overview of four different and excellent theoretical frameworks, which were considered as alternatives to the chosen one adopted from Dr. Whitehead. In my view however, only Bourdieu's "*habitus and field*" and possibly Etienne Wenger's Communities of Practice qualify as actual theoretical frameworks, solidly grounded in pedagogy or sociology. Senge's five disciplines and Royal Dutch Shell's Scenario Planning, while excellent practical action learning models, seem to be either too vast or too general and are themselves connected to a myriad of theoretical frameworks. They are indeed therefore more immediately applicable to curriculum development, whereas the other two bona fide theoretical frameworks (Whitehead and Bourdieu) require considerable "operationalizing" to render them into a useful curriculum format. Those two bona fide theoretical frameworks could, however, provide a rich, deep and invaluable foundation on which to build a wonderful curriculum for executive education, or any other learning for that matter.

Scenario Planning

Invented by Royal Dutch Shell as a thinking person's alternative to the bureaucracy of traditional strategic planning, this organizational learning process is designed to permit organizations continuously to adapt more easily, and even joyfully, to an ever-changing world. It is a process, which, in its very essence, is already quite similar to the Whitehead model. Principally for the training of executive level managers, this practice promotes a process of strategic conversations concerning "what if" scenarios, in which the participants see the world through different lenses. It involves more of an exploration of scenarios than any specific analyses of them. It is designed to prepare senior managers to react calmly, positively and confidently to whatever befalls the company. This is not so much because they might have discussed a possible answer to an eventual problem, but rather because they have acquired the knack, understanding and experience of having such discussions together. In other words, the process, not the outcome is key. Choosing the right scenario among the many is not the issue. Testing the validity of the whole firm's business idea is the *raison d'être* of this process. Management expert Peter Drucker stated that "Whenever a business keeps on going downhill despite massive spending and heroic efforts by its people, the most likely cause is the obsolescence of its business theory" (Mitroff et al., 1994)

Van Der Heijden (1996) stated that, "scenario planning distinguishes itself from other more traditional approaches to strategic planning through its explicit approach towards ambiguity and uncertainty in the strategic question" (p. 7). Creating a unique insight is the ultimate success criterion of all strategy work. The not-so-obvious objective is to challenge rigorously the "Business Idea" (the organizational self) or vision of the firm, through testing it against various scenarios. If the Business Idea cannot withstand a reasonably likely scenario, then it should be altered so that it can. Thus, Scenario Planning is the laboratory for continuously upgrading a firm's Business Idea. A side benefit of this process is that it provides the company with improved peripheral vision, because the exercise looks *around* issues, and often concerns itself with some fairly unexpected scenarios. Although they did not specifically mention the corporation, Bleak and Fulmer (2009) were complimentary about Shell's Scenario Planning when they commented that, "The best firms in leadership development have moved from events to process" (p. 11).

Pierre Bourdieu's Theories of 'Habitus' and 'Field'

The recognized and respected model of the great French sociologist, Pierre Bourdieu (1930-2002), could have been quite useful in understanding the political realities and power relationships that flourish in corporate contexts. The situational aspects of Bourdieu's description of social interactions being similar to game theory, particularly that of the game of chess, lend themselves nicely to understanding the wily realities of a corporate hierarchy. *Habitus* refers to:

> the symbols, ideas, tastes, and preferences that can be strategically used as resources in social action. [Bourdieu] sees this cultural capital as a 'habitus', an embodied socialized tendency or disposition to act, think, or feel in a particular way. By analogy with economic capital, such resources can be invested and accumulated and can be converted into other forms.

(Scott and Marshall, 2005, p. 129)

Wikipedia interestingly stated that, "For Bourdieu each individual occupies a position in a multidimensional social space; he or she is not defined by social class membership, but by the amounts of each kind of capital he or she possesses" (http://en.wikipedia.org/wiki/Pierre_Bourdieu). Bourdieu disagreed with the rational action theory in saying that social agents do not continuously calculate according to explicit practical logic, but rather according to their "feel for the game" (where the 'feel' is the *habitus*, and the 'game' is the *field*).

It is not difficult to imagine how the use of this Bourdieun model might help to understand and explain the executive persona, which is likely in play within corporate executive ranks. This model could also have been used in my research to better inform creation of interview questions and subsequently to interpret the results of the data gathered, in terms of what kinds of educational events might be the most effective in enhancing executive learning in playing to the individual executive's *habitus*.

However, although exotic, Bourdieu's theories are complicated, and their use might, at least in these hands, result in too negative an approach to my research topic – an approach I would not have enjoyed, and one which would have cast an unfair and unnecessary pallor on the fine work of many executives. For, characterizing social interactions as being part of a selfish game, in which the principal currency is the social capital of certain kinds of special knowledge and behaviours, could dictate a shocking direction for executive curriculum development, albeit a rather interesting one.

Communities of Practice

Wenger (2003) described the existence, since the beginning of history, of communities that shared cultural practices reflecting their collective learning. He includes in that description a tribe around the cave fire, a medieval guild, a group of nurses in a ward, a street gang, and a community of engineers. He stated that "participating in these communities of practice is essential to our learning. It is at the very core of what makes us human beings capable of meaningful knowing" (p. 80).

One of the hallmarks of a Community of Practice (CoP) is that its organization is not generally hierarchical, but rather one wherein everyone's individual expertise and contribution is sought towards a common endeavour or project of interest. Its creation is task oriented and transcends corporate silos, and hierarchies. Its membership crosses all functional boundaries and comprises the people who need or want to be there in order to make positive results happen. Power is not an issue.

Although longer-standing CoPs, with the luxury of time on their hands, may achieve wonderful states of revelation through processes such as dialogue, less lengthy versions of the CoP are still quite valid. Those more modest communities may lack available time to delve deeply into issues, formulate plans, and implement change, but they still bring like-minded people together to work in concert in synergetic ways that help. There is huge working efficiency to accomplish meaningful tasks available to a CoP that is organized around common goals and is populated by mature, like-minded individuals – like-minded in their intent, but possibly of divergent types of expertise and points of view, in order to spark creativity and to cause innovation.

It would have been possible to centre my research around CoPs, but once again that would have restricted it to inquiring about a specific model rather than using a general educational theory, like that of ANW, from which to research a variety of practices being used in the corporations and at the schools I researched. Nevertheless it will be *à propos* to see in Chapter Five that in one of the interviews (Case No. 6), that company's whole education program revolves around Communities of Practice.

Peter Senge's Five Disciplines

Dr. Peter Senge has become quite famous in management circles, and on the speakers' circuit, for iterating a system for enhancing organizational learning through the development of five critical disciplines, which organizational members, especially managers, need to learn and practice. These include personal mastery, mental models, shared vision, team learning, and systems thinking. Each one of these could also represent a stand-alone model in its own right, but the whole five disciplines package would cover a full and relevant general curriculum for an executive or an organizational learning program. The essence of this work is contained in two Senge books, *The Fifth Discipline: The art and practice of the learning organization* (1990), and *The Fifth Discipline Fieldbook: Strategies and tools for building a learning organization* (Senge, Kleiner, Roberts, Ross and Smith, 1994).

One might wonder why there are only five disciplines, and whether the five chosen are the most important ones for a learning organization to possess. Perhaps they are the ones which are so general that they permit the author to cover an enormous amount of territory, actually and by inference.

A researcher could adopt this model, and then frame data gathering around it (interviews, surveys, questionnaires, focus groups). Indeed, a colleague from the Royal Roads MA Leadership Program did that very thing, in his thesis concerning whether these five disciplines were "valid, real, and actionable" (Howe, 2005). As an interesting aside, one of Howe's (2005) conclusions was that "four of the five disciplines are relevant disciplines.... The practice of personal mastery is intuitively appealing but poorly conceptualized by Senge insofar as it does not translate well into a practice that is implementable into a highly complex, dynamic environment". Howe also reported from his discussion groups that "At an overarching level, there was a general sense that Senge's approach was more complicated that it needed to be" (p. 117).

Chapter Four – Methodology

Introduction

The Case Study

Parameters for case study research are not set in stone. This, however, is not an invitation for sloppy procedures, or for a less than rigorous expectation of quality in all facets of the research process. Case studies are noted for their ability to achieve a good degree of depth of understanding emanating from rich data that can be gleaned from an often limited but specific sample. At the simplest level, Cousin (2005) said, "case study research aims to explore and depict a setting with a view to advancing understanding of it" (p. 422). Yin (2003) described the case study method as one that "allows investigators to retain the holistic and meaningful characteristics of real-life events" (p. 2) and he gives organizational and managerial practices as examples. Stake (1995) described three categories of case study: *Intrinsic*, in which an understanding is sought; *Instrumental*, in which attempts are made to generalize; and *Collective*, in which more than one case is studied in order to obtain better representation than in a single case, and thereby to make some degree of generalization more credible. That said, Stake (2006) cautioned that "the power of case study is its attention to the local situation, not in how it represents other cases in general" (p. 8).

I believe that the case study is somewhat akin to the participatory feeling of Action Research – a process I used for my Master of Arts thesis about a leadership program at Royal Roads University, five years ago. Cousin (2005), in citing Adelman and Stake, described the case study as "capable of giving readers the vicarious experience of 'being there' so that they can share in the interpretation of the case, adjudicating its worth alongside the researcher" (p. 424). The presentation of the data in Chapters Five and Six is presented in a way that makes it possible for the reader feel part of the interviews, and a fellow-interpreter of the data from the universities.

From the participants' viewpoint, this highly participatory aspect of those interviews was exactly what was necessary to encourage executive level corporate managers to want to contribute to this study, for that interview process resembled the familiar problem based or action learning motif, with which executives are familiar, and were therefore likely to feel more comfortable. Without such personalized sharing of views, any valuable unfolding of truly held beliefs and ideas about executive education simply would not have been forthcoming. In the absence of actually doing an Action Research style of intervention, which I had considered doing with a single firm, I opted more appropriately to do a collective case study involving contacts with ten firms, but no interventions into any of them.

It is worthwhile to remember the meaning of "case study" in conjunction with a business school like Harvard that invented it as a teaching method 83 years ago, or like so many other universities around the world that have followed suit. Yin (2003) pointed to the possibility that some may confuse case study academic research with the case study teaching device. As it turned out, corporate executives, many of whom had completed MBAs at business schools, were not that interested in how I labelled my research process. Although I carefully explained the details of my research intentions in an introductory letter, an information sheet and in conversation before conducting each interview, I sensed that participants just wanted to get on with the conversation.

The Multiple or Collective Case Study

In an unpublished contribution to the *Encyclopedia of Case Study Research*, University of Calgary Professor Pam Bishop (2008) wrote a conceptual overview and discussion paper. In it, she described the multiple case study as one that "offers a means of understanding an individual, event, policy, program, or group via multiple representations of that phenomenon" (p. 1). She added that, "by illuminating the experiences, implications, or effects of a phenomenon in more than one setting, wider understandings about a phenomenon can emerge" (p. 1). Within a multiple case study, the individual cases or case sites have the dual purpose of describing what is different and what is similar about the phenomenon (in this instance: executive education) among the sites studied.

A multiple case study calls for the researcher to focus simultaneously on both the individual cases as well as the overall collection of cases – or the *Quintain*, as Stake (2006) labels such a collection. This means that discrepancies among the cases are to be expected, accepted and even welcomed. In multiple case studies, outliers do not really exist, and therefore cannot be rejected because they are not the norm. Therefore, as shall be seen in the next chapters, interview and institutional data analyses are done individually and then again for the Quintain or collection of cases as a whole.

My Research Design

My research used a collective or multiple case study format within a qualitative framework to gather and analyze data from the field, from web-based documentation and from my own experience.

The fieldwork research segment took the form of interviews about executive education and learning with 14 leaders connected with 10 firms in Canada. Individual interviews with executives within those firms were "the unit of analysis" as far as the fieldwork was concerned.

A secondary unit of analysis comprised the presentation of data from providers of open enrolment and custom executive programs at nine universities.

A third solitary unit of analysis comprised some of my own stories about executive learning, based on my experiences as a participant in corporate learning programs or events.

Acquiring Participation for Interviews

Invitations to participate in one-on-one interviews were sent out to the Chief Executive Officer or President of firms in Canada, representative of the major sectors of the Canadian economy. That letter briefly described some of the details of this doctoral research study, and it expressed the hope and expectation for a lively and mutually beneficial discussion with participating firms about their executive learning philosophy and programs, and about executives' experience in them.

Original intentions were to send out invitations for participation to a large number of corporations, based on a list of the top 200 corporations in Canada (ranked by number of employees), kindly provided by *infoCanada*, and related to my membership in the Vancouver Board of Trade. (The *infocanada* website can be found at http://www.infocanada.ca/main_page.aspx?aspxerrorpath=%2fservi ce%2fca%2fcontact.aspx).

The non-existent response rate from an initial fairly large mailing caused me to rethink this whole approach, especially in view of the horrendous worldwide financial disaster that had taken place in October 2008, only a few months prior to sending out these letters.

When I was bewailing to a friend and business owner this lack of interest demonstrated for the project, he wisely advised me by e-mail, as follows:

> Sadly, the non-response does not surprise me. These days CEOs are under tremendous pressure given the rapidly deteriorating economy in the US, sensitivity to CEO wages and bonuses, corporate performance and all the other challenges you can imagine in this environment. I have an assistant that screens all my mail and telephone calls; my direct line and

email are blocked for random contact as well. Otherwise, I would never get any work done from cold calls, requests similar to yours, guest speaker, board participation, interviews, charities, the latest inventions or gimmicks, soliciting for services, ...I guess that is why the burn-out rate is so high with CEO's. I hope you get more responses but I can see why it is a challenge with the people you are after. I think you will need a direct introduction similar to what you have here otherwise your request will never make it to the guy you are after. (personal communication, February 17, 2009)

As a result of this wise advice, I proceeded to contact people I knew in the business world. I also contacted a total of four very senior executives recommended by friends, family and business associates. Those recommendations also came with introductions supplied by those who had provided them.

Actual Response Results

Thirty-two executives from firms in Canada were then contacted by letter and invited to participate in one-on-one interviews. Fourteen individuals accepted; fourteen refused and four never responded. The refusals varied widely, but the most common ones were along theses lines:

- "We have received your letter requesting our participation in your doctoral research study. We thank you for your interest in our organization but unfortunately, we will not be able to participate. As you probably know, times are very difficult in our industry at the moment and we need all hands on deck at the moment. I wish you the best of luck in the continuation of your project".

- "I had a discussion with my boss and we have decided not to participate in the study. With all the current issues with the economy, our executive team is very focused on dealing with the economy and how it has impacted our business. I wish you all the best in the study".

Some of the more startling refusals included:

- "It will be impossible to participate at your study for our executives. I am the person responsible of Organizational Development and I can't because my English is too bad to discuss during 2-hours interviews. I am sorry".

- "Mr. X thanks you for your interest in ....., but must unfortunately decline your request, as our company policy is to not participate in any kind of studies or surveys".

- "XXX receives several requests from students, universities, governmental agencies, consultants, third parties, etc... every week and it becomes very difficult, if not impossible to accommodate so many requests, even if many are of interest. We apologize for any inconvenience caused by our delay to respond to your request".

Research Perspectives - Theoretical Validity

Interpretive Research Stance

In today's corporations, reality is often still perceived objectively as being separate from the observer, "out there", concrete, and more meaningful if it can be measured. According to Prasad and Prasad (2002), interpretive inquiry, a subset of qualitative research, has emerged out of its awkward adolescence into self assured adulthood, and it has made a complete break with its former blood relative known as qualitative positivism. Again according to Prasad and Prasad, contemporary interpretive research "refuses to play by the rules of positivism, or to be confined, policed, and disciplined by outdated notions of its limits" (p. 8). Rather, it belongs to a philosophy of social construction "which sees social reality as a constructed world built in and through meaningful interpretations" (p. 8).

The still daunting task of my employing a non-positivist approach to research within large corporations is partly assuaged by Prasad and Prasad's (2002) contention that interpretive inquiry has "steadily affirmed its relevance to management and organizational studies by addressing questions that cannot adequately be answered by traditional experimental or survey methodologies and by enhancing our understanding of, among other things, the symbolic dimensions of organizational life" (p. 4). This represents a shift, however slight it may be, toward a softer management approach to learning and away from what Regnier (1995) described as a western materialistic worldview associated with "distrust of holistic approaches to knowing, a distrust engendered by the dominance of epistemologies that emphasize the separation of mind and matter, humankind and nature, fact and value" (p. 392).

In the past, and still now to some extent, purists of the interpretive stance have promoted a type of arms-length "observe and report" *modus operandi*, in which it is not appropriate to intervene through participation or engage through critique. However, in preparation for my adopting a kind of business-friendly, participatory and critical interpretivism in my multiple case study of executive learning, I befriended the more evolved and recent style of "interpretivism-with-teeth". In this respect, Prasad and Prasad (2002) asserted that "the act of drawing interpretive thinking to its full potential practically demands some form of fundamental questioning that is not very far from an overtly critical orientation" (p. 8).

As it turned out in the interviews, executive participants did not seem concerned or perhaps did not care whether I was using a positivist or interpretivist approach. Once again, they just wanted to get on with the conversation, because they were interested in it. They also seemed concerned about time constraints, and graciously worried about my getting all I needed in the short space of an hour long interview.

Triangulation of Evidence and External Validity

Creswell (2007) stated that, "the purpose of the triangulation design is to obtain different but complementary data on the same topic" (p. 62), and Olsen (2004) argued that triangulation "is not aimed merely at validation but at deepening and widening one's understanding". My study comprises the triangulation of three sources of evidence about executive learning: what executives said in interviews, what is stated in web based documents and other materials about the availability and content of executive open enrolment and custom programs at universities, and what was gleaned by reflecting on what I have experienced as a learner during my business career as a practising executive.

Data Gathering Methods

Semi-Structured Individual Interviews

<u>Interview Statistics</u>

Ten firms and fourteen individual executives within them participated in the interviews

- Of those 10 firms, two are privately held; 8 are publicly held

- Of those 10 firms, seven are Canadian and are headquartered in Canada; and three are multinational with subsidiaries in Canada

Seven private sector segments were represented by these ten firms as follows:

- 2 x banking and financial services

- 1x natural resources

- 2x transportation

- 1x engineering

- 2x distribution

- 1x manufacturing

- 1x high tech

Three executive levels were represented among the fourteen participants interviewed:

- 5x Level 1 (CEO, Chair, or President)

- 6x Level 2 (Executive, Senior or Divisional Vice President)

- 3x Level 3 (Director, Senior Manager, Department Head)

Of the fourteen individual executives interviewed:

- 3 were 3rd level female executives (one of the 1st level female executives contacted was unable to participate because of too busy a schedule)

- 11 were 1st and 2nd level male executives

- 2 of the 14 were recently retired from their corporations

Interviews by Region

- 7x British Columbia

- 1x Alberta

- 4x Ontario

- 2x Quebec

Conducting the Interviews

For the semi-structured interviews, I attempted to design what Stake (1995) referred to as "load bearing issue questions" as an alternative to hypothesis-led questions. In that way, I was seeking not just information from executives, but also their first hand narrative portrayals, opinions, evaluations, and even individual hopes and fears about their corporate learning experiences.

A few days prior to each interview, I sent out a list of 24 questions by e-mail to the participant, with a strong message that they were only to serve as guidelines to the conversation. I stated that the discussion could take place around any topic related to executive learning and education, and that I was especially interested in hearing about participants' own personal experiences, opinions and stories about programs they had attended.

Each interview was planned to last one hour, a period estimated to be the maximum senior leaders would have time for. However, in a few cases in which the conversation was clearly of great interest to participants, they went beyond the allotted time to as much as two hours. Initially I had intended simply to take notes, in the belief that this would be less invasive and more akin to executive expectations. However, it became clear that for accuracy it was absolutely necessary to record the proceedings. As a researcher, I considered it was important to remember that the emphasis needed to be on getting the information required for the research, and not on changing the design to accommodate the perceived preferences of participants. The interviews were transcribed verbatim, except for needless repetitiveness. The format used for presenting the data and its analyses is explained in detail in the next chapter.

Web Based Review of Executive Programs at Universities

Sources for this segment of the research consisted of institutional websites, speeches, articles, video clips, audio bites, and podcasts from university websites, as well as information from Wikipedia, because some information there was more current than that available from the institutions themselves (for instance, the number of students enrolled for a senior executive program in 2009/2010; and the meanings of the acronyms INSEAD and IESE). Twenty-two universities were looked at for their excellence in providing open enrolment and custom executive programs. These were narrowed down to presentation of data from nine universities.

Selection of Universities

The universities were selected based on 2007-2009 rankings from *The Financial Times (FT)*. There are all sorts of rankings for business schools: *McLean's, The Financial Times, The Wall Street Journal, Business Week, Dow Jones, Environics, The Economist,* and *Expansión,* just to name a few. However, the most revealing source I found dealing with custom and open enrolment executive education programs was *The Financial Times.*

In addition to overall results shown for the universities chosen to be included in this research, it is worth mentioning for the use of other researchers that this *FT* ranking permits sorting by 17 individual criteria, and the ability to compare up to ten schools for each criterion. This is available at:

http://rankings.ft.com/businessschoolrankings/charts?ranking=executive-education---customised&field=1728&entities=&fromtablecompare=1

The criteria included such items as teaching excellence, program design, partnerships, and global reach. These were similar to the analysis categories used in my research and detailed in the next chapter. As will be apparent in the list that follows, all but one of the nine universities, whose data is presented and analyzed in the next chapter, figure in the *Financial Times* results. Beyond that, the nine institutions selected for review are superb examples of the best there is for open enrolment and customized executive learning programs.

Furthermore, six of these nine universities were mentioned at least once by the executives interviewed, due to the fact that they had some form of positive liaison with them. McGill was not ranked in the *Financial Times*, but was honoured in the respected *Environics Research Group's* 2006 Report on Executive Education in Canada. Based on this group's survey of opinions from 400 senior executives in Canada, the best five MBA degree and non degree programs (http://business.queensu.ca/about_us/docs/Environics_Report.pdf), were the same five Canadian institutions selected for profiling here. The selection of McGill was particularly pertinent for my research, because of its famous open enrolment Advanced Leadership Program, that features managers learning while doing.

The Financial Times Global Rankings (average for 3 years 2007-2009)

(http://rankings.ft.com/businessschoolrankings/executive-education---customised)

(http://rankings.ft.com/businessschoolrankings/executive-education---open)

In the following list, the first set of brackets indicates the rank among the top 55 schools in the world for Open Enrolment Executive Education, according to *FT* (2009). The second set of brackets indicates the rank among the top 65 schools in the world for Customized Executive Education, according to the same source and for the same three year period:

- Duke Executive Education, Duke University, USA (-) (1)

- Harvard, USA (1) (3)

- IESE, Spain (7) (6)

- INSEAD, France/Singapore, (16) (14)

- University of Western Ontario, IVEY, Canada/China (12) (25)

- University of Toronto, ROTMAN, Canada (27) (42)

- Queen's School of Business, Canada (18) (51) 2009; not ranked in 2008, nor 2007

- York University, SCHULICH, Canada (40) (54)

- (McGill University, Montreal, Canada – not included in this ranking, as previously indicated)

My Own Professional Experience of Executive Education

A third data gathering segment of this research comprises descriptions of executive programs, which I have personally experienced as a participant, while in middle and senior management positions in the pulp and paper industry.

Chapter Five – Presentation Of Findings And Analysis (Part 1)

Introduction

In the next three chapters, I will present and interpret data findings from three sources: interviews with executives, web-based material about universities, and descriptions of my own experience as a participant in programs during my business career. Field Interviews provided the principal data base, as well as the first and therefore the guiding method of analysis for the other data.

Let us recall from the methodology chapter that *Quintain* refers to an overall collection of cases. According to Stake (2006), a researcher needs to analyze both the peculiarities of each case separately, as well as the collective of all the cases, because these two views can be complementary or even different. This dual presentation will provide a full picture of the findings; it will not minimize either the rich data of each case, or the overall flavour of the Quintain.

I will attempt to make some connections between the educational philosophy of Alfred North Whitehead and discoveries from executive interviews and university executive programs along with the conclusions and recommendations in the final chapter.

The Interviews – Primary Unit of Analysis

Process of Analysis for the Interviews

Robert Stake (2006) has developed an excellent process to progressively and effectively move through analysis of the data for collective case studies. Essentially, this involves:

1. Creating a worksheet of five to seven Quintain themes, which are similar to the research questions themselves. The themes evolved into the first worksheet as shown in Table #1, with keen attention being paid to their alignment with the research questions. These six themes concerning executive education became the ones used to guide my consideration of the data from the interviews, the university presentations, and my own narrative about executive learning during my career:

Theme #1: Formal or informal learning plan
To what extent was there a formal executive education or learning plan in place? How formal or traditional were executive programs, and to what degree were they flexible?

Theme #2: Relevancy
How relevant were executive learning programs to the senior manager's job? What does relevance mean in terms of executive education and learning?

Theme #3:Learning Affiliations
How prevalent and how important were creation of learning liaisons between firms and institutions concerning executive education?

Theme #4: Individual cf. Group Learning
To what extent was executive learning experienced as an individual, compared to as a group or team process? What were the preferences in that regard? What, for instance, was said or written about the one-on-one processes of mentoring and coaching?
Theme#5: Electronic Communication and Social Media
To what extent was it important for executives to learn about, and become skilled in, electronic communication and social media?
Theme #6: Curriculum Issues
What were the curriculum preferences and concerns regarding executive education and learning? To what extent were executive education programs off-the-shelf or customized?

Table #1: Quintain Themes for presentation and analysis of data

2. For the interviews another special worksheet, as depicted in the next table, was created to record conveniently in note form all the major findings from each interview (F1 – F12, or more as the case required). At the right-hand side of page were six columns marked T1 through T6, representing the six themes outlined in Table #1. For every finding in every interview, its relevance to each theme was scored L (low), M (medium), H (high), or 0 (non existent, or not at all relevant). In the presentation of the interview data later in this chapter, the findings appear without my assignment of the L,M,H, and 0 scores. As well as saving space, it permits readers to come to their own opinions about relevance weighting. As Stevenson (2004) stated, "The researcher conveys what she [sic] has learned that she believes is important, while providing material for readers to learn or discover independently what the researcher may not have deemed important" (p. 46). Furthermore, how the weighting was applied is subjective; the significance is that there was a mechanism in place to

filter the vast amount of data into a manageable form for analysis.

Relevancy to Quintain Themes

Individual Interview Findings	T1	T2	T3	T4	T5	T6
F1. Each finding about interview data and quotes from verbatim transcripts were entered on these tables						
F2.						
F3.						

Table #2: Sample Worksheet for Recording Relevance to Themes

3. Admittedly the assigning of relevancy levels was a subjective exercise. It was, however, tempered in its subjectivity by close adherence to the previously chosen themes. From the relevancy scores, there emerged a hierarchy of significance in relation to the themes, which themselves were created due to their alignment with the research questions. The result was that high-ranking "relevancies", taken from all the interviews together, provide what Stake refers to as Quintain Assertions. For analysis or interpretation of each interview separately, this rather laborious process is not necessary, because the researcher and readers can see and digest that relatively limited amount of data, without the help of the relevancy hierarchies.

This albeit cumbersome process does an excellent job of clarifying and organizing in an unemotional, hierarchical fashion one's thinking about the abundant array of data available in verbatim transcriptions. For this segment of my research, transcriptions of the 14 interviews totalled over 50,000 words, and those focused interview sessions were teeming with useful data. During this process of analysis, items that once seemed so significant faded, while others surfaced as more relevant and of greater concern than was originally anticipated.

I have used segments of this charting process from Robert Stake, but not only as an analytical process. I have expanded it to present as well as to analyze the findings for each case. What the reader will see in the following pages concerning the interview data includes:

1. Major findings presented as described above for each interview;

2. An interpretation and appreciation of the findings from each interview.

3. A summary of Quintain assertions from the collection of interviews as a whole, developed from the relevancy ratings.

Narrative Style in Reporting on the Interviews

Although there are many quotes peppered throughout the interview descriptions, most of the narrative is in the form of paraphrased synopses of what each participant said about executive education, and about their own executive learning experiences. None of my own opinions is expressed in these descriptions. Therefore, the ideas expressed in the findings of each case are those of the participant, whether or not they are prefaced by such phrases as "This executive said...", or "According to this participant....".

It bears repeating that the individual case finding charts represent a complete synopsis of the verbatim transcripts, and they permit readers to "be present" in witnessing what was said, and to form their own opinions about what is important. The relevancy ranking to the interview questions is simply a way to give the researcher some guidance regarding which elements of the individual interviews deserve the status of quintain assertions.

The Interview Questions

1. For you personally: What types of learning or educational practices or events, related to your job as an executive, have NOT been a waste of time for you; which ones have been?

2. Who should decide about executive education in a corporation (about its flavour and style, its context and content, its delivery and scope, its participants)?

3. Is executive education an issue of succession, leadership development, general development, personal development, professional development? Regardless of how it is categorized, who should be responsible for it happening and how should it unfold?

4. To what extent are executive education and learning planned or orchestrated in any formal manner in your corporation?

5. To what degree is formal education (and related university degree or other certification) prized in your corporation, compared to other forms of accomplishment, style, or personal history?

6. What is your impression of how executive education and the process of executive learning are viewed within your corporation? Are they considered as individual or group pursuits; as a personal or a corporate responsibility in the pursuit of excellence; as potentially capable of providing a competitive edge? Is there accountability regarding executive education, and if so, where does it lie?

7. In this corporation, to what extent do you characterize executive learning as formal or informal? Is this any different for other levels of managerial learning within the company?

8. Formal or informal, stellar, mediocre or non-existent: What has your own individual experience of learning been in preparing you or solidifying you in an executive job and/or in preparing you for advancement? Would you please provide some actual examples of or stories about your individual learning experiences that have occurred while you have been an executive.

9. In your view, should executive educational programs be restricted to developing learning skills that are directly

applicable to enhancing an individual's on-the-job performance (for example, mentoring and coaching, public speaking), or should they/could they also address more general areas of learning (for instance, learning a new language, critical thinking techniques, learning about community service)?

10. What is your take on the educational value of interdisciplinary and inter-company "think-tanks" (for example, similar to those orchestrated by The Aspen Institute in Colorado), at which senior executives get together for two or three days, to discuss global issues of general concern to business and to the world (for instance: poverty, sustainability, philanthropy, education & literacy, leadership, the global economy, the relationship of politics to business, or education to business)?

11. What is your opinion about the potential value to executives and to your corporation of having senior people attend those well-known three-month top management programs – the likes of which are provided by Harvard Business School, Stanford Business School, INSEAD in France, or IMEDE in Switzerland? If you have attended such a program yourself, what is your opinion of that experience?

12. Given that your corporation intends to spend some resources on executive learning development, and given equal costs: Would you prefer to use existing curriculum from consultants, or from universities (leadership, communications, networking skills, coaching & mentoring, public speaking), or would you prefer to have curriculum designed in a customized fashion for your particular company and in synch with its priorities? Or is there a better way of educating executives?

13. Different individuals have different learning styles. Do you think it is important to cater to individual learning styles when crafting an executive learning program?

14. In the following list of potential curriculum items for your own executive learning or development, which ones (if any) strike you as more or less useful? What items are missing?

(a) Scenario Planning	(b) The KAIZEN	(c) Journaling & Reflective Practices
(d) Appreciative Inquiry	(e) Dialogue & Conversation	(f) Systems Thinking
(g) Public Speaking	(h) Cultural Diversity	(i) Philanthropy
(j) Media Relationships	(k) Wikinomics	(l) Mentoring and Coaching
(m) Preparing for Retirement	(n) Wealth Management	(o) Succession Duties
(p) Public Service	(q) The Art of Listening	(r) Boardroom Behaviour

15. Whatever type of curriculum you decide upon, would you be willing to see executive "internal graduates" (who have already completed a program) take the time to serve in a subsequent educational event, as learning leaders or facilitators? Would you have been interested or willing to devote some of your own time to acting as a facilitator in executive training within your firm?

16. What, in your opinion, is the value of the MBA degree? Please also comment on your appreciation of the value of any other formal degrees or diplomas in executive and management education.

17. To what extent can Universities (and particularly Business Schools) provide any meaningful executive learning to corporations?

18. Why do you suppose (if indeed you do) that corporations and academic institutions do not see each other more 'eye to eye'?

19. Is online learning an attractive delivery option for executive learning programs? How do you personally feel about this option for your own learning?

20. Looking to the future, in which we will see members of the 'NetGen' becoming the next class of executives: How do you foresee the use of online delivery of learning and networking, and use of collaborative spaces (e.g. facebook, my space) affecting executive education?

21. Who are your business heroes, and how have they deserved or earned that status with you?

22. What is the best book you have read, which helped your learning the most while you were working at the executive level? What are you reading these days?

23. Do you have any favourite authors whose writing has helped you in your business learning? Who are they and what have you learned from them?

24. Please describe a sports analogy regarding the training or behaviour of individual elite athletes or whole teams of elite athletes that might be applicable as a possible model for executive education.

As described in the last chapter, this list of 24 questions was sent out to each participant a few days before each interview. The use of these questions as guidelines only was emphasized in a covering e-mail, and participants were encouraged to feel free to tell their own stories, or to deal with other issues in which they were perhaps more interested, or felt were more important regarding executive education and learning. As it turned out, only two of the 14 interviewees had read these questions prior to the interview, and it was necessary to let the other 12 participants read them before we started the conversations. Ironically, it was arguably the most senior executive I interviewed who had most carefully read the questions beforehand. In fact, he was very familiar with them, pointing out throughout his conversation how his comments related to this or that question, and indeed sometimes quoting parts of the questions from memory, before proceeding with his opinions.

One of the questions asked of most participants was one that was both fun to talk about and one that might be quite useful, or at least interesting, to readers. It was to ask what participants were reading at the moment: whether directly, indirectly, or not at all related to business. This data about executive reading habits is not part of the analysis, nor are titles listed in the reference list, unless they happen to have been cited elsewhere.

I am not as concerned with demonstrating the differences and similarities among the different cases, as I am in presenting rich data of important insights from each one of these senior practitioners.

Interview Case Study Findings – Case No. 1A

F1. *Sponsoring of executive events for clients, at which famous guests* speak on subjects such as leadership or change management, is a regular occurrence.

F2. *Inclusiveness (diversity).* There are seminars dealing with bias, and there is an "inclusiveness champion" present at all performance reviews.

F3. *A 'Stratified Apprenticeship' learning model.* Also recognized at this firm as a promotable recruitment – double bottom line – advantage, as are all learning initiatives. This model demonstrates the firm's insistence on not separating executive learning from the overall learning of the organization.

F4. *Corporate University & Executive Learning.* This firm actually boasts a corporate university, which provides one-size-fits-all courses that are customized as you move up the chain: At the lower levels courses are obligatory; at the higher levels, there is more "optionality", but still with some control to help address weak points. There is also a "train the trainer program' afoot here, and there are some elements of online learning especially at lower levels. Some of this material is facilitated internally; some externally.

F5. *Mentoring and Coaching.* There is a specific plan in place that connects high potential candidates to board members. There exist what are called "Career Watch" (annual structured dialogues with top executives), and "Pathways" to [top executive positions], involving an individualized learning program.

F6. *Micro & Macro points of view:* The importance for an executive to learn an ability to be simultaneously capable of viewing a situation from up close and from afar is stressed – "the sea level and the 35,000 ft. views".

F7. *Learning Regrets:* Finding the time for all the necessary and beneficial learning, and wishing to have learned more about the "softer" skills such as mentoring and coaching.

F8. *Curriculum Preferences of this executive:* scenario planning, public speaking, diversity, mentoring and coaching, computer issues (wikinomics)

F9. *Reading Preferences:* John Kotter's books (*A Sense of Urgency*, 2008; *The Heart of Change*, 2002; *What Leaders Really Do*, 1999), as Kotter is often the Harvard professor facilitating learning events with this firm's executives; "*Playing to Win*" by David Sirlin (2006), which this executive found particularly *à propos* when he was on the National Team of a major Canadian sport, but also terribly relevant today in his business.

Interview Case Study Findings – Case No. 1-B

F1. *A Learning Organization.* "Everyone is required to do a certain number of learning hours per year, because last year's knowledge just won't cut it in doing your job this year". The training at this firm is technical at the lower levels and is conducted mostly in-house, because "you cannot wait for the new stuff to be developed externally". A good deal of learning at the senior level has to do with showing people how to build relationships with senior executives. The company is vigilant about inclusiveness, for instance about ensuring that women and minorities have access to executive development programs. Webcasts are used at all levels to get the message out (information and learning). It is difficult to maintain the learning passion, because "every hour you spend in personal learning is an hour you are not committing to clients".

F2. "*Fierce Conversations*". One of this company's many learning programs around communication is called "fierce conversations" and comes from a US provider. It deals with teaching people how to have "real" conversations, which do not shrink from getting into important and often troublesome issues.

F3.: *Feedback.* The big question is to figure out what to do with inspiration when it occurs; how to bring it back into the workplace and make the benefits of a good learning event more long-lasting. This executive suggested creating "small tasks" related to learning that should/could be required from participants after they return to the workplace – those that would facilitate or at least open the door to more similar learning. Furthermore, perhaps there is something that can be done to change the performance measurement equation not just to include revenue generation, but also to favour the incidence of learning.

F4. *Performance Reviews.* These take the form of round-table discussions, in which the people who work together talk about their performance together. Joining them is an "inclusiveness champion" who has been taught to listen for and to positively intervene when unreasonable, biased, unfair or inappropriate comments are made.

F5. *Life/Work Balance and Time Management.* Maybe you *need* to work 12 hours, but you need to learn to take breaks and to not think about work after those 12 hours. This firm has an energy program, which is a one-day optional course on eating properly. It is possible for executives to work part-time and this translates to their working with an 80% client load. They may still put in a ferocious number of hours, but their overtime becomes more manageable.

F6. *MBA Program:* I mentioned to this executive, who had originally been working on a PhD in English literature, that the switch to an MBA program must have been quite a radical one. The response was, "I found that it gave me quite an advantage. I could write, and I could speak. Frankly, those attributes are among the most useful in becoming successful in business".

F7. *Reading.* This executive was very well-read, and had a low opinion of most business books, feeling that most of what they contained of any value could be distilled into a few pages. The 'Heathrow School of Management' was mentioned: whereby the CEO picks up a business book at the airport for the long flight to London, and then returns to the company and tells someone in HR to implement what they have read about – an utter waste of time, according to this executive. This person liked to read *The New Yorker*, because of the high quality of the writing, and to read mysteries for diversion. Also mentioned was a current book about Darwin and Lincoln – people from very different backgrounds, both with great and creative minds, born on the same day and having had a huge impact on the world.

Narrative Appreciation

This firm provided an opportunity to interview a second tier male executive and a third tier female executive from different branches of the same organization. It is significant that only three of the 14 interviews were with women executives. Other very senior women executives had been approached, but had refused participation because of the huge demands on their time. One might wonder if this is because women executives actually have more demands against available time, or if they just feel that way about them; or perhaps just these individuals did. Upon hearing of this discrepancy concerning the lack of women participants, the executive from Case 1A arranged for me to contact one of his colleagues in another city to see if she would be interested in talking to me. She was, and we met for a one-hour talk (Case 1B). This action was a vivid example of this firm's genuine concern about issues of diversity and inclusiveness.

There was no question about this company's very serious commitment to learning through formal programs, which are in place at all levels of the organization. Indeed, this executive resisted most of my attempts to separate educational programs, so as to focus merely on executive learning.

Relevancy to and Resonance with Themes

The "T" numbers in brackets refer to the theme number to which major findings relate (the six themes were outlined at the beginning of this chapter):

- Formalized, carefully planned learning programs are important to this firm, and they are in place for all organizational levels, not just for the executive group (T1).

- Learning programs are a mix of just-in-time skill-based training, especially for the lower organizational levels, and of longer term "softer" skill development, especially for the higher levels (T2).

- Learning affiliations are with individuals with particular expertise, as well as with institutions, with which the firm has had a long relationship (T3).

- Most of the training happens in groups; some coaching happens, but it does not seem to be a priority except for a few high potential leaders (T4).

- Learning more about electronic communication was a curriculum priority for these executives, and some of the technical training at this firm is done through online materials, but it is not particularly interactive (T5).

- Many of the educational programs at this firm are customized either in-house for technical skill training of lower management levels, or from outside providers for the developmental material destined for more senior people (T6).

- The theme permeating most of these two conversations was about the value of diversity in leadership, and the implication that this had to be a topic that was front and foremost in every aspect of the organization's life: from hiring and firing practices, to performance reviews, to the conducting of meetings, to succession plans. A memorable quote from the first interview was:

> [There is] some interesting literature, particularly in the current environment [worldwide financial collapse], that if there had been more

women in leadership positions, the problems we have might not have happened; because some of our decision making would have been different. So, it's a pretty powerful argument: You can't refute the mess we're in; and you can't refute the fact that it was mostly white males that got us here.

Standout Items

- Fierce Conversations: The topic of a specific learning program, which teaches people how to have real conversations and get to issues.

- Life/Work Balance: Maybe you need to work 12 hours a day. The trick is to do it in a healthy, less stressful manner.

Interview Case Study Findings – Case No. 2

F1. *Multi-faceted program for all levels of this corporation:* (1) At this firm, there is an Emerging Leaders Program (six modules, of four days over one year) plus an ongoing development plan for each individual, including expectation that participants will change jobs within 12 months after completion. (2) University Administered program: Graduate Diploma in Business Administration (seven MBA level courses) with 200 graduates in the last decade. (3) Last year 25 GDBA grads have embarked on a four-year continuation program which will give them an MBA degree, after they complete an additional six courses, plus a job related thesis.

F2. *Online courses* have had bad reviews with participants saying they much prefer face-to-face (f-t-f) work as a group and in groups. The executive interviewed has never taken an online course, and dislikes working online.

F3. *Consultants* are generally not used by this firm. It is felt that it is very difficult for any meaningful learning coming from outside to take root; so almost everything is created and delivered either inside, or else in conjunction with, a local university – one which has become familiar with this firm.

F4. *The best learning* personally experienced during the career of this executive was during "stretch challenges", in which he had to tackle a new project, a new job, or a new function in a different division and region. Before anyone gets to the GM level at this firm, they have to have worked in a different region or product group.

F5. *Executive education:* Other than the Emerging Leaders Program, there is currently nothing specifically directed towards very senior managers; and it was felt that the proper thing to do was to consult those senior people about what they wanted to see happen for their executive learning, and compare that to a profile of what experts (in HR) think is required. But the implication was that the impetus for this should come from the executive users themselves. They realize they must do something about senior development, and will target the VP and GM group, which comprises 40 people. There is not much interest in sending senior people to such events as the long (three month) programs at Harvard or Stanford.

F6. *International Curriculum:* For an international company, there is not enough course material or learning happening in the area of international and global issues. Most learning is happening in conjunction with a local university. There is a need for material on cultural diversity, and for learning to take place in other parts of the world where the company is located.

F7. *Coaching and Mentoring:* Some individual courses are provided in coaching, but mentoring has proven difficult to implement. Mentoring works better on an informal basis, and some people are good at giving or receiving it, and others are not. Regarding overall learning in an organization, but with specific reference to mentoring, this executive stated: "An organization that encourages development generally (spending time thinking about how to develop people and that have programs to do it) rewards managers for developing their people, and for putting candidates forward for succession, and all that good stuff…. In those organizations, people will see mentoring as an important behaviour".

F8. *Electronic Social Communication Platforms:* These may be important, but probably not for the senior people. This senior HR executive said that the best thing to do here was to ask those senior people if they saw any need in this respect, and to provide it if they did.

F9. *The Basics:* "We must tell people what they are expected to do; Make sure they get regular feedback; focus on a few areas in the development plans where improvement could happen. We need to ask what individuals are interested in doing with the company over the longer term. We need to give supervisors the necessary tools to do all this".

F10. *Curriculum Preferences:* This executive favoured scenario planning, public speaking, cultural diversity (especially for an international firm), and media relations where experience was lacking. This person asked about Appreciative Inquiry, and after finding out about it, expressed interest in possibly using it. This participant expressed critical concern about the uselessness of many among the array of programs hitting the market in the 80s and 90s, such as Quality circles, Total Quality Management (TQM), Statistical Process Control (SPC), Japanese-style Quality Assurance Programs (Kaizen), Performance Management Systems, and Leadership Models. Some of these had merit, but in most cases, even if they had merit, too often management used these programs as an excuse to relinquish responsibility for organizational learning to consultants. "Every time I hear about something new on the horizon, I become nervous. The latest one is *Courageous Leadership* around safety issues".

F11. *Reading Preferences:* This executive was another person who was critical of business books taking hundreds of pages to unfold fairly simple ideas. He mentioned favourites being *In Search of Excellence*

(Tom Peters); and *What They Don't Teach at Harvard Business School: Notes from a Street-Smart Executive* (Mark H. McCormack).

Narrative Appreciation

As for Case No.1, this firm also appears to have fairly energetic learning programs in place for all ranks of employees. As predicted in Chapter One, it would seem logical that if a firm did not have at least some semblance of educational development for its employees, then it would have been unlikely to grant me an interview to discuss executive learning. Although there is nothing particularly designed for the senior executives (those reporting to the CEO), this Vice President of Human Resources said that he would be interested in looking at creating something for them, in consultation with them. This individual was quite interested in hearing about my post graduate experience after I had taken early retirement, and he is seriously considering doing similarly when he retires.

Relevancy to and Resonance with Themes

- Several formalized learning programs exist for middle managers (T1).

- There are no programs afoot for senior managers *per se*. There is a program for Emerging Leaders (T2).

- There is a strong affiliation with a local university for the design and delivery of programs for middle managers (T3).

- Coaching and Mentoring seem to be absent from the learning practices at this organization. There are, however, some coaching courses given as part of major development programs (T4).

- Online courses have a bad reputation at this firm, and are not used very much at all. It was felt that middle managers needed to know about electronic communication and internet issues more than do the very senior people (T5).

- Curriculum preferences were especially strong in the area of cultural diversity, because this is an international firm doing business in many countries. "We are an international company, and one of the things that I think is absent from our programs is that we don't have enough international content – most of it happens around here through our affiliation with [a local university]" (T6).

- Having a formalized learning system in place, such as the one for middle managers at this firm, can serve as a deterrent to fly-by-night offerings from unscrupulous corporate education providers: In other words, having structure as a foil against chaos (T1).

Standout Items or Ideas

- Despite the absence of senior management programs, there is the compelling idea that this firm is perhaps quite wise to continue concentrating on the proper underpinning of programs for middle management, and that this will be fertile ground in which to develop something for senior management later on. Perhaps the one needs to come before the other.

- According to this executive, formal mentoring is not the sort of thing you can create in a structured format, because people may not be any good at giving it or receiving it. It causes jealousy, and it is inherently unfair. However, informal mentoring - people with experience helping people with less experience – works well. "I think that every successful person will talk about someone who has helped them, and I bet research would bear that out".

Interview Case Study Findings – Case No. 3

F1. *Executive learning through visibility:* The CEO and all members of the executive team spend time regularly on the floor (cafeteria, lounges, foyer) of the corporation to permit employees of all levels to join them and ask questions.

F2. *The Multi-tiered organizational education program that is inseparable from the specific part of it that addresses executive learning:* Executive level learning includes leading self, leading others and leading the corporation. A modular based program specific to each of these levels has been introduced.

F3. *Leading the Corporation:* Sixty-five executives attend bi-annual global leadership two-day retreats that deal with the direction of the business as well as some development work. For instance, sessions were given on how to deal with board members. These global leader sessions are organized and developed by an external consultant in close consultation with the firm. This executive believes that a higher level of current expertise than can be developed internally is required in dealing with the learning of the most senior people.

F4. *Educational Programs:* These are developed and delivered mostly by an internal corporate team of instructional designers and facilitators. "The one problem I have found over the years regarding training programs is getting good governance into them, and I have never been a big believer in centralizing training".

F5. *External Educational Affiliations:* In forging these, the first order of business is to have such outside experts train our own organizational development team on the content of any learning program, before it goes out into the field. Universities generally do not appreciate this approach, and that is why this firm rarely deals with them. "We've had discussions with many universities on content, and it has been an absolute unmitigated disappointment". The executive explained that this was principally because universities seemed to want to control most aspects of the educational programs, and that they lacked flexibility to update content easily or in a timely fashion. He also stated that, in his experience, consultants did a better job of initially presenting material to clients.

F6. *Electronics and Social Platforms:* The relatively young workforce at this firm (even the senior group's average age is the mid 40s) realizes the importance, effectiveness and popularity of modern systems of communication, and has developed podcasts to ipods, blogs, employee forums, and some web-based learning materials. It was explained that these are excellent and current communication methods, but that they are not the principal tools for learning. That said, the executive thought that they should be leveraging more use of electronic social platforms for a whole myriad of business reasons in addition to education.

F7. *Curriculum Preferences:* From the list in the interview questions, this executive chose Scenario Planning, Kaizen "which is the continuous improvement process", dialogue and conversation. He emphasized his belief in developing conversation among employees, and stated that doing business is really just a series of conversations. He went on to say that executives must ask themselves what they are doing as leaders to shape the conversations happening in their area of the company, and stated "Conversations to me are one of the most important drivers of the organizational culture". Concerning education for the corporation, he added that they like to do what is needed and not what is fashionable; that whatever is done must be very current and must fit with the business model.

F8. *Business heroes:* Jack Welch, Sam Walton, Warren Buffet and a former CEO of this firm.

F9. *Reading Preferences:* On the business side, Jim Collins (*Good to Great*, 2001; *Built to Last*, 2004; and his articles in the *Harvard Business Review*); Markus Buckingham's *First Break All the Rules*, 1999; Ken Blanchard who was a personal mentor for this executive (*Situational Leadership and the One Minute Manager*, 2005). David Armstrong's *Managing by Storying Around* (1992, currently out of print); and Malcolm Gladwell (*The Tipping Point*, 2000; *Outliers*, 2008).

Narrative Appreciation

This Executive Vice President of Human Resources serves, in his spare time, as thesis advisor for MBA students at a major Canadian

University. He has spent three weeks doing the Ivey Executive Program (IEP) at the University of Western Ontario. In a preliminary phone call that this person requested in preparation for our interview, great interest was expressed in this research. Following this interview, this participant asked for a copy of the dissertation, once it is complete (as have all the other participants without exception).

I arrived for this interview several hours early, and was able to experience life in the common areas of this corporate headquarters, which included a gourmet cafeteria and a magnificent lobby. The atmosphere was electric, exciting, happy, engaged, and it was actually a pleasure to be there. While sitting in the foyer in one of the many very comfortable seats provided there, I watched the firm's CEO who had come down himself to sit in that area. For a whole hour, he sat there meeting with those who would come up to chat with him, and many did. After that, he went to the cafeteria and spent another half hour talking with a couple of his senior team members.

Relevancy to and Resonance with Themes

- Informal learning takes place through the visibility of the senior most group; this is part of the culture (T1, T2, T4).

- This is a learning organization that has specifically developed educational programs for all employee levels. Learning is valued, expected and combines very technically oriented, just-in-time skill enhancement with leadership development and communication programs (T2).

- Help in developing senior management programs is provided exclusively in concert with consultants and not at all with universities. A corporate team of instructional designers and facilitators develops other programs internally (T3).

- Formal, group learning events, particularly for acquiring technical skill sets are the norm. However, informal learning happens all the time in pods of conversation, informal mentoring and coaching, and in story telling (T1).

- Knowledge and facility with the internet, and electronic social communication platforms are expected to be priorities with all employees at all levels of this organization, including top management (T5).

- "We'd like to see more of partnership, in which academic institutions would partner with businesses, but that they would allow those businesses to adjust curriculum and [share] some ownership of it" (T3 and T6).

- Regarding curriculum, "We do what's needed; not what's fashionable. It's got to fit within the business model. We watch our operating costs very carefully. If I'm gong to be bringing 60 people together for a day or two of training, it's a very expensive proposition, and we had better be ensuring that we are getting value out of that. That's part of just-in-time training, to deliver what's important at that time" (T6).

Standout Items

An excerpt from this interview:

> The leader needs to recognize that conversation is going to happen anyway, so he/she needs to set the example by setting the stage for the types of conversation that are going to happen, as they engage with other people. There needs to be some expectations set around not having political or negative, gossipy or argumentative, conversations. So, for instance, let [the leaders] set the example of catching themselves in conversation, when they begin a complaining streak or a negative one; catch and help a colleague when they do it, and move the conversation into a new and better direction.

Interview Case Study Findings – Case No. 4

F1. *Top Executive Learning:* At the senior level, learning is very much along the lines of, "if you think you need something, figure out what it is, and then go out and get it for yourself". It is a very individual thing whether senior people ask for help in discovering learning opportunities, and it is rare that they do. They are much more interested in talking about the training of their own teams of senior people. Nevertheless, there are some provisions for senior executive learning that include internal leadership dialogues, which are arranged on an ad hoc/as required basis.

F2. *Senior Manager and Junior Executive Learning Programs:* Programs are provided by outside consultants and universities around succession planning, leadership development, high potential candidate development, improving on management strengths, and dealing with weaknesses. Often senior executives will work in tandem with professors to deliver "leadership dialogues" to the top 200 executives, who in turn disseminate that training to the next 300 senior managers.

F3. *Balancing Private and Professional Life:* Executive level employees are expected to know how to do this. If help is sought about achieving a better balance, then it will be provided, and there are policies, practices and resources available, which address life/work balance. However, executives who work the long hours are likely still to be honoured and rewarded for doing so.

F4. *External Learning Affiliations:* A deliberate strategy at this firm is forging relationships with individual professors from several universities who possess special expertise, rather than to develop relationships with specific institutions. A good number of these professors now come from the USA. "We feel that we do not have to align ourselves with an institution in order to prove that we are a learning organization". Responsibility for creating and delivering learning programs is never entirely given over to an institution or a consultant. "We are always involved at every step of the way".

F5. *Relevancy:* All educational programs underway at this firm must equate time spent learning with a measurable return, and there is scepticism about many potential programs lacking such "tangibility".

F6. *Electronic Communication and Social Platforms:* There is considerable pressure from the CEO for everyone to become familiar with and to begin using Facebook, blogs, and other current social platforms, which a whole client generation is using (not to mention future executives). There is the absolute belief corporately about the utilization of social media, that "we've got to go in this direction and understand it better; We're trying to bring an aspect of social networking into the company, so that it will lead to business networking as well". When I asked this executive if he himself were on face book, he replied, "Oh, absolutely; and on Linked-In as well". He mentioned that the company Facebook included 8,000 adherents so far. He likened an executive not being on Facebook to a parent not watching television while all their children did.

F7. *Online Learning:* The firm has a preference for face-to-face learning at all levels. The only exceptions seemed to be for regulatory courses or highly technical material.

F8. *Executive Visibility:* An experiment is underway at one of the large divisions to have no offices, but rather an open concept in which everyone works together, and meeting rooms can be reserved for special gatherings. Some executives are resisting this, but others say it has provided better access to them for employees, and that this is improving communication and teamwork. [This was tried at MacMillan Bloedel 20 years ago].

F9. *Cultural Diversity:* Some courses and personal coaching (1-4 participants) are available for this, given the international nature of the company.

F10. *Reading Preferences:* There was no time to ask this question.

Narrative Appreciation

The initial participant for this case was a Vice President responsible for recruitment and learning for a major corporation. In setting up this interview, we had a 40 minute preliminary telephone conversation, the data from which are included here, along with the two-hour face-to-face interview. Because this individual had a prior commitment, he asked two of his colleagues to sit in for him for 45 minutes prior to his arrival. This provided the welcome opportunity for me to interview two additional third level female executives, whom I interviewed separately from the vice president to whom they reported.

Although learning events such as strategic conversations, executive team alignment and development are provided for very senior people in this firm, the thrust of their educational programs is directed further downstream, towards more junior executives and senior managers. Those programs deal with succession, leadership and team development, and specific skill strengthening. Indeed, there are several vice president-level executives in this firm whose specific responsibility is for areas of succession, emerging leader strategy, leadership agility, and employee engagement.

This firm's senior people attend a great many conferences at which they might be keynote speakers. They are involved in *pro bono* charitable activities, and they sit on corporate boards. They are constantly networking with their counterparts in other business sectors in Canada and around the world. Attendance at long duration programs, such as the senior management program at Harvard, or even think tank sessions hosted at such venerated venues as the Aspen Institute, would not be on the agenda for executives from this large Canadian corporation. As this executive stated: "Most senior people at this company find that they can get a lot done here over four days [let alone over several weeks or months], and unless there is a specific value that we can get out of it – after all we're paying for it – we're not going to attend".

Relevancy to and Resonance with Themes

- On the one hand, the philosophy here is that if you need some training, ask for it and it will be granted unto you; On the other hand, there is a vast offering of programs available for every level of management within this organization (T1).

- Senior executives are active in participating as facilitators at major management training events (T1, T4 & T6).

- There is a strong requirement to evaluate all educational program learning benefits with a measurable return, and a psychological "tangibility" (T2).

- Learning affiliations exist with both universities and consulting firms (T3).

- Most programs are designed for large groups or small teams, rather than for individuals. However, coaching of one to four people is available for acquiring special skills, or for dealing with perceived managerial weakness (T4).

- There is considerable pressure from the top for everyone in this organization to keep up to date and become knowledgeable about all electronic communication, including social media platforms, as well as the internet. There was not much understanding about the potential power of online learning to foster interactive and collaborative learning, as well as to simply disseminate knowledge (T5).

- As to senior management programs, there are learning events specifically directed at the top 200 executives. Cultural diversity subjects are key, because this is an international corporation (T6).

Standout Items

- Outside institutional affiliations are more with individual professors, with whom the company has forged meaningful ties, than with a specific institution.

- The notion of leaders leading leaders: The top executives get together on an annual basis to go through a leadership dialogue that is co-facilitated by the CEO and his team, along with experts from academia. Topics are dependent upon the areas of expertise required at that point.

- A quote from this executive:

> Let me tell you, as head of learning, what I do when I run into an executive (regardless of age) who doesn't feel that there is any value in such things as facebook: I try to understand that way of thinking in order to find a way in to a discussion about it – A particular 40 yr old exec was one such person; I know his 14yr old daughter is on facebook all the time, so I told him that I had a 15 and a 17 yr old, and that my advice to him was that if they're on, you'd better be on too; [snaps his fingers] He signed up the next day.

Interview Case Study Findings – Case No. 5

F1. *Every Company is Different:* Educational programs, and especially those for executives must be tailored to the company itself, and to individuals themselves; they must be customized to relate to what is currently happening in the business and in the world at any given point. "There is no such thing as a typical company. Every [learning] approach must be *sui generis*".

F2. *Executive Programs off-the-Shelf or Specifically Designed:* There are executives who would thrive and benefit from the three-month program at Harvard, or from going to the Aspen Institute, but others may require something very specific and different from those.

F3. *Learning Affiliations:* It can be of significant value for a corporation to have a privileged relationship with a good [university] institution. Through such connections a continuity can develop, in the way the faculty people involved follow what the firm is up to, and begin to understand its culture. This executive, however, also firmly believes in tapping the best people in the field in a completely unstructured fashion, and that when you meet with someone who is intelligent, you always learn. For instance, he once invited Jack Welch to speak to his team, and stated "That was difficult to plan, because you cannot script Jack Welch".

F4. *Use of Consultants:* Good results were achieved via an in-depth look at the executive group's strengths and weaknesses. The payoff was finding out that in terms of focus, drive, sense of urgency, they were off the charts, but that they did not listen to their people, nor allowed them to make the contributions to the firm that they were capable of making and wanted to make.

F5. *Powerful Conversations:* Phil Harkins (CEO of Linkage) led a retreat for 45 executives from this firm. It dealt with creating better communications 'Powerful Conversations' (also the title of a book that he wrote). http://www.linkageinc.com/Pages/default.aspx

F6. *Collective or Individual Learning:* "You have to define your needs precisely, at a given point in time; Then you have to decide whether this training should be collective or individual".

F7. *The role of Human Resources in Executive Training:* Too often the HR group is a training shop wanting to promote its various programs. The HR group needs to be the watchdog about learning; the head of HR needs to have the ear of the CEO, and needs to act as a confidant (or confidante) for that leader.

F8. *Balancing Work and Personal Life:* This leader believes that when you run an organization, or part of an organization, you need to share the stress. However, in business you are always accountable and usually immediately so. Therefore, the tendency is to push people (and yourself) to the limit, and vigilance is needed to realize that, under those circumstances, people can lose their balance, marriages can break up, and children will be neglected. Leaders need to know how to pull back and set an example of balance. Nevertheless, if you actually tell a senior person that he has to "get professional help and has a problem with balance", that person may well tell you to "go and fly a kite".

F9. *Curriculum Preferences for Executive Learning:* This leader said that public speaking and media relations were areas often badly ignored, even though they are absolutely crucial. Often there is the assumption that new leaders already possess expertise in these things, but that might not be so. Media coaching is important to teach people how to communicate effectively: "It's got to be lively and interesting to capture their attention; and it should last 20-25 minutes; not an hour!"

F10. *Reading Preferences: Powerful Conversations* (Phil Harkins, 1999); *Good to Great* (Jim Collins, 2001); *Warlord: A Life of Winston Churchill at War, 1974-1945* (Carlo D'este, 2008).

Narrative Appreciation

This individual, arguably the highest level executive of all the senior people interviewed, was the one who had carefully read through all the questions, and had prepared carefully for our chat. He often referred to the questions individually, explaining how what he said was related to them, and asked several times whether he was on-track in helping me to acquire the data I needed for my research. Therefore, it is not surprising that relevancy to theme scores of this interview were much higher than for all other participants, except for Case No. 6 which was slightly higher still. That said, I had invited participants only to regard the questions sent out as guidelines, but I had not expected that this would mean that many of them simply would not read them.

As requested in the preamble to the interview questions, this participant told stories of his own personal experiences as an executive learner. He has served in the CEO job at several large Canadian corporations, and is acting in the roles of chair or board member in others. He has been awarded honourary doctoral degrees from five Canadian Universities, and has served on the advisory board of a well-known Business School.

This executive's philosophy regarding executive education is extremely flexible, based on his belief that every situation is different as to its individuals, what a firm is currently dealing with, and the external factors at play. His philosophy is flexible regarding curriculum content, affiliations (universities and/or consultants), corporate educational requirements, and individual learning preferences. Based on this executive's own experience, he said that he had "a good deal of scepticism about grandiose executive development programs", and that they really had to be tailored to be effective and relevant.

Relevancy to and Resonance with Themes

- As every company, every executive, and every situation is different, it is impossible and inadvisable to choose between formal or informal learning plans (T1).

- Everything you do in training and learning must always be utterly relevant (T2).

- Privileged relationships with universities, in which those institutions become very familiar with a corporation (their client) can bring significant value. In addition, though, relationships with current and practising experts in their field are crucial, whether or not they hail from a university (T3).

- Use of good consultants can also pay off handsomely, and this executive has used their kind of service successfully (T3).

- Most of the learning described by this senior executive was designed for small or large groups of senior managers, although he had a completely open mind about using individual training, whenever it might be necessary (T4).

- There was no mention about electronic social media or the internet (T5).

- Curriculum preferences for this individual were around public speaking and media, relations (T6).

Standout Items

> In my experience, too often you have Human Resources acting as a training shop, and of course they want to promote their programs. The people at the top of the company have said that they want to spend, say (pick a number) 3% of the payroll on training; so therefore they run a session for 20 people and HR comes to you and says "Hey Bruce you didn't send anyone for this; how about sending so-and-so?"

The comments from this executive regarding the HR function were quite novel and fascinating. In order to have the HR group regarded as more than simply one that does staffing functions, it has to be able to bring added value to the corporation. One of the pathways to bringing that value is for the HR group to become more involved and expert in things that are important rather than urgent. In other words, HR must become involved in longer term concerns.

Specifically, this executive told the personal story of having been blessed with an HR leader who was also his confidant in terms of watching over the learning and team workings of the senior group, for things like customer focus and relationships. That confidant virtually forced his CEO to "think through whether there were any weak links in the chain of command".

Interview Case Study Findings – Case No. 6

F1. *The Learning Vision:* To create a company approach, and way of doing things, that relates to a history of best practices – one that can be continually built upon by future generations - and to propagate that throughout the firm. This vision attempts to take advantage of the good things learned through the practice of Distributed Leadership (entrepreneurship, accountability, empowerment), and to jettison the bad elements (silos that do not use best practices, repeating of mistakes, "reinventing the wheel", and a suffering of innovation).

F2. *The Expertise and Product Differentiation Paradox:* Despite possessing such divergent product groups, and having related areas of world-class expertise, 90% of managing these things is really the same exercise (project management, health and safety, project controls). "Pipe building is needed to join up the different silos, so that the same beautiful coloured liquid can flow among them".

F3. *Bringing It Together: Communities of Practice* will be created in which like-minded individuals can begin to compare notes, tell stories, create understanding, build respectful relationships, and begin to put together best learning practices around what they do. They have common interests, and they want to learn together, and to solve problems together.

F4. *The Communities of Practice and How They Function:* (1) As part of their regular job, and as an excellent training process itself, a corporate leader is permanently assigned to put some structure around a problem or challenge in the form of a Community of Practice (CoP), and he/she is judged on the success of that CoP. (2) Each year, a three-day event is scheduled with all CoP teams in attendance, at which progress reports are presented and celebrated (30 such teams are functioning currently within the company). (3) On an ongoing basis, individual teams work online and face-to-face on these challenges, which are inherently common to many of the companies different locations and issues. For instance, every second month, there is a conference call for each CoP to do follow-up. (4) A Share Zone on the intranet, overseen by the Leader, is available for each member (coded access) of each CoP for blogging, asking questions, airing concerns, describing lessons learned and best practices. (5) Common Tools: A selection process by which the CoP membership can acquire tools (e.g. software packages off-the-shelf or commissioned) to facilitate their work, and then promote use of the tool by other groups.

F5. *Internet Zones:* These exist to present the current workings and findings of all CoPs. This is a communication tool to encourage engagement about the company, and also a recruiting function from the general work population for the CoPs, and for inciting creation of new CoPs. Currently CoPs are created from the top down, but eventually they hope to have them bubble up from where the action really is. Already individuals are beginning to ask about the mechanics of setting up these groups.

F6. *Top Executive Team and The Management Committee as Communities of Practice:* The top 100 or so executives of the company are in fact considered, in this company's learning philosophy, as being a Community of Practice, or actually several CoPs. This executive, member of the CEO's natural reporting team, is also the COP "leader" of two such groups: the Management Committee, and Global Procurement.

F7. *Launching of The Corporate University:* Initially this will house the various Communities of Practice currently in operation within the company. These will be supported by a portal on the Info Zone for the learning of all employees. A listing of all training opportunities will then ensue and will include seminars, workshops, learning modules, and courses through affiliations with external institutions. Much of this training is already taking place in the various divisions, but it is hidden from view. The corporate university will unveil and add to those offerings. The Corporate University will also serve as a best practices sharing vehicle for managers and training professionals throughout the organization. Finally, actual curriculum will be created, which will be adapted to the different parts and levels of the company, including a curriculum for executives. "I want this (executive curriculum) to come from the people who will be using it, as opposed to us inventing something and forcing it through".

F8. *The Harvard Connection:* Most executive team members have been to one of the three-month Harvard programs for senior executives. This executive reported it as having been a wonderful and very valuable experience, that took place just before he assumed his new role in charge of strategy for the company, and after having found and trained a replacement for his previous position. With that smooth succession assured, he was able to concentrate totally on his Harvard experience, and to return from it with a virtually completed learning plan for this organization. His recent attendance at the Harvard program consisted of case study work with 161 other executives of the same level from around the world. (A class photo of the same program shows the Class of '82, with only 29 participants). Top notch professors put on a great show, and were very motivated to deliver the goods to such a relevant, focused, and lucrative audience of senior practitioners.

F9. *Work/Life Balance:* The regular employee safeguards for this are in place (assistance programs and flex time arrangements). The firm's culture, however, does not address life/work balance for executives, and it is expected that they know how to deal with that themselves, otherwise they would not have ended up as an executive. "We think this is a personal issue, which is really up to the individual executive to deal with". If an executive requests specific help in balancing work with their personal lives, then of course the firm will do everything to help.

F10. *Mentoring and Coaching:* A mentoring process was attempted but was not successful, due to high expectations and false assumptions about being on the fast track. "We didn't get it right, and it didn't work". On the other hand, this executive brought in individual coaches to the firm, and it is now regarded as a badge of honour, not as a stigma, to have a coach.

F11. *Reading Preferences:* There was not time to ask this question.

Narrative Appreciation

This senior corporate executive is a regular guest lecturer at a well-known Business School in the city where the corporate headquarters are located. This was a very timely interview, because this individual had just been appointed to a new position in charge of strategy for the company. One of the assignments connected with that strategy was to come up with a plan for learning within his multi-national organization, that will bring value to all the components of the organization.

His is a decentralized, product driven organization with divisions all over the world, therefore tending to operate in silos, both geographically and in terms of expertise (centres of excellence). The company uses a Distributed Leadership operating model, in which accountability and responsibility lies with those people who are closest to the clients, their communities and their industry. Local managers are empowered to make decisions, and are responsible for their own financial results.

A healthy and pragmatic flair for self-criticism permitted this executive to reflect on current learning shortcomings within the firm: operating in silos; not bringing enough synergies of best practices to the divisions, which should be the result of belonging to a larger worldwide organization; learning in one division not being easily transferred to another; investing in training not being optimized due to decentralization; freeing up of executives' time, thanks to varying product cycles, not being taken advantage of in using their expertise elsewhere.

Relevancy to and Resonance with Themes

- The recent and company-wide introduction of Communities of Practice (CoP) as the foundation for organizational learning, is indicative of a highly organized and formal educational program (T1).

- The Communities of Practice are in fact learning pods which are not only relevant to the business at hand, but they *are* the business at hand (T2).

- Learning affiliations exist with several local universities, at which members of this organization have created whole programs which they facilitate (T3).

- The essence of the learning is in groups, which are the CoPs (T4).

- Multi-faceted use of electronic communication, intra and internet is apparent, and it includes Share Zones for the work of the CoPs, some web-based online learning for technical courses, and blogs (T5).

- Curriculum is developed on an ad hoc basis and delivered just-in-time, in direct relationship with the demands and requirements of the many CoPs operating continuously within the company. Curriculum for the most senior people is along the lines of retreats, at which strategic issues are discussed, and at which guest speakers may present (T6).

Standout Items

- Communities of Practice: Executives must all become familiar with the reasons for and the running of CoPs, and they are expected to support them actively, and eventually to participate in them. At this corporation, through the creation by the employees themselves of Communities of Practice (30 currently operating within the company), learning has become a way of life. This executive's description of organizational learning via CoPs was nothing short of remarkable in its scope, cohesion, completeness and far-sightedness. This development is carefully orchestrated, and involves every level of the organization. This initiative has been instituted by the leaders, but will eventually be created from the ground up. Silo-breaking CoPs will be populated by like-minded individuals in fields of expertise from all areas of the company. "They will love the relationship that causes them to talk to their colleagues around the company all year round. They have a leader who stimulates them; there is buy-in and there is interactivity". Learning happens because 80% of it is generic in nature (learning to learn, communication, networking, problem solving, being entrepreneurial and innovative) with the other 20% being particularly adapted to the project in hand of each CoP.

- A Corporate University has been announced: Initially, this will be a shell to house the Communities of Practice, but eventually it will be expanded to include the educational skill feeds for those CoPs, in terms of courses and other major learning programs. The Corporate University educational unit will corral into one place the many useful training initiatives in play at the company's various sites around the world. It will develop programs for all levels of the organization, including for executive ranks.

Interview Case Study Findings (F) – Case No. 7

F1. *Executive Education:* There are not many executives at this firm – more because of leanness than size. The principal learning happens through a constant rotation which sees each of the top five people presiding over manufacturing operations of the company in Asia during several weeks per year. The CEO sends individuals on special formal courses as the need arises. For instance, he sent three of his senior team on a personal development course to hone people skills, facilitated by a consulting firm out of Seattle.

F2. *Organizational Learning:* All employees are encouraged to take university courses towards certification. Candidates' tuition fees are paid by the company upon successful completion.

F3. *Learning Affiliations:* The only formal learning affiliation is the strong one that the CEO personally has as a member of the graduate advisory board of a major Canadian University. That board has been quite responsive to his critical advice, despite its often being controversial. This advice is mostly about the MBA program, which is the backbone for other offerings, but it also sometimes delves into general and customized executive learning programs.

F4. *Relevancy:* This executive has shown concern about how to bring greater relevance into existing business courses, and into those which are being developed. For instance, if students are learning about doing business in Asia, he suggests they should go to Asia. He wondered how to react constructively to the large number of professors teaching business who have never been exposed to real world education formats, and he therefore asked "Are we in fact preparing our students to go out into the real world, as opposed to just getting the academic learning experience; to make decisions that are relevant, and not simply academic?" All that said, this executive is pro universities, and he will not hire anyone into his company, regardless of level, who does not have a university degree.

F5. *Using Universities or Consultants for Executive Programs:* The CEO feels that universities seem to do a good job with the generic off-the-shelf programs, including such things as information technology, which can be used for large groups of people coming in from corporations who are big enough to be able to afford them. For the mid-sized company, or for specialized needs for any corporation (e.g. international or global business logistics, manufacturing offshore, or dealing with regional rules and regulations), consultants might have better expertise stemming from their actual experiences.

F6. *Mintzberg's International Practicing Managers Program:* I wondered whether this type of academic program that includes spending five two-week stints while shadowing a student colleague in his/her native land, in five different countries/cultures would fit the bill as far as the practicality test was concerned. This executive responded that it was certainly closer to the mark, but that "I can't give up one of my executives for three days, let alone for 10 weeks!" He added that people are expected to do more now than ever before, and when they fall out of sync with what is going on, even for a few days, it takes them a week or so of extra work to get back on track.

F7. *Technology:* This firm is well versed in technology regarding electronic communication, social networks (blogging, Q&As, Facebook, e-commerce, real-time sophisticated search engines). There is a VP in charge of client services, which is heavy on the side of information technology. Young people have grown up with technology and may have then furthered its practice at university.

Older people are less familiar with technology and need to learn about it. When he joined the company seven years ago, this executive personally developed a complete online learning program regarding management/supervisory skills in times of turbulent change. It comprised 12 modules for all employees to take. "It was voluntary, but everyone took it, and *said* that they got something out of it", he commented with a smile. This online program however did not contain any interactivity (blackboard discussion groups, smaller work groups etc), and was really an "info dump" of reading materials, notices, individual exercises to confirm participation and learning.

F8. *Curriculum Preferences:* Public Speaking ("I have seen so many times where an executive is representing a company, and it is not done well. Or else, the poor people are so nervous and it has to be absolute torture for them"); Dialogue and Conversation ("Businesses which do not have both great formal and informal dialogue and conversation are definitely destined for failure"); Cultural Diversity, especially for international or global companies; Media Relationships and skill to handle them. This executive also said he would add topics on International Business, Global Operations and Logistics (e.g. tax issues and avoidance, regulations; procedures that might be illegal "here" but not "there").

F9. *Coaching:* The participant said that these days, everyone seemed to be a coach (just as everyone seemed to be involved in "green" products) and that, "The whole idea of this coaching thing to me has lost its spark". At his firm, coaching took the form of creating internal redundancy among all senior executive positions through cross-training. Specifically, every executive is trained and coached to be able to function in another senior job should the need arise. He said that this form of coaching could simply be regarded as succession planning or risk management.

F10. *Reading Preferences:* This leader believes in staying very well informed about what is going on in the world. He is a self-declared avid reader of business related and informational material, and does not read fiction. He reads regional, national and international magazines (*Business Week, The Economist, Time, McLeans*) and three or four newspapers daily. He mentioned as favourite business authors Jack Welch and Peter Newman; thought Covey was a little outdated. He reads weekly research material, and daily updates from the likes of the TD Bank, as well as daily batches of industry related reading.

Narrative Appreciation

This executive partly owns and runs a multi-national company, which manufactures and sells consumer products. As such, it is very well electronically connected to its distributors and end-use customers, and has substantial technological knowledge and practice. This leader serves on an advisory board for graduate programs in business at a major Canadian University. He holds an MBA, which he earned later in his business life, and he is currently completing a graduate degree in law while he continues his demanding job as CEO and President of his mid-sized firm. The value of this interview comes mostly from this individual's ideas about executive learning based on his vast business experience, his own formal MBA learning, and his advisory capacity about graduate business programs already mentioned. The executive learning taking place within this firm is of lesser significance for this particular case.

This leader is a strong believer in formal education and will not hire anyone who does not have a university degree, regardless of job entry level. There is therefore an *à priori* indication for all potential employees that the constant pursuit of learning is a respected, expected, and encouraged part of this company's culture.

Relevancy to and Resonance with Themes

- There is a good mix at this firm of informal executive learning on-the-job, in the form of a rotation of senior people through company operations in Asia; personal development of senior people with the help of consultants, and attendance by lower level managers at regular local university programs and courses (T1).

- No program, course, or learning intervention is used, unless it has a very high degree of relevancy to the job (T2).

- The only learning affiliation used for people development is the one with a consulting firm. Employees who attend university courses, as they are encouraged to do, choose their own institutional affiliation. However, as stated earlier, the executive interviewed sits on a university advisory board for graduate business education (T3).

- Education at this company used to be in the form of a whole program of intense learning as a group, which this executive was hired to develop and deliver 12 years ago. He did that through lunch meetings, seminars, as well as online learning segments. More recently, learning has become an individual affair, and it mostly happens on-the-job in real time (T4).

- This company is highly technical in its connectivity to the rest of the world through the internet, which it monitors closely. It is knowledgeable about all social electronic platforms, search engines, and it makes use of them. Its connection to suppliers, customers, and the general public is all electronic and automated. There is a senior executive in charge of this technology and of keeping it current. (T5).

- Other than general programs which employees are encouraged to attend at local universities, curricular emphasis is on just-in-time skill acquisition, and on arranging learning to overcome specific individual learning or communication shortfalls in a remedial manner (T6).

- As to specific curriculum, this executive emphasized the importance of public speaking and media relations; dialogue and conversation; and cultural diversity for any company that deals outside North America (T6).

Standout Items

This executive's recommendations regarding improvement of graduate business school offerings included:

- More relevance in planning for learning to happen where it physically should happen to be most effective. In other words, if a course is on doing business in Asia, have the students go to Asia.

- Professors must have practical experience in the areas in which they are teaching.

- Universities do a good job in subjects that are generic, off-the-shelf skills concerning professional items such as accounting, finance, technology; but for the highly customized, urgent, very specific requirements, consultants are better. The implication here is that universities could learn by looking at what consultants are doing.

- Forget the programs that take senior people away for two-week stints, let alone longer than that: "I cannot afford to have those people away for more than a day or two".

- Too much talk about coaching. Everyone you meet is a coach. It feels like a fad, similar to the "green" craze. Universities should be cautious about jumping on these bandwagons unless they really mean it.

This executive, also a personal friend, offered to ask a few questions on my behalf at a high-level executive seminar he was invited to attend in the United States. He filled out some question cards, but the moderator (Charlie Rose) changed the wording slightly from the original request. Participants were not allowed to ask direct questions of Welch & Nardelli. They wanted the questions screened, probably because the event was to be reported world-wide. It should be noted that this event occurred only days before the Congressional hearing into the automobile industry, which Bob Nardelli of Chrysler was about to attend.

The original question: How important do you think executive education is within a corporation?

This exchange occurred in which CR is moderator Charlie Rose; JW is Jack Welch (ex Chair of General Electric), and RN is Robert Nardelli (CEO Chrysler):

CR to JW: How do you develop your executives, how do you train them?

JW: It's all about learning. Sessions should be modest food fights; you need to dig in, have fun, debate, argue. Forget the slide shows and the presentations...that's stupid. You need to take an idea, decide if it is a good one and then go after it. Hire people smarter than you are. Don't hire weaker people than yourself.

CR to RN: What do you think about Executive Education and MBAs?

RN: Charlie, it is very important. Over half of our top three hundred executives at Chrysler hold an MBA. We strongly encourage graduate education for our executives, and we are an educated lot.

Interview Case Findings – Case No. 8

F1. *Leadership and Strategic Planning:* This firm has a fairly elaborate senior managers' program, which was created by an external consulting firm. This executive has been closely connected with these programs, running sessions in the leadership program, and facilitating strategic sessions for the senior executive team of the parent firm.

F2. *Mentoring and Coaching:* Mentoring at this firm is not a formal process, but rather one of ad hoc coaching. That seemed surprising, given the size of the corporation and its other very active training initiatives. This executive thought that, in the parent corporation, executives seemed to be finding less and less time for this terribly valuable and nurturing function of taking people under their wing, and generally becoming involved in the educational programs of their employees. This participant does not think that it is a cost problem, but rather one of managers finding time to put one more thing on their plates. Nevertheless, during his own career, this executive has considered coaching and mentoring as a crucial and rewarding part of his job. He now sees the mentoring and coaching process as one of helping quality employees out of a rut, so that they can get on with, and ahead, in their careers. It is complicated, though, because one has to draw the line between coaching on professional matters and being compassionate, versus becoming involved in the woes and challenges of their personal lives. He felt it was important to leave protégées with the idea of passing on the torch: that at some point in their career, the student had to become the teacher.

F3. *Internal and External Facilitation:* These are important items that could be "taught" through giving a good example, and through practice. He said that the best coaches for this kind of thing, therefore, come from inside – just like in sports, he added. Those internal people understand better and more urgently what is important; what works and what doesn't work. This kind of learning from the inside can be supplemented with external coaches who can deal with the more generic aspects.

F4. *Developing "Hard" cf. "Soft" Skills:* Most senior people already have the "hard" skills when they reach the executive level (for example, letting go underperformers, firing an account that is just killing you, resolving credit situations). "The thing we have to be careful about is that we don't become too crusty once we get there", and that is when there may be a need for learning or re-learning some of the "softer" skills, and becoming more compassionate. That style works with managing from in front; being with the people (employees and customers), and not hiding in your office asking for some report. "I think that the current generation of business has lost the knack [of doing that]". They have become just too busy through things like downsizing, having to keep many more stakeholders happy, and therefore having more on their plate; and they "manage from behind the blackberry".

F5. *Curriculum – Strategic Thinking Process, Public Speaking and Writing Skills:* This executive, who was involved in facilitating the parent corporation's strategic plan with the executive team, felt that this process was a most valuable management learning activity. It was a three-day process, which brought the senior team together, getting them to think together and come up with a plan, which was then rolled out in a similarly participative manner throughout the company. In that way, everyone felt "buy-in": It was their plan to create, and to deliver. The process did not end there; there were quarterly updates. It was a simple, non-elaborate plan, which everyone could understand and contribute to. This executive said that public speaking was also important as a remedial action for those who needed it, based on seeing them speak at senior management gatherings and presentations. Similarly, this executive would read e-mails from his senior people, would arrange writing skill enhancement help for them as required. Writing is a skill that one expects from leaders, but one which they do not necessarily have.

F6. *Custom and Open Executive Programs:* This firm preferred custom designed programs, or generic ones given by experts in their own industry, who had a portfolio of success in that area. It was felt that such programs would likely be better put together and delivered by consultant groups than by universities. For topics such as technology, science, or specifically academically oriented topics like economics, or risk management, an open enrolment university course or program might be just the thing. However, for specifically oriented, industry-specific, flexible programs, consultants would be the better way to go. "What I have found with consultants is that they have some pretty interesting practical experiences in their own lives".

F7. *Feedback from Learning Programs:* This was in the form of a survey, filled out on the last day of the program – but with a difference. The last day of the formal program was not the last day of the offsite meeting. There was always a dinner held on the last night, with participants scheduled to leave the following day. Thus, when the formal program ended, nobody was rushing out of the room to catch a plane; and the feedback was approached with due care and attention, with more useful results.

F8. *Life/Work Balance:* With the help of an external consultant and a good deal of funds, this firm had a major initiative created around balancing work life and personal life. The HR group held high-level meetings with the senior group to present its strong view that this balance would improve performance; that it would keep people healthy and around for the long haul. However, the corporation just kept on cranking up the workload and the expectations. "These two things did not mesh, and the program failed completely". Regarding how to help people balance life and work, one size does not fit all. A balanced life for one family is not necessarily balanced for another family. "Telling somebody who works 70 hours per week, and somehow manages it all, that they must now only work 40 hours per week, and that they have to spend more time at home just doesn't work". This whole issue of balance has, of course, become more complicated now, because often both spouses are working. It was simpler when one spouse was working at home.

F9. *Valuable Executive Teaching and Learning Behaviours:* (1) Setting the example (walking around, face-time); (2) The strategic planning process (learning and creating together); (3) Treating people differently (not being afraid to single out and honour, or celebrate, certain behaviours).

F10. *Reading Preferences:* "These days it's mostly Motor Home and Boating magazines!" This executive reads a number of current business books to stay informed. He added that the publishers that put out those books do a good job using the fear tactic that many executives are afraid of being out of the loop, and simply have to get hold of the latest must-have volume by the corporate gurus, for use at their next cocktail party. He favourably mentioned Jim Collins (*Good to Great*, 2001) – not earth shattering, but simple, practical and useful stuff: getting the right people on the bus and in the right seats; and getting the wrong people off the bus.

Narrative Appreciation

Recently retired ex president of the Canadian operations of an international firm, this executive had a sales and general management background. He was also an excellent facilitator, and had been used in that capacity on many occasions, in order to work with senior leaders of the parent organization in their creation of system-wide business strategies.

Relevancy to and Resonance with Themes

- There was a formal company-wide leadership program for senior managers (T1).

- The strategic planning exercise is one of the best senior management learning processes there is. It is a cohesive team-building event, which causes buy-in regarding company objectives, because they are co-created during the process itself. (T2).

- According to this executive, the best coaches and facilitators come from inside, and should be developed from there. Nevertheless, the senior managers' education program was put together by an external consultant (T3).

- This executive had a strong belief in the value of coaching, and the obligation of senior managers to do it. In the overall operations of this large firm however, there seemed to be less time available for this apparently valuable activity. (T4).

- Very little conversation took place about the internet and electronic communications, except for the comment that too many people were managing from behind their blackberries, rather than being in front of their people (T5).

- The strategic thinking process, public speaking and writing skills were mentioned as the most important curriculum items (T6).

Standout Items

Acquiring useful feedback on learning programs:

> There was no rushing away at the end, because (from an idea I picked up from my strategic planning process) we did not permit people to fly home on the final day. There was a closing dinner that night that the CEO always attended, and the participants left the next day. So there was one more opportunity to get together socially on that last night; one more time to let hair down, [but also a likelihood that the surveys would be answered with due care and attention]. I thought this worked very well.

Interview Case Findings – Case No. 9

F1. *Internal Executive Programs:* These were offered at a central location by the Corporate Training Centre. There was, in particular, an eight week business course for senior managers from around the world. The program content included financials, HR, computers, manufacturing, logistics, and some, but not much, on "soft" skills. There was a great deal of reading to catch up on each night, as well as study groups; there were team-building courses designed to find people who might excel in senior management. Surprisingly, although these people came from many different countries and spoke many different languages, all the training was done in English. The foreign participants used to record the sessions, and then have them translated when they got back home. Despite this being an internal program, they relied on a number of outside professors from the local university to facilitate the program.

F2. *Annual Executive Meetings:* These comprised 110 individual senior management presentations about favourite best practices, over three days. The "take-away" was that each divisional manager had to adopt one of the best practices that he/she had heard during this meeting, and follow-up on the success of its implementation with individual bosses.

F3. *Best Practices:* The model that this divisional VP presented to the group (which was used by others subsequently) involved colour coding their entire organizational chart: white for "great soldierly type but limited for advancement"; yellow for "getting into trouble, and having a skill deficiency. We should take positive action by sending them off to do some courses"; red for "remedial action required, because they were in trouble and were on an exit track unless the issue were resolved"; green for "movers and shakers who could advance through the company, and who should be sent on specific educational courses to facilitate that happening". The follow-up, a case in point, might be sending a person who had trouble relating to others to attend a Dale Carnegie course. That actually did wonders, but five months later he reverted to his old unsociable behaviours.

F4. *Feedback and Follow-up:* After the eight week senior program, there was a reunion six months later, at which each participant had to present a thesis about the learning that had occurred, and how it had been used in a practical on-the-job manner, during the intervening months. On the everyday side, however, feedback was terribly lacking in this person's opinion. For instance, during his 34 years with the company, he had never had a performance review.

F5. *Expectations about Executive Learning:* These were informal, and, for example, the firm was not happy with the relative disinterest this executive had for these programs, or for obtaining any external accreditation (such as the MBA). This person had little respect for formal learning such as that demonstrated by the MBA degree. He praised "street smarts" as being the relevant, experiential learning that really mattered.

F6. *360 degree Feedback:* This process, facilitated by an outside consultant upon recommendation of the board, was adopted by the corporation and was compulsory for the top 200 executives. There was a perceived problem in the organizational culture of the firm. This individual said he fared rather well in it (peers, subordinates, customers and boss all gave him positive feedback). Although a few of the senior people were let go because of this review, many who did not fare so well in this exercise openly stated that they couldn't care less, and continued their own old habits with impunity. When the results came back, with many of the senior group faring so badly, the consultant apparently stated that it would take 10-15 years to make a dent in the current, relatively unhealthy, culture.

F7. *External Learning Affiliations:* This executive would opt for a relationship with a university before a consultant. His experience with consultants was that they tended to get too close to the company, whereas the relationship with a university was more professional and businesslike.

F8. *Life/Work Balance:* This person said that he had managed a very good balance, but it was one that was not aided by his company's edict about generally not including spouses in corporate and customer entertainment events. Including spouses, in this executive's opinion, is a way to help balance work life and personal life. This leader was not at all sure whether senior people cared much about the life/work balance question; and that, therefore, it might be rather a waste of time to be worrying about it, and trying to come up with a helpful learning program around it.

F9. *Technology:* This person felt that some of the technology helpers were invaluable, permitting him to travel as much as he did while still remaining in contact with the office, and personally with the family. However, he felt that e-mail was mostly a waste of time, because its use was utterly out of control, misused and abused; for example, in the way people two offices apart would e-mail each other, rather than visiting personally with each other. Slightly related to technology, but of a different ilk, was this person's decision early on to (a) take typing lessons and to (b) learn shorthand. He felt that these old-fashioned "technologies" had served him well.

F10. *Reading Preferences:* Surprisingly, this executive said that he did no reading whatsoever. He got all he needed from news, documentaries and public affairs programs on TV. He said he religiously watched BBC World News, and CNN and that's all he wanted/needed.

Narrative Appreciation

Most of this corporation's executives were internally promoted and worked their way up through the ranks, and were therefore more elderly than was apparent with the competition, or in other major corporations. The company had trouble introducing a new wave of educated executives into their ranks, because their outdated policies were unattractive. They did manage to hire people with MBAs, but found it very difficult to keep them. There was a great wall between management and labour within the company, and there was an attitude of not intermingling these two factions.

This executive, a senior vice president, had retired from this company a few years ago. He is the perfect example of a street-smart, customer-oriented, pragmatic and successful, leader who was close to his people and had a common touch. He was somewhat jaundiced regarding his corporation's fancy plans to "educate" people, especially those who had learned most of what they know through practical lessons on-the-job. I felt that this large firm had a better overall executive education program in place than this senior executive person appreciated, underlining once again just how personal or individual learning preferences really are.

Relevancy to and Resonance with Themes

- This firm had a corporate training department, the type typical of large corporations in the 1970s and 80s, to orchestrate formal training courses and programs for all levels of the organization. Annual executive meetings for the top 100 executives were held to deal with strategic issues and best practices (T1).

- Internally and centrally organized training ensured that most material was relevant to the corporation's interests. There was a surprisingly good follow-up, for instance for an eight-week senior managers program: It consisted in getting the learning group back together again six months later to have each participant present a "thesis" about how the learning had been put into practice (T2).

- There was some remedial learning through liaisons with schools such as The Dale Carnegie Institute; and 360 degree feedback exercises administered by professional consultants were *de rigueur* for all executives. This executive felt that "the 360" did not change any behaviour, and yet it did result in the firing of some senior people. This VP preferred working with what he considered the more professional universities over consultants, whom he felt tended to be less professional and businesslike (T3).

- Most training was done in large or small groups, and there was no mention of individual learning such as coaching (T4).

- This executive loved advances in technology, which had permitted him to stay connected with his office and family while travelling. However, he felt that e-mail was mostly a waste of time, and was abused by most, who overused it (T5).

- Not much interest was shown in curriculum issues by this executive, because in his view the content did not seem to produce good enough results. As he stated, "We don't need the pinstripe suit guy who doesn't understand the system, doesn't understand unions, doesn't understand people, including customers". Concerning another colleague, he stated "You could educate that guy until you were blue in the face; he was not going to change" (T6).

Standout Items

Comments about retirement:

> We all change when we retire, and we go through phases, and we need to figure that out. [It's as though we're searching for the kind of variety in retirement that we had when working]. Part of the training that we took involved feeling comfortable in your own skin, and I felt that way;.... and I loved my work. But when I retired, although I still felt comfortable, I had to figure out who I [now] was, and that took a little doing. I'm not sure that a training or educational program around that would have helped me.... No matter what training you give someone [about this], if the spouse is still working, then you have a real problem, because the one who's retired has to figure out what to do on their own [and that is doubly difficult].

Interview Case Findings – Case No. 10

F1. *Executive Success:* These leaders felt that the most successful executives are those who are most conscious, meaning that they can identify patterns and behaviour in their subconscious mind, and recognize them for what they are, rather than letting them control the person. Fast moving current business requires leaders who are conscious.

F2. *Executive Learning:* This needs to be consistent and continual personal development – whatever form that may take. It applies to the whole corporation, and not simply or specifically to the senior levels. All levels must go through the personal development courses that are staged regularly. Otherwise it's only all about the leaders, which, of course, it is not. People need to learn how to help each other out, how to better serve. There are five or six mandatory development courses that the senior people go to; there are group courses for the next level of about 40 people who take sessions together – one just last month.

F3. *The Neurological Point of View about Training:* "Training is all about nerve structure". Learning is repetition in doing something, and this improves the operation of nerve pathways and develops the myelin sheath (electrically insulating material that forms a layer) around those pathways. The result is that the nerve conducts faster – up to 200 times faster – leading to a major improvement: consistently thinking faster, and reacting faster, in a given area of expertise. No matter how much talent someone may have [gave the example of Tiger Woods], their myelin sheath pathways need to be provoked over and over again. Now, this would happen naturally, simply by doing. However, this needs to be done particularly by working on the mistakes – on things that aren't quite right - otherwise nothing changes. In business this particularly applies to innovation.

F4. *Company Goals:* To grow the company and to grow oneself. "A business is a collection of many different individuals, but we come together as one entity; so the growth of the entity really depends on the growth of the individuals".

F5. *Curriculum:* These two executives believe that people can learn all the business tools and strategies they want, but if the underlying structure of individual identity is faulty or wanting, then there will be trouble. So the learning culture of an organization recognizes this and develops people accordingly. The learning person is someone who begins to understand how to put themselves in the shoes of others (fellow employees and customers, among others). Nevertheless, you need a formal educational plan for personal as well as technical development for all your people. The focus needs, however, to be on how to grow each individual personally. Learning is best done collectively, frequently and in an environment of immersion offsite. This is not contradictory because individual growth needs to be in the context of relating to others.

F6. *Coaching and Mentoring:* As a business leader, it is not about you; it is about all the people who are working with you. Mentoring and coaching are critical in certain situations. These executives pointed to the long and rich history of guild apprenticeship during the Italian Renaissance, before it became too powerful to be accepted by the Nation States ("It was a good 50 year run"). This firm is actually already using the apprenticeship model that will be crucial due to their phenomenal growth plans. However, they realize that everyone is not a good teacher or model, and that the right master and the right apprentice are both required for this transfer of knowledge to work.

F7. *The MBA, Harvard, and The Aspen Institute:* These executives stated that they would not send any of their people to any MBA program, nor to the Harvard three month program for senior managers, because they felt that these offerings were irrelevant to the kind of personal development learning they wanted for their employees. They might send them to a three to five day think-tank event at the Aspen Institute, which often deals with world issues, with thoughtful exercises and networking with like-minded, caring people.

F8. *Attitude:* "If people at any level of an organization are unhappy in their work, they are stagnant. If they are stagnant they are not learning; if they are not learning, there is no talent development; if there is no talent development, then they will inevitably just sink. The skill rests in finding ways to empower and grow people. Everyone learns a little differently. There is no perfect system to teach everyone. People can arrive at the same [learning] destination via different routes. You need to find ways to stimulate and encourage the growth of every individual".

F9. *Learning Program Design:* People learn best in concert with each other, not in isolation ("not by Coaching-101"). That is the way people find out about themselves, and about exactly who they are. The content is secondary to this relationship learning. Therefore, sending people to high impact, off-the-shelf courses (rather than in-house customized programs) is the way to go, so that they can interact with others from all different kinds of backgrounds. The exception would be for massive companies, for whom customized courses would still involve enough participants to have ample interactions happening, because people might never have met each other, even though they work with the same firm.

F10. *Culture:* This smallish firm has the luxury of starting small and being focused, with a culture that mirrors the mindset of the founders: one of technology, growth, innovation, passion and trust. "Our long-term goal is to have a global community espousing this culture". They hire for personality traits, which are in sync with this culture. The learning (personal development) curriculum is clearly spelled out to all potential employees. Once hired, seeing these new people learning together is another way they have to check out the rightness of the fit.

F11. *Reading Preferences:* Both men were clearly extremely well read. However, the only book that was mentioned was Jim Collins' *Good to Great* (2001).

Narrative Appreciation

These two executives were a fascinating team: an older, wiser PhD in Physics, who is also a practising medical doctor with huge entrepreneurial leanings, teamed up with a much younger, energetic, well educated visionary devoted to learning every minute (says he is away 26 out of 52 weekends during the year in some kind of learning environment). He stated within the first minute of our conversation, "Doc here can attest to the fact that I have basically two goals: to grow the company and to grow myself.... So the whole corporate culture here is one of growth for the company, and personal growth for the individual".

Hiring practices in this start-up, high-tech firm underscore finding passionate people who believe in learning and self-development as a way of life. They are hired and serve as teachers for subsequent hires within their areas of expertise, so that the firm is able to expand quickly into other North American and world markets.

Relevancy to and Resonance with Themes

- This firm insists on intense, internal, practical, skill-based education in the form of an apprenticeship model, combined with consistent and continual personal development courses externally. This requires a formal learning structure that is clearly spelled out for all employees to understand (T1).

- The skill-based learning is obviously closely and urgently connected to the job. Personal development courses are also utterly relevant, but in a more sophisticated way: these must enhance an executive's consciousness or awareness so that they can identify, understand and use patterns and behaviours of their subconscious minds (T2).

- Learning affiliations are mostly with any excellent providers of personal development programs, but with an apparent preference for the non academic variety. For instance, these executive entrepreneurs would not send any of their people to any MBA program, which they feel is irrelevant to what their senior people need to know and should be able to do. Neither would they send them to the longer, strategic programs such as the one at Harvard for senior executives. They might however send people to the Aspen Institute's three to five day think-tank style forums, which deal with world issues such as poverty, famine, technology and business. (T3).

- These men believe that there is no perfect system to teach everyone, and that people can arrive at the same learning destination via different routes. Therefore, learning can just as easily happen individually or in groups. However, the best learning includes a component of relationship building, hence there might be a preference for team learning to provide a superior or a more complete result(T4).

- Being a firm that uses very high-tech manufacturing processes, and given the youth of one of the partners and most of the operating staff (all of whom will eventually be among the firm's leaders), there is a great deal of knowledge present about technological platforms. This includes use and familiarity with electronic social media, search engines and web-based research (T5).

- Curriculum content is secondary to the relationship component of learning. The relationship component is the one that awakens people to who they are. High-impact off-the-shelf courses, rather than in-house programs, is the way to go; it affords people the opportunity to interact with others from all sorts of different backgrounds, and industries or sectors. (T6).

Standout Items

- The New Executive Curriculum: the new way that should dictate curriculum is for a senior manager to ask his/her boss what it is that the supervisor particularly needs; then that executive should implement it. If certain skills, or understanding are missing for its delivery, then the executive should go out and acquire them, wherever that can be best accomplished. "Basically wherever you are in the food chain, you need to go up to the next level and ask how you can better serve, and this needs to percolate all the way up through an organization".

- The Neurological View of Training and Development: for the purposes of this presentation, the important elements of this fascinating idea were explained in F3 of this Case's highlights.

- This Firm's Surprising Culture (A direct quote from the interview):

> I know that you have already interviewed 13 people, but you are the first person to interview us, and you certainly won't be the last. The environment that we are creating here is one that does not exist. You are not going to find a reference for it among the 13 whom you have interviewed. When it's built, everyone from Harvard and Stanford is going to be teaching courses around it. I am not expecting you to have a reference for what I am talking about. One of the great things here is that we get to structure the company the way we want and need to for long-term growth from the outset. The goal is to create an enlightened company. It is not a job anymore for those that come to work here. We are creating an environment in which people are constantly learning and growing, and the company is as well. We will never stop creating products and services, which are going to constantly challenge people to do things they have never done before. We do not assume that the position that a person is in right now is the only one that they will ever hold within the company. We want to

grow our leaders from within. So the people at the bottom as well as those at the top will go through the personal development courses. It is not the same as in a set industry like steel or forestry or mining. We will have a lot of product innovations that we can deploy over the next twenty years. We believe in taking people in here with a raw foundation, and developing them into people who can achieve amazing things. That requires a process of constant learning and growth in addition to the everyday tasks that they need to perform in their jobs. These deeply loyal, committed and passionate employees will be with us forever.

The Interview Quintain

The Themes (Items of Highest Relevance)

Case	Custom Open C or O	Formal Y or N	Coaching Y or N	Consultants Universities Internal C,I or U	Centralized Decentralized C or D	Tech. Usage H,M,L	Learng Org. Score H,M,L
1	C & O	Y	<u>Y</u>	I & u	d	M	H
2	O	Y	N	U	C	L	M
3	C	Y	N	<u>I</u> & C	C	H	H
4	C & O	Y	N	U	C	M	M
5	C & o	Y	n	C & U	C	L	M
6	C	Y	N	<u>I</u> & u	<u>**D**</u>	H	<u>**H**</u>

7	C &o	Y	n	I & c	C & d	H	M
8	C	Y	y	C	C	L	M
9	C &o	Y	y	I & u	C	L	M
10	O	Y	N	U et al	C	H	H
all	C x 8	All Y	Y x 3	C x 4	C x 8	H x 4	H x 4
	O x 7		N x 7	U x 7	D x 3	M x 2	M x 6
				I x 5		L x 4	L x 0

Table #3- Interview Statistics: Themes used for some of the following analyses

Note: special emphasis in the use of upper cf. lower case, and of **bold** (For example, C&O means both custom and open enrolment programs are evenly emphasized; C&o means that Custom programs are emphasized more than open enrolment programs)

For the Quintain of Interview cases, the following items were the most highly relevant to the research themes:

Formality or Informality of Learning Plans and their Design

Learning plans for executives may have been informal in style and even expectations, but in every case, they had structure. Each one of the ten cases could certainly be considered as having a formalized learning program in place. It is possible that those people who agreed to be interviewed did so because they had a formalized learning system to talk about, otherwise they might not have agreed to do it. Although there was structure, there was very little talk about accountability regarding funds spent on executive learning. In several cases (four of the 10), there seemed to be a healthy reluctance to separate executive learning from overall learning in the organization. These firms had clearly delineated programs for their executive ranks, but they only wanted to talk about them in conjunction with their company's overall learning efforts. This seemed in keeping with what one might expect from what is called "a learning organization".

In a subjective exercise, based on the tenor of my conversations and the passion with which these executives talked about their learning programs, I have presumed to put a High, Medium or Low designation about the degree to which the firms appeared to me to be so-called "learning organizations": Four scored HIGH, six scored MEDIUM, and none scored LOW. Of the four HIGH scores, two of them were remarkably so, and could easily serve as stellar examples (in some future study) of what a modern day learning organization should look like.

The firm that could be considered the best example of a learning organization had an absolutely decentralized, although formal, company-wide learning program: Readers may remember Case No.6, which boasted Communities of Practice being created at the grass-roots level in operations around the world – a veritable poster for decentralized learning. The other nine firms had highly centralized programs, which were conceived, designed, and tested at headquarters, and then rolled out to everyone else.

From the design perspective, there was a slight overall preference for custom over open enrolment (off-the-shelf) learning programs. Most executives said their firms liked to use a combination of the two, weighted towards the custom design, over which they could exercise greater control. Two firms used open enrolment type programs, with no customization.

Relevancy and Learning Affiliations

Issues of relevancy according to the executives interviewed refer to learning providers delivering to clients the desired tight connection between subject matter and business priorities, a flexibility in adapting to the wishes of the client, facility in changing curriculum quickly with minimum of fuss, a predilection for expecting and wanting the clients' input at every step of the way, a closeness to the market in terms of practicality versus theory, and a sense of urgency similar to the burning sense of urgency that the client, who is paying for the service, possesses.

In the interviews, it was almost universally assumed that a requirement for educational programs was that they should be utterly relevant to, and aligned with, business objectives. There was the typical hue and cry about relevancy from most participants. Consultants, generally presumed to be closer to the ground as far as relevancy matters are concerned, were not, however, more popular as education program designers/providers to the firms represented by interviewed executives.

In fact, the most popular providers were universities, closely followed by some of the firms themselves, who liked to set up their own programs, thereby assuring and controlling relevancy, sometimes with the help of outside advice (from both consultants and universities). As mentioned in the previous section, there was a slight preference for custom designed over open enrolment programs, and this certainly speaks to this relevancy issue.

Preference for universities could be explained in part due to interview participants' continuing relationships with their *almae matres*, being on university advisory boards, being guest lecturers, or feeling that universities could better relate curriculum to learning principles. One variation on this academic preference was that it took the form of a preferred relationship with individual professors, regardless of which institution they were connected with.

Nobody in the interviews specifically mentioned accountability concerning the huge amounts of financial and other resources spent on education. If relevancy is so important to firms, then one has to be very curious as to why there is so little accountability. It could be that such things are just too difficult to measure. As mentioned in the literature review, it could also be that - especially for very senior people - accountability means a lot more than just money; and this "more that it means" is often intangible, but no less valuable for being so.

Individual and Group Learning Formats

There has been a great deal of talk and activity around coaching in business circles. Many universities offer coaching courses, programs and accreditation as well as actual executive coaching services. It was therefore quite surprising to find so little interest in it during my conversations with executives. Coaching was used for remedial situations, where an executive needed help in a specific area, or where a change in behaviour was warranted, but generally there was little interest shown in coaching as an integral part of executive learning. There was slightly more interest in mentoring, but really only as an expected executive behaviour: that senior people should help junior people – a process that could buttress a firm's overall succession plans. One executive was a firm believer in coaching and had a formalized plan in place for it to occur at his company; two others had some form of coaching that could be used as needed; and seven executives showed little interest in coaching as a learning tool. One executive believed strongly in mentoring, but only as an informal process, and two had tried it and did not like it at all, because both mentors and mentees varied widely in their abilities to give and to receive mentorship; and because it caused jealousy among junior executives.

Balancing work and personal life was a question asked of most participants, and it dealt with a highly individual learning item. It was largely believed that help in this regard should be provided if asked for, or even offered if an obvious problem was apparent. However, it was also generally stated that this was a personal matter, and that, especially for senior people, it was absolutely inappropriate to intervene in the matter of balancing personal and professional life, and that it was none of the firm's business.

Electronic Communications and Platforms

In general terms, the 14 executives from the 10 firms interviewed included four firms that were very knowledgeable about all aspects of electronic communications, social platforms, web-based research, use of intranet and internet resources; and they made wide use of these. Two firms were represented that had a good working knowledge of this usage, and executives of four firms were not very aware of them. However, perhaps of greater interest for this research is that only one interviewed executive seemed to be aware of, or to have experienced, the power of the collaborative aspect of online learning: the huge potential and substantial track-record of its use when working in teams; the interactive synchronous, real-time discussions and/or flexible timing, asynchronous online discussion groups that can be used for so much more than merely sharing information.

Curriculum

- Custom curricula must be flexible in their ability to be changed quickly in sync with what is constantly changing in the life of the firm. The firm must be involved in curricula design at every step in the process. Where possible, senior managers should be members of the facilitating (teaching) team.

- All curricula, whether open enrolment or custom, must contain a sense of urgency in the way they are excitingly connected to burning and current business issues.

- In most instances, curricula segments should unfold in one or in several short segments, probably no longer than a couple of days each, with at least a couple of months between each segment.

- Feed-back from learning events should be more than just finding out whether participants enjoyed themselves. Rather than rushing to fill out forms in the program's waning hours, participants might stay over one final night after the program, to celebrate the learning. Participants should carefully and conscientiously complete a detailed questionnaire before final celebrations. Quality feedback might also involve participants incorporating a few "small tasks" as to what they learned into their practice when they return to the office.

- Avoid fads in all curricula. To accomplish this, make sure that topics have "legs" and are clearly described: For example, personal mastery might be preferable to emotional intelligence; leadership principles are preferable to courageous leadership; and managing resources might be better than upsizing, downsizing, and right sizing.

- Public speaking, dealing with media, and the creation of Communities of Practice might be valuable additions to any executive curriculum.

- Given that most large corporations have operations in many different countries, executive curricula should include aspects of cultural diversity, as well as other global concerns.

Chapter Six – Presentation Of Findings And Analysis (Part 2)

The Providers: University Data on Open Enrolment and Custom Executive Programs – Second Unit of Analysis

Introduction

Eleven theme categories (plus two description categories: testimonials and websites) are used in this next section to display data about executive learning programs at nine universities. Each institution is scrutinized separately, and then the results are further analyzed as a Quintain (or collective), as was done for the interviews.

Cases are numbered A through I, and the institutions are named, as all of this data is readily available to the public on the internet. The raw data for each institution is presented along with a featured program, which I have subjectively chosen as being exemplary of that institution's best or most interesting executive offering. The means of selecting these nine universities was explained fully in the last chapter on Methodology. Following each featured program is a Narrative Appreciation.

Case A - McGill Executive Institute, McGill University, Montreal, QC., Canada

1. Scope of Executive Offerings

There are 26 programs offered by McGill's Executive Institute, including six senior leadership programs. Customized programs are available and have had a successful history with an impressive list of clients.

2. Customized/Open Program Objective, Design and Style

Fees vary from around $1600 for two days, $2000 for three days, $2700 for eight days (2x four days). The International Masters in Practicing Management (IMPM) takes place during five modules of 10 days each in five different countries, and the tuition is US $55,000 (not including travel, accommodation and other living expenses). There is an option to write a thesis and obtain a masters degree for an additional fee of US $6750. The Advanced Leadership Program (ALP) is delivered in three modules, each one in a different international location, and each lasting one week. The cost is $120,000 per company "table" of six people. The fee includes lunches and refreshments, but is exclusive of travel, accommodation and other living expenses.

Custom programs can take the form of an existing off-the-shelf offering delivered to a specific organization, or can be developed as a new program from scratch. Such programs can be delivered at McGill or at any site anywhere in the world.

3. Curriculum Elements (soft/hard skills)

Core themes include leadership and strategic change; managing others and yourself; functional business competencies; and customized solutions. Some of the learning themes delivered in executive programs include: advanced interpersonal business communications, business development strategies, energizing and leading teams, influence and assertiveness, presenting with confidence and power, global asset management, credit risk management, managing your workload, health and stress, innovation and entrepreneurship, strategic planning and execution.

4. Face-to-face /Online Delivery

Blending tailored e-learning modules with other existing programs is an option that can increase flexibility in accommodating busy executive schedules.

5. Individual/Group Learning

In the longer courses, such as the ALP and the IMPM, group learning is the main ingredient of the modules which take place in different international locations. Between modules, the work is individual and online as participants reflect and report on what they have learned from the previous segment, and as they prepare for the next one. In the shorter courses and seminars, which take place at McGill, group learning is the main activity. Team and individual coaching are also available through the Institute, and seem to be recommended as a precursor and as a follow-up to individual or team attendance at the major executive programs.

6. Philosophy

Action-based education is the norm. The participants are the ones who are the main players, and facilitators must retreat after getting the process underway to let the learning unfold: "The participants bring their experience, and the faculty introduces cutting edge concepts. The learning takes place where these meet, in an atmosphere conducive to thoughtful reflection for changed action". Dr. Henry Mintzberg is the original power behind this philosophy of learning by doing.

7. Specialty or Differentiation

Action learning in its most literal sense is best described by what unfolds in the ALP: There, real problems and challenges are addressed in real time by a team of executives from each of several participating firms. This process is similarly used in most of the customized and open enrolment programs and courses offered through this school. Participants attend as teams from different firms, rather than as individuals. "The ALP sells tables, not chairs".

8. Faculty

It was very difficult to find any information about the faculty at this business school, in respect of the executive offerings. Of course, Henry Mintzberg is featured, along with his latest article in the Harvard Business Review entitled "Rebuilding Companies as Communities" (*HBR* July 2009). The website highlighted that there is a solid core team of English, French and bilingual faculty. Most faculty have worked on faculty projects abroad.

9. International Factors and Diversity

McGill has an international dimension which is "unsurpassed in North America" (*The Financial Times*, 2004). Two-thirds of the faculty comes from outside Canada. Participants in ALP spend time learning in three different countries, and participants in the IMPM do so in five countries. 75% of PhD, 50% of MBA and 25% of B.Com students come from abroad. In the 2004 and 2005 editions of the Princeton Review's Best 357 Colleges, McGill ranked first overall in North America for racial harmony on campus.

10. Relevance (to Executive Learning)

"You can't create a leader in a classroom. Management is not a science, nor a profession. It is a practice – it has to be appreciated through experience, in context" (Dr. Henry Mintzberg).

11. Connections to the Outside World (partnerships, alliances)

The face-to-face modules for major programs for senior executives (The ALP and the IMPM) are delivered by McGill in conjunction with other universities: The Indian Institute of Management, in Bangalore, India; Lancaster University in the UK; Korea Development Institute School of Public Policy and Management in Seoul, Korea; and INSEAD in France.

12. Testimonials

"Because we wanted to help our professionals reach their full potential and develop their entrepreneurial spirit, BCF has developed a long-term partnership with the McGill Executive Institute. We have been highly satisfied with the comprehensive program design, quality of instruction and impact on our team" (Jean-Pierre Huard, Lawyer - a Montreal-Based law firm).

13. Website Quote and Website(s)

"If an executive program is to develop insight and innovation, its own design must be insightful and innovative".

http://executive.mcgill.ca/ (McGill Executive Institute homepage). This was not an easy website to navigate. This researcher was constantly losing his place and covering the same ground several times.

http://www.mcgill.ca/desautels/executive/ (senior executive programs).

Featured Program

The Advanced Leadership Program (ALP) is for senior executive teams, one to three levels below the CEO, depending on the organization. The program has two contexts to choose from: Global or North American. It is a shorter-form offshoot of the International Masters in Practicing Management (IMPM), originally developed as a Masters program 16 years ago by Professor Henry Mintzberg. The ALP has the same insistence as its predecessor about the need for learning to happen while doing; while actually experiencing on-the-job, real-time leadership and management activities, rather than by merely covering cases and doing simulations. It is a program for leadership development, embedded in a process of organizational development. The program takes place in three different international locations, hosted by schools from Asia, Europe and North America. Firms send a "table" of six participants to the ALP, and these teams work with faculty and the other member teams as "friendly consultants" to develop action plans about a specific strategic issue or challenge required at each firm. This makes the ALP both a learning community, as well as a company-specific program. The learning benefits thus accrue to the firms, the teams and to the individuals.

The ALP is segmented into three one-week modules in each of the three different countries: (1) **Reflective Leadership** in Montreal Canada (McGill University) deals with topics such as personal challenges in leading others, organizational challenges, reframing the team challenge, and understanding corporate culture; (2) **Change Leadership** in Bangalore, India (Indian Institute of Management), deals with topics such as myths about change, the cultural aspects of change, and designs for change; and (3) **Action Leadership** in the Lake District, England (Lancaster University), which deals with topics such as the levers of change, the emotional dimension of change, renewing an organization and its culture, and catalytic leadership.

The tuition is €100,000 ($150,000) per company "table" of five or six participants, and it includes tuition, all course materials, most program lunches, but it does not include transportation and accommodation.

The ALP deals with working through the current organizational challenges of participating firms, rather than with case studies which, per the website, are considered "simulations of other people's problems", and as such have a varying degree of relevance to participants. There are three major learning inputs in this program: The first comes from the nucleus of the organizational team of five or six people, who attend as one of several team pods from various different firms. They work together both at the program and between modules back at their firm. The second is an academic input, whereby faculty act as facilitators, advisors and coaches for learning that is co-created with participants. The third input is from "Friendly Consultants", as a result of the creative sharing that takes place among the different teams who act throughout the three modules as quasi boards of directors, and non-competing friends, in listening to offer insight and experience into each other's organizational challenges. Thus, as the program overview suggests, "The ALP combines the best of two worlds, the power of internal task forces and the insights of outside consultants".

Appreciation

The Advanced Leadership Program, and its lengthier cousin the International Masters in Practicing Management, are wonderfully conceived action learning events which can be attended as a pod of individuals from one firm, or as an individual. The learning benefits are immediately applicable to the job, because they are all about the job's challenges all the time. Participants from different firms act as a type of Board of Directors to help and advise colleagues throughout these programs. Friendships are forged and networks are strengthened.

There is a great deal of attention paid to McGill's Dr. Henry Mintzberg who has attained almost rock-star status for his contrarian opinions about management learning, which have become thorns in the side of many business schools. His insistence that most schools are wrongly teaching practical skills in a theoretical manner is a relentless and constant refrain in the many books and articles he has written – several of which were mentioned in the literature review. His ideas are valuable and compelling, and I personally have a great deal of respect for them. However, perhaps visitors to the website should be reading more about what the other professors and Business School leaders at McGill's Executive Institute are saying about the excellent executive programs available. There is simply too much about Mintzberg, and not enough about everybody else.

Mintzberg has already left his valuable imprint on the teaching style and philosophy of this Institute. It is one that insists on action learning in the most urgent sense of learning outside the classroom, in the trenches, while doing one's job. This invaluable legacy lives on in the world-class, highly respected and successful flagship programs: The Advanced Leadership Program and the International Masters in Practicing Management. It also permeates the degree programs at McGill's Desautels Business School.

The executive programs at this Institute recognize better than most schools, even among the other eight illustrious institutions discussed here, the need for international diversity and content. Indeed McGill has been recognized as having an international dimension unsurpassed in North America for diversity among students and faculty, and for program style and content. The scope of McGill's global outlook is certainly equal to that of Harvard and INSEAD, also featured here as giants of international connectivity, which simply must be part of any learning program involving executives of international or multinational firms.

Case B: The Richard Ivey School of Business, University of Western Ontario, London, ON., Canada

1. Scope of Executive Offerings

Custom Programs feature Strategy Development (for example, strategic renewal), Talent Development (for example, for individuals or groups) and Organizational Development (for example, culture change). Firms choose among four categories: tailored topics, custom programs created from scratch, consortium programs designed for a group of six to eight different non-competing firms that face similar challenges, and corporate academies, to build comprehensive management development partnerships with specific organizations. In 2008, Ivey was rated the #6 provider of custom programs in the world *(The Financial Times)*.

Open Enrolment Programs: In addition to an executive MBA, there are only seven on-campus open enrolment programs at Ivey listed for 2009: (1) The Ivey Executive Program for senior executives is a three week program in two modules, which can be taken in flexible (2x 10 days) or continuous (1x 20 days) formats and costs $23,995. There is also an option to do a four day add-on Financial Analysis Tutorial for an additional $2,950; (2) The Ivey Management Development Program for emerging leaders is a two week program in two modules (in flexible 2x seven days) or continuous 14 day formats, costing $14,500. There is an option for a two day accounting and financial analysis tutorial for an additional $1,950; (3) The Ivey Leadership Program for managers, executives and entrepreneurs in any area of an organization is a six day program costing $9,100; (4) The Ivey Financial Analysis Program for executives and managers with little or no financial experience is a six day (flexible 2x three days, or continuous) program costing $7,950; (5) The Ivey Influence and Persuasion Program for managers at all levels of an organization who want to work on their leadership communication style is a three day program costing $4,900; (6) Quantum Shift™ for Entrepreneurs (CEOs and business owners) is a six day program by invitation only, with candidates being nominated by KPMG Enterprise, and selected by Ivey's Institute for Entrepreneurship, costing $8,000;

(7) Reconnect™: career renewal for returning professional women, who are considering their career options and have been out of the workforce for two to six years, is a two-module (1x five days and 1x two days) program costing $3,500.

2. Customized/Open Program Objective, Design and Style

The focus is on leadership, and specifically on what they refer to as "cross-enterprise leadership". Ivey promotes the importance of fostering a cross-enterprise understanding which defines their approach to business. Case studies are used that cross all functional areas in a variety of industries. Other learning methods incorporate group discussions, role plays and simulations, as well as informal out-of-class discussions.

3. Curriculum Elements (soft/hard skills)

Ivey's insistence on broadening perspectives, seeing the whole organization beyond its parts (that is, Systems Thinking), and growing beyond functional skills, implies an emphasis on "soft" over "hard" skills. However, Ivey's traditionally respected teaching of functional and analytical skills is still an integral core competency requirement of their new programs.

4. Face-to-face /Online Delivery

I could not see anything mentioned on the website about online learning with respect to executive programs.

5. Individual/Group Learning

Participants become engaged in a truly interactive, learn-by-doing environment. The collective experience is underscored. The case method is used extensively.

6. Philosophy

"Our interactive learning experience is designed to make an immediate impact on the way you think, act and lead, and enables you to elevate your performance in your current role and in all future career assignments" (Ivey Executive Development 2009, Program Catalogue). A propensity for action is considered an ingredient for executive success.

7. Specialty or Differentiation

Ivey's Cross-Enterprise Perspective is one in which participants are coached in thinking, acting, and leading across an entire enterprise; They approach opportunities with an organization-wide point of view.

8. Faculty

Faculty members are often referred to as facilitators rather than professors. Ivey boasts an unparalleled access to faculty over lunch and during consultation sessions. Faculty members are renowned for their research, and case writing; they are in touch with best practices from leading companies.

9. International Factors and Diversity

The Financial Times (2008) recognizes Ivey as #3 in the world for international participants. There are campuses in London, Ontario; Toronto, Ontario; and in Hong Kong. Course content described in the Ivey Executive Program brochure reflects little international or global content, however. Of the 34 topics mentioned for the three major open enrolment executive programs, only one topic deals with a global subject. In the Executive MBA brochure, there is mention of expanding global perspectives through working with people from different cultures, and developing understanding of global business.

10. Relevance (to Executive Learning)

Participants leave with an action plan. They are given a *Return on Ivey*™ (ROI – a play on words relating to the more common "Return on Investment") journal at the beginning of the program, which, in conjunction with related faculty consultations, is the basis of that action plan. Case studies are used throughout the programs to feature actual company challenges.

11. Connections to the Outside World (partnerships, alliances)

Ivey was the first North American Business School to set up a permanent facility in Asia. Ivey's professors have been guests at Beijing's Tsinghua University since 1985, and Shanghai Fudan University since 1986. Ivey's Asian Management Institute develops and disseminates Ivey's award winning case studies in Asia.

12. Testimonials

"I learned the value of broadening my perspective and seeing things from different viewpoints. That helped me analyze situations more fully once I got back to my job" (Scott Donald, COO Western Surety, Regina).

13. Website Quote and Website(s)

"Functional knowledge is always necessary but never sufficient for career success. We want to make sure you can become more than just a functional player" (Tony Frost, Ivey Professor).

http://www.ivey.uwo.ca/Executive/ (Ivey Executive Development)

This was not the easiest website to navigate; There seems to be a disconnection between what is on the site and what program descriptions are downloadable.

http://www.ivey.uwo.ca/executive/Videos/MichaelPearce1.mpeg

(Dr. Michael Pierce's video clip on Learning at Ivey)

Featured Program

The Ivey Executive Program has existed for 60 years, and it is targeted for accomplished executives and senior managers with ten or more years management experience. It is a three week program in two modules, which can be taken separately for more flexibility, or else in a continuous format. There is an optional four day add-on tutorial in Accounting and Financial Analysis. The cost, including tuition and all expenses (meals and lodging) is $23,995 for the three weeks, and another $2,950 for the additional tutorial.

Ivey talks of a "cross-enterprise approach", which focuses on the core competencies of the strategic leader, rather than on individual management functions, and participants return to work having each developed a personal action plan. Emphasis is on the integration of functions rather than on the functions *per se*.

The two modules comprise these core themes: Strategy and Value Creation, Leadership and Organizational Excellence, and Leading Change. They contain topics similar to individual courses. These include 17 topics such as: understanding the global business environment, value creation and capture business unit strategy, mergers and acquisitions, the executive leadership role, leading high-performance teams, leading large-scale change, and project leadership.

The case study method is the principal learning vehicle, and most cases use a format whereby the individual participant reads and considers the case, then works in a small pod of colleagues to discuss the case, and finally deals with the case in class the following day with the facilitator.

Appreciation

In May 2008, *The Financial Times* ranked Ivey as the #1 executive education provider in Canada for the ninth consecutive year; and #10 in the world for its open enrolment programs. This is especially intriguing, because there seem to be only seven open enrolment programs being offered. One must assume a strategy in this regard which focuses on quality, and one that has in fact successfully built up a strong following for these few programs. Ivey's use of business experts as teachers in executive programs, alongside their regular professors, demonstrates a close connection to the business world. Furthermore, the fact that their professors are closely connected to research and consulting engagements with many organizations enhances their credibility in the classroom as well as with designers and implementers of Ivey's much sought-after custom programs.

Facilities include Ivey's home-based Spencer Leadership Centre at the University of Western Ontario in London, Ontario; The ING Leadership Centre in Toronto's financial district; and The Cheng Yu Tung Management Institute in Hong Kong.

There is a good deal of commentary about the overall, total organizational view, and about the importance of curriculum beyond mere functional skill. However, in the executive program's curriculum, for example, arguably well over half of the 17 learning subjects (under the major themes of Strategy and Value-Creation, Leadership and Organizational Excellence and Leading Change) are "hard" rather than "soft" topics.

Ivey's Cross-Enterprise Perspective, which they refer to as their own, sounds very much like the holistic Systems Thinking approach to business, touted previously by such luminaries as O'Connor and McDermott (1997) in their *The Art of Systems Thinking: Essential*

Skills for Creativity and Problem Solving, and by Oshry (1995) in his *Seeing Systems: Unlocking the Mysteries of Organizational Life*.

Ivey campuses in London and Toronto, Ontario, as well as in Hong Kong, perhaps explains Ivey's 2008 *Financial Times* award as #3 in the world for international participation. Nevertheless, there is little international content in the courses shown. For instance, in the 34 topic content descriptions for the Ivey Executive Program, The Ivey Management Development Program and the Ivey Leadership Program combined, there is only one topic about global or international considerations (understanding the global business environment). The Executive MBA Program contains comments about global themes, but I cannot find enough mentioned along these lines for the open enrolment programs. For instance, there does not seem to be any content around cultural diversity in these open enrolment programs for executives.

Ivey is the second largest publisher of cases in the world after Harvard, and the largest publisher of Asia case studies. The use of the Case Method is a respected, quasi action learning method to teach participants about management issues. I suspect that it is more pertinent for young university students doing an MBA than for seasoned executives returning to school to refresh their skills. Seasoned executives are already facing those kinds of challenges every day, and they may or may not agree with the way a case is supposed to unfold. Ivey describes the case as "a real problem and challenge faced by a real company at a critical management decision point. You're placed in the role of decision-maker, asked to analyze the data, develop alternatives and make and defend your recommendations". However, although it may be similar to "your" company and the challenges that it may be facing, it is not in fact your company and the challenges that you are facing. One of the executives interviewed stated that he attended a two week program that used case studies almost exclusively, and he was emphatic about reporting that they "covered" fully 85 cases in that two week period. I do not know if that was a criticism or a compliment about that learning experience. There is no doubt that the Case Study is a hands-on learning method, which is clearly relevant to what has happened in real business situations, but is it the most hands-on approach that can be employed? Should one be looking for something even more action oriented, along the lines of what McGill espouses?

It was a pleasure to see and hear the dulcet tones, and yet the still great passion, of Professor Michael Pierce in several of the Executive Development Video clips which so adeptly promote life and learning (especially the relevance of the material and the use of case studies) at this excellent school. He was one of my professors 25 years ago, when I attended the three week Marketing Management Course (MMC '85).

Case C - Queen's Executive Development Centre, Queen's University, Kingston, ON., Canada

1. Scope of Executive Offerings

Queen's Executive Development Centre (QEDC) has been providing executive education for the last 30 years, and now operates campuses in Kingston, Toronto and Dubai. It is recognized as one of the world's largest and most respected providers of open-enrolment programs – teaching more senior managers and executives than any other Canadian business school. In 2009/2010, the Centre will offer 17 one to three week open enrolment programs, with most coming under the heading of Management Education Programs, and two of them under Executive Programs (the three-week Executive Program, and the two-week Public Executive Program). Custom Programs are designed in conjunction with clients to address a specific and well-defined organizational development need. Emphasis seems to be more on the Open Enrolment Programs than on the Custom Programs, and it is claimed that fully one third of all Canadians who pursue university-based executive development choose Queen's. In 2007/2008, sixty-six custom programs were delivered to 34 different organizations impacting close to 2,000 participants at client-chosen sites across North America. More than 10,000 managers from over 1,400 Canadian organizations have participated in management education and development programs at QEDC.

2. Customized/Open Program Objective, Design and Style

Queen's terminology here is "Programs for Individuals and Custom Programs for Companies". Tuition fees for the open enrolment programs range from an average of $2,000-2,500 for the shorter two-day courses; $8,900 for one week programs such as the ones in Finance and Strategy; $15,700 for the two week programs such as the Public Executive Program; and $23,900 for the flagship Queen's Executive Program. There is also a new Professional Development Series comprising two two-day programs entitled Tackling Challenging Conversations and Project Management. Case method and classroom discussions are the mainstay of the residential programs. Queen's approach to custom programs is their slogan "You set the agenda". Programs are flexible as to location (at Queen's, at the client's workplace, or other offsite locations), as well as to the timeline, which is determined by the client.

3. Curriculum Elements (soft/hard skills)

All programs contain some elements of both "hard" and "soft" skill learning. Nevertheless, of all the Open Enrolment programs, well over half mostly feature the teaching and learning of "hard" skills. This is of course particularly prevalent in such offerings as finance, planning, IT, strategy, and operations, in which participants learn to use tools, and to understand, analyze, and interpret information. In about one third of the offerings, learning about and practising "soft" skills predominate in such programs as the ones dealing with leadership and communication. For instance, these "soft" skills include use of the PRESence model for leadership (present, reaching-out, expressive, self-knowing); developing acting and story-telling skills; practising authentic communication.

4. Face-to-face /Online Delivery

Most of the action learning and teaching methods used to replicate the business environment are face-to-face. Queen's By Your Side™, is a website for executive education alumni. It provides webinars on updated content, articles, and an ability to consult with Queen's faculty members. Queen's Executive Decision Centre is Canada's first electronic group-decision support laboratory.

5. Individual/Group Learning

Queen's Executive Development programs use a variety of teaching tools, which are said to replicate today's fast-paced and ever-changing business environment. These include class discussions and seminars, case studies, simulations, small group exercises, and one-on-one coaching. In 2007/2008, 19 executive coaching partnerships were established. The case study method is used extensively in degree as well as executive programs.

6. Philosophy

"Often just getting out of the way and letting the students take over" is a stated teaching philosophy at Queen's. There is a highly promoted lifestyle component to most programs, by which positive attitudes, balance in all aspects of one's life and commitment to one's goals are all stressed.

7. Specialty or Differentiation

Consultants in Residence™ provides participants attending programs with the opportunity to discuss business issues in confidence with session leaders. There is also an Executive Coaching Service, by which Queen's contracts to coach executives individually concerning their goals, for six months with an option to extend. Participants interview potential coaches before deciding which one they want to work with. One of the newest programs being offered is the two-day Tackling Challenging Conversations, which offers a roadmap for navigating those kinds of encounters, and involves the disciplined use of specific communication skills.

8. Faculty

Session leaders include senior Queen's School of Business professors and experts from the private and public sectors. It is a faculty renowned for its business experience and academic credentials.

9. International Factors and Diversity

In their titles, as well as in their content descriptions, none of the programs or courses emphasizes global or international topics or connections. In the section "Why Queen's", there is no mention about international or global concerns, or content for executive education programs, except for the statement that offices are located in Kingston, Toronto, and Dubai. There are 12 executive open enrolment programs offered in the cities of Dubai (UAE) and Muscat (Oman). International program content and collaboration with other universities for exchange programs (64 in 2007/2008) are part of the regular graduate and undergraduate degree programs, but not of the executive programs. Aspects of international experience are included in several of the academic programs, and indeed 75% of the regular students venture abroad during and as part of their degrees. Furthermore, there is the 12-month Queen's Master of Global Management for regular graduate students (with no previous work experience required), which features studying in Canada and abroad.

10. Relevance (to Executive Learning)

The flexibility of the custom designed programs is touted as providing timely relevance to learning content, and these programs have as much relevance to their business as clients want to design into them; and as much of a mix of "hard" skill development, which will be eventually relevant, and "soft" skills, which will be immediately relevant.

11. Connections to the Outside World (partnerships, alliances)

Queen's Centre for Corporate Social Responsibility, Queen's Executive Decision Centre, The CA-Queen's Centre for Governance, Queen's Centre for Business Venturing, are some of this university's outreach connections. There is also a joint executive MBA program with Cornell University, from which graduating students receive an MBA degree from both institutions.

12. Testimonials

"Queen's Executive Development Centre delivered on their promises and deadlines. Their professionalism, flexibility, and commitment to making our program truly customized were very impressive" (Kelley M. Oke, Manager, Planning & Operations, Wealth & Estate Planning Group, London Life).

13. Website Quote and Website(s)

According to one of its executive participants, the custom program Queen's developed for Canada Post "was an opportunity to network with colleagues that I wouldn't normally interact with and really understand first hand what their business challenges are".

http://business.queensu.ca/execdev/index.php (Queen's Executive Development Centre) This site is easy to navigate and is very logical in its format. You feel in control of where you need to go while you are on it.

http://business.queensu.ca/execdev/index.php (introductory video about the executive programs)

Featured Program

The Queen's Executive Program is intensive, and it takes place during three consecutive weeks. It is designed for senior managers and executives from all functional areas, who have at least ten years of management experience. Tuition costs are $23,900 for 2009, including all learning materials, use of recreational facilities, and accommodation and food at the Donald Gordon Conference Centre. Participants receive a certificate of achievement upon completion, and they become part of the alumni network. The program content includes:

- Strategy in Week One: Strategic Planning and Implementation, Leading Change, and Strategic Collaboration (internal and external, to achieve a competitive edge). Within these themes, some topics include looking at best practices from leading organizations, learning about intricate relationships across functions, developing structured and disciplined frameworks for planning, creating coalitions to drive change, managing communications and motivating people, forming alliances to leverage key resources, and identifying criteria for selecting partners.

- Management in Week Two: Finance, Marketing and Sales Management, and Information Management. Within these themes, some topics include sensitivity analysis, break-even analysis and scenario analysis; linking marketing and sales strategies to the overall business strategy; and recognizing and preparing for emerging technologies that will have an impact on your business.

- Leadership in Week Three: Developing a Leadership Plan, Creating a High Performance Organization, and Negotiation and Consensus Building. Within these themes, some topics include developing a personal leadership plan; understanding the elements of a high-performance environment; and examining the underlying structure of negotiations.

The Consultants in Residence advisory service enables individual participants to discuss opportunities, business, and challenges, in confidence with Program session leaders. In keeping with Queen's balanced approach to educating executives, guests are encouraged to join participants on the two weekends during the Program.

One participant stated: "I looked at a lot of programs across the world, and I think the Queen's program is unique. The content is really well balanced and worked in a logical sequence. You're getting the most up-to-date perspectives on strategy, leadership and management" (Hamish Riddell, General Manager, Organizational Change and Development, Sensis Proprietary Ltd., Melbourne, Australia).

Appreciation

The program brochure goes to some length explaining that this three consecutive week model has a demonstrated effectiveness in permitting participants the necessary time to reflect properly on the learning, and to develop relationships and networking. This format differs from some similar programs at other institutions which favour the flexibility of several shorter modules, while seemingly maintaining the benefits, perhaps to a lesser degree, of networking and reflection. In recognition of the substantial three week time commitment, Queen's boasts daily sessions ending at 3:30 pm permitting participants time (several hours before the evening sessions) to reconnect with their offices, adding that there is a 24-hour onsite business centre for participants' exclusive use, as well as other resources such as video conferencing, administrative support and courier services. Thus, the three-week design which promotes the benefits of being truly disconnected form the workplace, and the availability of time for daily contact with work seem contradictory as compared, for instance, to INSEAD's four-week Advanced Management Program, which admonishes participants to stay completely away from the office, and to dissuade colleagues from contacting them.

Occasionally, this three-week Executive Program seems too much like an MBA for students without business experience. For instance, it proposes to deal with identifying and implementing the drivers of shareholder value, and considering sources and threats to sustainable competitive advantage, or creating value with product/service bundles. While all these are important concepts, most senior managers and executives with ten years experience in upper level management do these things every day. They themselves should be teaching such subjects.

"With offices in Kingston, Toronto, and Dubai, Queen's Executive Development Centre is capable of offering programs anywhere in the world". It is difficult to understand what this means, given that coverage is not really all that vast. As mentioned in the chart, there does not appear to be much international or global content in the executive program material. Of the 17 open enrolment courses including the Queen's Executive Program, for instance, there does not seem to be any mention of global or international concerns or issues. Subject matter on cultural diversity, international regulations and regulatory bodies, and something generally about doing business around the globe might be of interest. Because the degree programs at Queen's *do* contain significant segments about global and international topics, it would likely be quite easy to transfer some of this material and capability over into the executive programs.

Case D – The Rotman School of Business, University of Toronto, Toronto, ON., Canada.

1. Scope of Executive Offerings

There are 25 open enrolment programs offered on Rotman's executive program list; and half of them are arguably destined for executives. However, a third of these are really for middle managers, managers and junior professionals. Of the 25 programs, fully eight of them focus on women in management, and half of those are for the executive level (for example, Emerging Leaders Program, and The Judy Project: An Enlightened Leadership Forum for Executive

Women). The Integrative Thinking Program is the topical flagship of the Rotman School of Business. Extensive availability of custom programs is described in the next section.

2. Customized/Open Program Objective, Design and Style

Open Enrolment programs mostly vary in duration from two to five days, with tuition fees for two days at $3000, and four days at $6000 (not including accommodation). The five-day Leading Strategic Change Program costs $12,000 and includes accommodation and meals; the flagship Advanced Program in Human Resources Management (4x five days over six months) costs $13,500 but does not include accommodation and meals other than class-day meals.

Custom Programs use "forming a learning partnership" as the value proposition. They boast a standard process that includes strategy review, competency framework alignment, gap analysis and needs assessment, program design, evaluation and follow-up. Types of customized programs comprise comprehensive programs, which are one day intensives for 30 executives, up to an extended modular structure for 200 people; an executive speaker series consisting of one day strategic conversations; one to two hour webinars, which are web-based focused learning events, which can be independently used or used as part of pre or post program activities; simulations; Strategy engagement workshops, which are "sessions designed to tackle wicked problems faced by organizations today"; and customized open enrolment programs. Many clients have a long-standing relationship with Rotman for the delivery of their custom programs.

3. Curriculum Elements (soft/hard skills)

The curriculum of many academic as well as executive programs is based on the mostly "soft" approach of Integrative Thinking™, which features an ingrained tolerance for ambiguity. However, curricula subjects listed as typical include the arguably "hard" topics of leadership, organizational effectiveness, leading change, finance, governance, negotiation, strategic management, innovation, and customer-centred marketing.

4. Face-to-face /Online Delivery

For executive programs, the format is mostly face-to-face. However, online web based webinars are used to support learning before and after the face-to-face events.

5. Individual/Group Learning

Lectures, simulations, case studies, and action planning are used. Executive programs have evolved from individual to team attendance comprising managers from the same companies, or else similarly focused companies who learn together.

6. Philosophy

In the last ten years, Rotman's philosophy has evolved very much around the theme of Integrative Thinking™, since its founder, Roger Martin came in as Dean. The "thinker of the future" will need this knack of building something new out of various possible options, rather than choosing among them.

7. Specialty or Differentiation

- There is a leadership course called Canada's Outstanding Principals Program for executives, which is a four-day dialogue for educational, social, cultural and business leaders to reflect on leadership issues along with award winning public education principals. That session is followed by a year-long online collaboration among participants.

- There is an emphasis on focusing several programs on women in management.

- The much touted Integrative Thinking™ model is the content of a three day program. Integrative Thinking™ is embedded in the Rotman School's curriculum and continues to evolve, earning it a global reputation as one of the world's most innovative business schools.

8. Faculty

An exhaustive list of instructors and their bios is provided on the School's website. Several Rotman visiting or permanent instructors do not have doctoral degrees, but do have extensive entrepreneurial and executive experience, and some are still actively involved in their own businesses or as consultants.

9. International Factors and Diversity

Rotman brings business professionals to Toronto from South America, Europe and Asia; It also teams up with international companies and academic institutions to offer programs in Toronto and overseas.

One of the eight key research institutes at Rotman is The Institute for International Business. The Institute's mission is to focus faculty expertise on research and its dissemination; also, in teaching and international exchange on sustaining Canadian competitiveness in this new global environment.

The Rotman School of Management has been asked to conduct a series of roundtables in Dubai in August 2009 with a focus on discussing business education in the UAE and the region.

10. Relevance (to Executive Learning)

Faculty expertise, supplementing academic credentials with current entrepreneurial experience, helps to keep the teaching relevant. "The Rotman School is a thinking environment. It's a training ground for business leaders. It's an energizing community where dynamic people come together to develop creative business solutions".

11. Connections to the Outside World (partnerships, alliances)

Learning partners include seven other Canadian business schools, two from central Canada, and (perhaps not surprisingly) five from BC and Alberta. International liaisons are with universities in France, Germany, Scandinavia, South America, China and Japan.

12. Testimonials

"Integrative Thinking has become an essential component of the training and development program for our most senior managers at P&G. Our executives are able to take the lessons of integrative thinking back to their jobs with them, putting the tools into action to solve the thorniest issues in their businesses" (Dr. Laura Mattimore, Director, Leadership Development, Procter & Gamble).

13. Website Quote and Website(s)

"We want to help you find new ways to solve the really tough problems. These are the thorny issues with no obvious solution that plague every manager, whether in business, health care, or the arts" (Dean Roger Martin on Integrative Thinking™).

http://ep.rotman.utoronto.ca/ (executive programs home page). Website is user-friendly and quite easy to navigate. Everything required for the researcher is one or two clicks away.

<u>Featured Program</u>

The Integrative Thinking Program ($6,000) is a three day program for senior executives and emerging leaders, designed to enable participant leaders to make better decisions more of the time. It equips them with Integrative Thinking tools and an understanding of their use in action. It has four major themes: (1) Salience – The idea is that integrative thinkers consider more features of the problem salient, and the resulting question for participants is: What do you see as important? (2) Causality – Those thinkers consider non-linear and multidirectional causality, and the resulting question is: How do you make sense of what you see? (3) Architecture – Integrative thinkers consider the whole problem while working on individual parts, and the resulting question is: What tasks will you do and in what order? (4) Resolutions – These thinkers search for creative resolutions of tensions, with the question: How will you know when you are done?

The program delves into fascinating and thoughtful considerations, such as how to deal with a colleague whose understanding of the world seems to be fundamentally at odds with your own; and how to resolve the kinds of problems that seem to change as you attempt to solve them. A *Business Week* video interview with Dean Roger Martin describes the program and process it its founder's own words: http:// feedroom.businessweek.com/index.jsp?fr_story=61d4d953876d380 a39f018b85cedc3d5c3f8a8ac

Appreciation

The Fee Structure

The fee information, only available by going to each program description, is confusing in its inconsistency of showing fees, sometimes inclusive and sometimes exclusive of meals and accommodation.

Integrative Thinking™

The website states that the Rotman School is redesigning business education for the 21ˢᵗ century with a curriculum built on Integrative Thinking ™. It states that because of integrative thinking, the school has grown substantially, doubling the size of most of its programs along with the number of faculty, staff and research institutes.

The Integrative Thinking model was created by Dean Martin from his consulting practice before joining the University of Toronto (Monitor Company, a global strategy consulting firm based in Cambridge, Massachusetts). Nevertheless, the website states that the content is proprietary and unique to the Rotman School.

In 2007 Martin was named a BusinessWeek 'B-School All-Star' for being one of the 10 most influential business professors in the world. Integrative Thinking, born from Dr. Martin's research on how leaders think, rather than on what they do, is used as a framework for many executive and academic programs at the Rotman School, and is a fundamental part of how the school teaches and conducts research. The philosophy of this model is well described by a statement from F. Scott Fitzgerald used in the website: "The test of a first-rate intelligence is the ability to hold two opposing ideas in mind at the same time and still retain the ability to function". It implies that when one adopts such a philosophy, one becomes adept at facing opposing strategies or ideas, so that instead of choosing one at the expense of the other, one creates a new model which is related to the originals, but which is superior to each. In other words, model creation rather than model choosing.

As readers will recall from the theoretical framework chapter, Dr Whitehead (1925/1967) espoused something very similar to Integrative Thinking when he commented on professionals and vocational trainees tending to see this or that set of circumstances, but not both sets together. Therefore, "the generalised direction lacks vision", and/or that "the whole is lost in one of its aspects", such that directive wisdom is lacking.

Integrative Thinking's process of how to think about models, without fearing a state of disequilibrium is also similar to Royal Dutch Shell's Scenario Planning process, in which practitioners hold several different scenarios in mind. However, in so doing, they are not attempting to choose the best route forward, but rather to test the business idea of the firm to decide whether that business case can withstand any of the imagined scenarios. Furthermore, the Integrative Thinking (IT) model mirrors the mechanics of the classical dialogue process. In that dialogue process, one learns to step back from an active conversation, and to suspend one's often too close involvement in it, in order to be able to see greater meaning and connections outside the melée of details. In this way one can re-enter the conversation with a fresh perspective.

Diversity and The Common Good

Among the executive open enrolment programs, the number of offerings specifically for women (eight out of 23, but the other 15 are for both women and men) is a glowing testament to Rotman's grasp of demographic reality, and of the benefits of diversity in learning.

The combination of IT's "soft" skill approach with "hard" skill curricula is a winning one which mirrors what businesses do every day, and executives will likely feel quite at home with what Rotman is offering them.

There is a statement on the website which promotes the idea that finding creative solutions to difficult problems will also make Canada a better place to work and live. This is also an appreciation of the place that executive education occupies in society: one that is connected to the profit motive, but also one with an obligation to make society better. This, along with a similar whisper on the INSEAD website, are the only mentions of "greater good" this researcher discovered among the websites of these excellent schools. Such statements do not, however, appear overly altruistic nor out of place.

Case E - Schulich Executive Education Centre (SEEC), York University, Toronto, ON., Canada.

1. Scope of Executive Offerings

The Schulich Executive Education Centre (SEEC) provides open enrolment and custom executive development programs annually to more than 16,000 executives in Canada and abroad. The custom programs are delivered to more than 100 organizations and 10,000 employees, from Canada and around the world, every year. (I have checked these stats out with SEEC administration and they are apparently correct, but one has to wonder if they really mean that 10,000 employees attended the programs or that there are that many employees in those 100 organizations?). The website lists 131 open enrolment courses, and the brochure boasts "over 100 learning choices".

There is a concentration on Open Enrolment over Custom programs at SEEC. The Open Enrolment Programs come under five headings and comprise 90 programs or courses for 2009/2010, of which 18 are certificate programs. The five segments include Business Operations, Executive and Masters Certificate Programs, Finance and Accounting, Management and Leadership, and Marketing and Sales. None of these programs is for senior executives, with the possible exception of Management 3. Most of the programs are targeted at middle and junior management levels.

2. Customized & Open Program Objective, Design and Style

Examples of course and program costs, exclusive of accommodation and meals other than lunches, in the Management and Leadership segment are: $1795 for a two day; $2395 for a three day; $3595-4595 for a five day course or program. Longer certificate programs are delivered in segments of one to three days for a total of 12-18 days over an extended period of five or six months, and cost $8,500-$10,950.

The customized programs are broken down into one or multi-day sessions in residential or non residential formats, delivered as immediate solutions, or over a period of several months. "Immediate solutions" bring off-the-shelf open enrolment programs to specific clients; and tailored solutions are specifically designed to the client.

3. Curriculum Elements (soft/hard skills)

The vast array of 90 open enrolment courses and programs are a smorgasbord for acquiring skills in highly focused subjects in a variety of formats. This selection is a sampling of their curriculum content: essential critical thinking and communication skills; five day coaching skills; 15 key skills for developing emotional intelligence in the workplace (3 days); developing a strategic mindset (3 days) executive program in leading sustainable strategic change (5 days); executive program in sales management (5 days); improving presentation effectiveness (2 days); a roadmap for leadership through teambuilding (3 days); mergers and acquisitions (2 days).

4. Face-to-face /Online Delivery

There may be elements of online delivery and follow-up, but most of the learning activity is face-to-face.

5. Individual/Group Learning

Action and reflection, role-play activities, real-work simulations and competitive learning strategies are used as learning methods. There is an inferred emphasis on group over individual learning methods.

6. Philosophy

Custom programs are said to offer highly focused training designed to give particular employee groups tools to drive organizational success. Also mentioned is a unique blend of theory and practice (academic rigour plus real-world experience of expert industry practitioners).

7. Specialty or Differentiation

Centres of Excellence in the form of 11 Communities of Practitioners have been formed, which invite executive participation. These communities offer short courses and action learning with the possibility of certification, alumni networking events, national conferences and forums, and sponsored research. Examples of these Centres of Excellence include strategic alliance management, municipal leadership, and enterprise risk management. SEEC operates a Sustainable Enterprise Academy that provides executive seminars on corporate sustainable development featuring leading edge thinkers and practitioners, in the form of four day residential programs for senior executives and public sector leaders.

"All programs are backed by a 100% Satisfaction Guarantee Period" (Director, Executive Education).

8. Faculty

Faculty is drawn from both practitioners and academia, and each is an acknowledged leader and innovator in their field. Professional activities, research and business experience allow them to bring a wealth of insight and cutting-edge knowledge to the development of the programs. In the classroom, each is a proven educator with excellent communication skills.

9. International Factors and Diversity

The Schulich School of Business pioneered Canada's first International MBA and BBA degrees, as well as North America's first ever cross-border executive MBA with Kellogg. Sales offices and business partnerships are located in six locations outside North America.

10. Relevance (to Executive Learning)

The huge number of programs and courses appear to be directed principally at middle managers, with the possible exception of the one program featured below called Management 3: The Leaders Program. All courses and programs boast relevance to the workplace.

11. Connections to the Outside World (partnerships, alliances)

Offices and partnerships around the globe, and relationships with over 50 of the world's leading business schools, means SEEC can draw the right faculty to meet a company's distinct learning needs. There are sales offices or partnerships in Moscow, Dubai, Beijing, Shanghai, Mumbai and Seoul. SEEC says it can tackle training challenges in Canadian, North American and Global contexts.

12. Testimonials

"Our partnership with SEEC has resulted in a great learning experience. Schulich brings to us a tremendous reputation, credibility and experience. They're flexible: they will customize their programs to the needs of the client, and in this case obviously American Express. It is a combination of theory plus real world business experience that they bring to the table." (Beth S. Horowitz, former President & General Manager, American Express Canada)

13. Website Quote and Website(s)

http://www.seec.schulich.yorku.ca/home/ (Schulich Executive Education Centre). The website is fairly user-friendly, but requires some back and forward clicking to get at specifically what one might be looking for. There is a great deal of information available, but you have to figure out where to find it. I cannot, for instance, find faculty members' bios on the executive programs website. The site includes PDF downloads of colourful, well-designed brochures for each program, as well as an overall 138 page brochure.

"If you need to use it now, learn it now."

Featured Program

Management 3: The Leaders Program ($4,950) is a new five day program developed exclusively for senior managers, VPs and executives who lead a growing number of business portfolios and employee groups. Management 3 is recommended to candidates with at least 10-15 years of leadership experience. The five day curriculum is broken into eight learning components that address current topics: ethics, planning, employee engagement and globalization just to name a few.

Component One: Coaching, Mentoring and Succession Planning
Component Two: Creating Sustainability in Today's Marketplace
Component Three: Ethical Leadership Strategies & Practice
Component Four: Effective Corporate Governance Practices
Component Five: Competing Effectively in The Global Economy
Component Six: Financial Analysis and Control
Component Seven: Corporate Social Responsibility: The Senior Manager's Role
Component Eight: Operational Leadership

To ensure maximum course value, the Management 3 program provides each participant with individual coaching sessions when they return to their work environment. Once each month for three months, participants are able to schedule convenient 15 minute facilitator coaching and problem solving sessions. This brand of personal coaching benefit differentiates the Management 3 curriculum from any other leadership program in Canada.

<u>Appreciation</u>

The Schulich Executive Education Centre offers programs in two central Toronto locations: at the Executive Learning Centre at York University's main campus, and at the Miles S. Nadal Management Centre, located in the heart of Toronto's financial district.

The emphasis at the Schulich School of Business is on graduating future business leaders from their academic programs such as the MBA. The Dean's message does not mention executive education. At SEEC, the vast number of programs and courses are almost all directed at middle managers and below, with the exception of the one program featured above, Management 3: The Leaders Program. But even that one, despite its name and judging by its content, is really for mid-level management. All courses and programs boast relevance to the workplace.

Certificate accreditation is a principal objective for these management programs, and it is likely a popular one with participants. There is a fairly unique and very flexible "Personalized Learning Path" option, which lets participants choose four courses (one foundation, plus three electives) in one of five learning paths: General Management, Strategic Leadership, Financial Management & Business Planning, Cross-Functional Management, and Business Operations Management. The four courses must be completed within three years, at the end of which a certificate in professional excellence is awarded.

The open enrolment offering is vast at 131 open enrolment courses listed on the website and 90 scheduled for the 2009/2010 season. One has to assume, given that several programs do not have scheduled dates, that they will be cancelled if any do not fill. Over time, this would cause a natural culling of programs in which executives had little interest. At 16,000 participants, the yearly attendance levels for the open enrolment and the custom programs would suggest that this blanket policy of over-supply makes sense.

Not providing programs specifically directed at C-level executives is likely an understandable strategy for this school: such programs are very costly to design and deliver; the human and other resources and time commitment are onerous; and passing on all these costs is difficult, unless the school's reputation is specifically established in this specialized area.

As the executive director of SEEC stated in the 138 page colour brochure, "The list of learning possibilities to stay ahead is boundless, and right here at SEEC, you have tremendous educational choices at your doorstep". Compare Schulich's 90 open enrolment executive/ management offerings for 2009/2010 with those of the other four Canadian schools presented here: seven at Ivey, 17 at Queen's, 26 at McGill and 25 at Rotman. Only Harvard Executive Education comes close, with 71 Open Enrolment Programs being offered in 2009/2010. It might be that the accreditation offered for so many programs at Schulich has proven to be an attractive incentive in choosing to attend Schulich. SEEC certainly seems to be enjoying a huge annual attendance for their open enrolment programs, and for their custom programs as well. All in all, this is a very impressive school, doing a great deal for middle management and junior executive learning in Canada.

Case F - Harvard Business School (HBS) Executive Programs, Boston, MA., USA.

1.Scope of Executive Offerings

Executive programs have been provided at HBS for over 60 years. For 2009/2010, there are 71 open enrolment programs under 12 major categories. There are three flagship open enrolment programs for executives who are at key transitional points in their careers: (1) The two month on-campus Advanced Management Program, for members of executive committees and heads of business units; (2) The General Management Program of four on-campus modules lasting four months, for executives with recently acquired, or significantly expanded, general management responsibilities; (3) For functional specialists, there is the Program for Leadership

Development comprising an initial 10-week individual learning off-campus module, a two week on-campus second module, a 14-week off-campus module, and a final two week module on campus. The off-campus segments feature personal study as well as both synchronous and asynchronous online work.

Custom Programs are available in the form of company-specific learning solutions. The goals of the custom programs include: preparing leaders to implement strategic change (merger or acquisition); enabling individuals to enhance specific management skills; and building new or greater organizational competence in specific areas.

2. Customized/Open Program Objective, Design and Style

The longer courses, such as the eight week Advanced Management Program, costs $60,000, inclusive of accommodation, meals and supplies. At Harvard, a week means six days of classes. The shorter courses vary in cost and duration, with some examples being: The three day Corporate Governance for Compensation Committees at $5,000; the four day Corporate Social Responsibility at $7,000; the six day Global Strategic Management at $9,500.

The Case Study Method is used in every program. It was invented here, and it is used by universities throughout the world (in fact, 80% of the cases used by other universities were written by HBS professors). Case studies are relevant, because they deal with actual, current business stories, and because they are often so similar to challenges facing participants in their own companies. "Case Studies open the window to actual business dilemmas in some of the world's most admired companies". Although the flagship general management programs are surprisingly lengthy (a few weeks to several months), most open enrolment executive programs are two to five days in duration. In the context of learning at HBS, everyone is a teacher, and everyone is a learner.

Customized programs are tailored to organizational needs and capabilities, but generally they happen in short doses of a few days at a time over long periods: "Custom programs are virtual windows into the rich resources of the Harvard University community". Examples provided of the custom programs which might be offered in a series of two and a half-day sessions demonstrate an understanding of time preciousness in executives' lives: a process for introducing a new management strategy to the top 300 business leaders in one corporation; in another, HBS was asked to create a leadership program for the top 250 executives.

3. Curriculum Elements (soft/hard skills)

The curricula assure that there is a global perspective on things. Open Enrolment Programs are available under the major "soft" and "hard" headings of: Comprehensive Leadership, Owner-Managed Firms, Business Strategy, Corporate Governance, Financial Management, Healthcare and Science, Leadership and Change, Marketing, Negotiation and Managerial Decision Making, Personal Development, Social Enterprise, and Technology and Operations Management.

4. Face-to-face /Online Delivery

Most open enrolment executive programs are conducted face-to-face, with only the ones of longer duration (more than five days) including distance learning elements. Most of the custom programs also tend to be face-to-face, with no mention I can see on the vast website about the use of online segments, although "homework", which could be online, happens throughout the process. The ten and 14-week off-campus modules of the Leadership Development Program include some online synchronous and asynchronous learning. Online information is offered for most programs.

5. Individual/Group Learning

During most sessions, the principal vehicle is the case study. This is a heavily facilitated process with much group participation, including breakout sessions and online simulations. Generally, the process includes working alone to read and think about each case; small group discussions the night before; class-time discussions with famous professors actively participating.

6. Philosophy

"Every HBS Executive Education experience is shaped by the School's cross-functional approach to general management, its innovative teaching methodologies, and a unique residential learning environment that promotes teamwork and collaboration".

We know that the case study learning method is paramount at this institution – the very one that created it. There is also an emphasis on alumni maintaining a long-term relationship with HBS, and this is a fact that everyone I have talked to who has been there will substantiate. An emphasis on international considerations and global impact must be mentioned as an integral part of program philosophy for executive learning programs at HBS. "Participants enjoy personalized service and expansive facilities that help them concentrate, interact and learn. They live, dine, and work in an enclave devoted to executive development". Learning diversity, in every sense of that word, is key at this school.

7. Specialty or Differentiation

HBS expertise in using Case Study as a practical learning tool; the global reach and fame, which constantly generate funding and make HBS the place to be as a student, a learning executive, a practicing CEO guest lecturer, or a faculty member.

8. Faculty

HBS faculty are involved in ground-breaking field-based research concerning management practice. Many are mainstream business authors. Each year "faculty members draw on their breakthrough thinking to write or collaborate on approximately 35 books, 600 case studies, 300 academic papers, and a broad array of articles for both professional and general business publications; and HBS creates a self-funded $70 million research budget".

9. International Factors and Diversity

Executive Program mix of participants is one third from North and South America, one third from Europe the Middle East and Africa, and one third from Asia. Having a broad geographical distribution of participants is fundamental to the HBS philosophy of having a global perspective in everything that they do. One quarter of the cases written each year by HBS professors are about international issues.

10. Relevance (to Executive Learning)

To this researcher, there is not one iota of program or curriculum content at HBS Executive Programs that is not absolutely connected and relevant to executive learning.

11. Connections to the Outside World (partnerships, alliances)

HBS maintains alliances with alumni, corporations with whom it has conducted custom programs, and with other universities for example, IESE (also among the institutions featured in this data) for the delivery of executive programs in other countries. HBS faculty have multiple global affiliations from previous international business experiences, and current board affiliations to research projects and consulting arrangements with organizations on every continent. In addition to their HBS roles, most faculty also serve as advisers, consultants, and directors of companies around the globe. HBS has set up six research centres worldwide.

12. Testimonials

One video featured the faculty view that professors loved to teach in these programs, because they were able to improve their own teaching thanks to what they learned from the experience of so many practising executives from all over the world. One participant from Australia stated that he found the networking experience utterly phenomenal, and boasted that he now had contacts in many places in the world whom he could visit for both personal and commercial reasons. Another person complimented the school for not having the predominantly American perspective on business matters which he had expected to witness.

13. Website Quote and Website(s)

HBS was founded in 1908 in the midst of a financial crisis that has striking parallels to the economic turbulence the world is witnessing today. The School now has an even greater opportunity and responsibility to deliver on its mission "to educate leaders who make a difference in the world" (2008 HBS Annual Report).

http://www.exed.hbs.edu/ (HBS Executive Education home page). There is an attention to detail in the website which almost certainly describes a similar attention in the HBS teaching and learning philosophy. The site is easy to navigate, and is wonderfully designed. If you spend an appreciable amount of time on the website, you are asked to do a short survey which asks questions about the site with a constant view to improving upon it.

http://www.exed.hbs.edu/assets/videos/202.html (video: case study)

Featured Program

Given the hue and cry from several interviewed executives about not having time to attend any but the shortest programs, it might have been interesting to feature here one of Harvard's shorter courses of the sort which could fit into executives' busy schedules. However, I have opted to feature the famous Advanced Management Program (AMP) to understand better the type of program to which so many executives were saying "no" because of its unwieldy duration.

The Advanced Management Program (AMP) is an eight week intensive learning opportunity for senior executives with 20-25 years of management experience, who come from organizations with annual revenues of at least $250 million. It is offered in the fall and spring, and tuition costs are $60,000, inclusive of course materials, accommodation, and most meals. Twenty thousand executive leaders have graduated from the AMP since it was founded in 1945.

Participants are organized into communities of eight learners who live together and discuss business case studies before going to classes, which are divided into three or four sections of 20-30 people in each. Thus, there is dynamic interplay among guests, participants, faculty, living groups and classes. For instance, there might be a case about American Express, and the CEO of AmEx might be a fellow participant. By its very nature, the case study approach invites a classroom marriage between theory and practice.

The program deals with Comprehensive Leadership, Business Strategy, Financial Management, Leadership & Change, Marketing, Negotiation & Managerial Decision Making, Personal Development, Technology & Operations Management. Leading strategically, responsibly, and ethically are hallmarks of this program's credo. The lofty objective of this program is immodestly to transform senior executives into indispensable leaders. "Soft" and "hard" learning aspects of the courses comprise self-assessment, learning new skills, and understanding innovation. Personal benefits include the creation of invaluable networks of contacts which not only become useful professionally, but can result in long-lasting friendships.

Appreciation

There is no question as to the excellence and fame of this Business School in delivering top-drawer executive programs. It was apparent, however, that most of the executives I interviewed had the opinion that any program which lasted more than a few days could not be in their plans in the current business environment, and perhaps never would be again. They simply did not have time to take anywhere near eight weeks away from their demanding jobs and careers to attend a program such as Harvard's Advanced Management Program. In fact, a couple of weeks was considered too long to be away from the real action.

The one exception was in Case No. 6 Interview in which that executive reported that all members of the senior executive team had attended one of these long programs at Harvard. The executive of the Case No. 6 Interview was selected to attend the Harvard International Program just before being promoted to his next job within the company. During those kinds of transitions, these very lengthy, top notch programs may still make sense.

Listening and watching some of the videos available on the website is a good way in which to experience the palpable passion, dedication, and excitement of participants and professors about Harvard executive programs.

Alfred North Whitehead's connection to Harvard University as a philosophy professor, and as a staunch supporter of the then new business school, led him to describe that institution (1932/1959) as being "on a scale amounting to magnificence" (p. 137). According to those several senior leaders with whom I have talked about their time at Harvard, that school apparently still possesses this kind of magic - this kind of magnificence referred to by Whitehead. Harvard has the wisdom and good grace to appreciate and respect the immense practical experience of the executives who attend its programs, and to weave that experience into the unfolding of everyday learning sessions that happen there. This mutual respect between business leaders and Harvard fosters strong and lasting alliances between the Business School and the business community, and particularly with individual alumni. Those alumni are extremely loyal to their alma mater, even if they were only attending a short course for a few weeks or days. That respect which faculty members display for executives who attend their programs stands out significantly for me. There is a clear recognition of a two-way street of learning by having front-line senior practitioners attend these programs. Faculty love the opportunity to facilitate these programs, which provide such close contact with relevancy, and which in turn enhances their teaching in other (degree) programs.

Case G - Duke Corporate Education (DCE or Duke CE), Durham, NC, USA.

1. Scope of Executive Offerings

Duke Corporate Education (DCE) was incorporated in July 2000 as a carve-out of the custom executive education practice of Duke University's Fuqua School of Business. Along with its parent, Duke University, as well as with institutional partners in the UK and in India, DCE is recognized for its innovative creation, and management of customized programs for executives around the world. It currently has clients in 62 countries across six continents. DCE provides only custom programs for executives and their firms. There are no open enrolment programs at DCE.

2. Customized/Open Program Objective, Design and Style

DCE uses non-traditional approaches such as Metaphoric Experience™ (see section 7 on differentiation), action learning, just-in-time coaching, and team-based learning. Design prices usually run from US$50,000 to US$200,000; after which delivery prices are typically US$400 to US$2,000 per person per day. DCE creates its custom programs around "three deceptively simple questions": (1) What do you want your people to **know** as a result of this learning experience that they do not know now? (2) What do you want them to **do** that they don't do now? (3) What do you want them to **believe** about themselves, their business, their customers, their world and their future that they don't believe now?

Duke CE states that its ability to listen, to collaborate, and to customize solutions which are unique to specific businesses and cultural contexts, are fundamental to their approach. Often, a client's senior team will help design, assess, teach and attend its customized program. DCE designs educational programs which can deliver specific, desired outcomes. As DCE's president has stated, "We design to outcome using any kind of learning method or technology that is appropriate to do that".

3. Curriculum Elements (soft/hard skills)

The curriculum is completely customized to corporate clients, and includes the mix of "soft" and "hard" skills appropriate to the educational project being created.

4. Face-to-face /Online Delivery

Programs are created as face-to-face or virtual, or a combination of both. All methods are acceptable in DCE's learning philosophy as long as learning is happening. Online learning through video games, or its classroom counterpart in the form of metaphoric learning, are used. But mostly it is learning while doing, on the job, regardless of whether that is face-to-face or online.

5. Individual/Group Learning

DCE has created and successfully tested an education and change process called Team-Based Learning (TBL). The mix of individual with group learning is designed in concert with exactly what the client wants and needs.

6. Philosophy

DCE's two founders are an assistant dean of Fuqua and the chief learning officer at Coca Cola. Their teamwork explains the ensuing radically new business model that integrates academic and corporate philosophies.

One size does not fit all in executive education, and variables include industry, location, culture, business needs, participants' learning styles and level within the organization. DCE's outlook on business is one of partnership and collaboration over one of competition and winning.

7. Specialty or Differentiation

(1) DCE is 100% focused on developing customized executive programs, which are taught and facilitated by professors, the executives themselves from client firms, retired executives, industry specialists, consultants, and other experts in their fields.

(2) Design Lab is a collaborative and hands-on two-week process in which Duke CE works face-to-face with a client's learning professionals to help them arrive at new program designs which can be implemented immediately.

(3) Metaphoric Learning: Duke CE's Metaphoric Experience™ learning method takes participants out of their familiar environments, forcing them to experiment with new behaviours, skills and perspectives in an unfamiliar but compelling context. For instance, executives at a global energy company have "become" tobacco executives facing a congressional sub-committee.

8. Faculty

The facilitators for these custom programs are selected from all sorts of experts in the field. More than 800 of these individuals have joined the DCE group since 2003, and have been involved in teaching its programs around the world. They are not trying to advance a body of knowledge, but rather to work on finding solutions for real-time challenges.

9. International Factors and Diversity

Partner schools in the USA, the UK and India permit DCE to be more local and more global at the same time. The affiliation with the London School of Economics is particularly "international", with half of its faculty coming from outside the UK. Small or large scale custom programs can be delivered in several languages, with complex logistical requirements, anywhere in the world.

10. Relevance (to Executive Learning)

Custom programs are created, managed and delivered in the context of building a company's capabilities. These programs are all about what is currently happening in a corporation's life.

Nothing about this learning is disconnected from the business itself. Everything is pertinent.

11. Connections to the Outside World (partnerships, alliances)

DCE has formal relationships with its parent, Duke University in Durham, North Carolina (Fuqua School of Business); with the London School of Economics and Political Science in the UK; and with the Indian Institute of Management in Ahmedabad, India. "Faculty" from all over the world have joined the DCE team of designers and facilitators, making DCE global through local involvements and expertise.

12. Testimonials

(1) VP Verizon: "Of course even though leaders would prefer it to be otherwise, few people actually thrive on change. The Duke CE program is helping" (from Client Stories).

(2) Emirates Bank Group: "By immediately applying the lessons they learn in the classroom to their team projects, the skills become real and are integrated into the way they work" (from Client Stories).

(3) President and CEO of Genpact Latin America, Steve Rudderham: "People are latching onto delighting customers versus satisfying them, the importance of finance, understanding personal and team goals and the dynamics of teams and functions" (from Client Stories).

13. Website Quote and Website(s)

"Executive Education shouldn't be about business people. It should be about business outcomes.... Your business outcomes are critical: highly customized education is critical" (Duke Corporate Education brochure).

http://www.dukece.com/ (DEC website). A wonderful website, easy and great fun to navigate. If there were an award for the best website among these nine schools, this researcher would award it to DUKE CE.

http://www.dukece.com/utility/watch.php (a most inspired and exciting series of four videos, which well describe the DCE learning philosophy through short clips from DCE executives and clients).

Appreciation

Duke Corporate Education (DCE) is not a university. It is a separately operating offshoot of Duke University's Fuqua School of Business. It designs and delivers custom executive education programs to organizational clients around the world.

In order to provide custom programs that have the right faculty and the right learning methods for each unique client situation, DCE draws on resources around the globe. This has resulted in a collective of coaches, facilitators, actors, consultants, industry experts, and retired executives from DCE's Global Learning Resource Network. As stated on the website: "Because we employ few faculty, we have unlimited faculty": this makes their faculty a non-fixed or a flexible asset.

Unlike most institutions, DCE does not spend much ink boasting about their awards. However, it could be mentioned that *The Financial Times* worldwide ranking of custom executive education providers placed DCE first in each of the last three years (2007, 2008 and 2009). *Business Week* also placed DCE first for customized curriculum in 2007.

Although Fuqua and DCE are operated as separate entities, there is a tight and meaningful connection between the two: many former business school faculty are on the DCE staff. The custom work which DCE does with its clients serves to connect The Fuqua School of Business to the everyday challenges and reality of the business world. As mentioned on the Business School's website in the Dean's message, "We begin by developing credible intelligence about business needs, working with information that our partner, Duke Corporate Education, accrues in daily practice with firms across the important regions and industries of the world". This connection is made even tighter by the fact that Blair Sheppard was one of the DCE founders. He went to DCE in 2000 directly from his job as associate dean at Fuqua, and then returned seven years later to the Business School, once DCE was well underway. Being in such close touch with business reality, DCE and Fuqua each possess the best of both academic and corporate worlds. Operating the business school separately from Duke Corporate education allows each to concentrate on separate but related agendas: teaching students and serving clients.

The terminology used on the website and in the videos captures the atmosphere of urgency and relevance which DCE espouses. For instance, from the vision statement come these words: "Adult learning is our expertise, executive education our business. Our vision is to be an institution that matters in the world.... We want to inspire and lead constructive, pragmatic change. We want to bring clients deep practical knowledge, diverse voices and critical perspectives that have real impact. We want to change mindsets".

DCE uses innovative teaching models such as Metaphoric Experience™, mentioned in the previous chart, and it may seem strange to foster the kinds of experience that this method proposes. However, these engaging metaphors are always linked to business outcomes. To do otherwise would be, as explained on the website, to have created some sort of parlour game.

Another DCE model is called Thought Partnership, in which advisory services help business professionals to create the architecture of their organization's own learning and development solutions. Thought leaders are brought in to share points of view and experiences, enabling collaborative creation of answers to challenges. Rather than consulting, it is about designing and strategizing together.

The Philosophy of DCE is very much that work offers the best place to develop capability. There is no mention of the case study method, for, in their opinion, clients' businesses are actual, live cases. DCE (along with McGill, as we have seen) is on to something new here: learning how to solve actual problems in real time.

Case H - INSEAD (Institut Européen d'Administration), Fontainebleau, France

1.Scope of Executive Offerings

Founded in 1957 by Georges Doriot, Claude Janssen, and Olivier Giscard d'Estaing, INSEAD is one of the world's leading business schools. INSEAD has two full campuses : in Europe (France) and in Asia (Singapore), an education and research centre in Abu Dhabi, a North Americas office in New York City, and a Research Centre in Israel.

INSEAD offers a full slate of 52 open enrolment executive programs: four in general management, three in top management, eight in leadership, 11 in strategy, eight in people and performance management, five in marketing, six in finance and banking, four in operations management, and two in entrepreneurship and family business; plus an executive MBA. Approximately 9,500 executives from over 120 countries undertake courses or programmes at INSEAD each year.

The three open enrolment top management programs showing tuition that does not include accommodation are: (1) The five day, €15,000, AVIRA Program: Awareness, Vision, Imagination, Responsibility, Action; (2) The 18-day in four modules, €30,000, Challenge of Leadership Program (Creating reflective leaders); (3) The two day, €7,900, International Directors' Forum (Effective boards in a changing world).

The four General Management Programs include (1) The five week, €32,000, Advanced Management Program; (2) The six week, €38,200, International Executive Program; (3) The six week, €47,600, Asian International Executive Program; (4) The three week, €20,200, Management Acceleration Program.

2. Customized/Open Program Objective, Design and Style

Fees, not inclusive of accommodation, for other open enrolment programs vary from €4,100-6,950 for 3days; €6,700-8,200 for five days; €11,700-12,500 for 10 days.

INSEAD has worked closely with a range of companies and firms of varying size across multiple industries and geographies to develop tailor made executive education programmes since the 1960s. Clients for these custom tailored programs are often those that require a rich intercultural component. INSEAD believes tailor-made programs should simultaneously achieve individual, group and organization-wide learning.

For the open enrolment programs, INSEAD offers to send CD-ROM highlights capturing main learning concepts, so that executives can share these with their teams when they return to the workplace. Live web casts, online programmes, follow-up workshops, interactive sessions with faculty and advanced program platforms offer a myriad of ways of helping executives continue to make the most of INSEAD before, during or after the classroom experience.

The Case method is largely used in the classroom as a teaching method. Business case studies, authored by INSEAD professors, are the second most widely used in classrooms by business schools globally, after Harvard Business School's case studies. Selection of participants for the major programs is rigorous in order to achieve the proper mix of talent, executive levels, and internationalism.

3. Curriculum Elements (soft/hard skills)

Each of the top management programs contains curriculum in most of the following competencies: leading people, leading change, managing across boundaries, strategic capabilities, decision making capabilities, customer orientation, value-based management, and fostering innovation.

4. Face-to-face /Online Delivery

INSEAD OnLine (IOL) represents an entire segment of the learning platform. It comprises courses and programs which can be entirely delivered online, and consist of interactive exercises. Online communities are also created to bring managers together before, during and after face-to-face sessions to leverage program investment, and to strengthen global collaboration. There is a stated preference for blended learning solutions, which combine face-to-face classroom sessions with the "virtual classroom online". There are corporate clients such as Bertelsmann, IBM, Rolls Royce, Johnson & Johnson and Shell that are IOL clients using a combination of e-learning, discussion, web seminars, conference calls, and some in-class sessions for the unfolding of their custom programs.

5. Individual/Group Learning

All programs and courses, whether they be online, face-to-face or a blended design, combine individual work involving reflection or personal study of stand-alone material with group sessions.

6. Philosophy

"It is not what you discover but what you **do** with your discovery that is important. It is not what you think, but what you **do** with your thinking that counts. It is not what you say, but what you **do** that makes a difference". (executive programs website)

Diversity as a source of learning and enrichment: INSEAD's global viewpoint and insistence on diversity for faculty and participants, makes it free from any dominant culture or prevalent dogma.

7. Specialty or Differentiation

INSEAD's principal differentiation lies in its global perspective and cultural diversity – the international outlook for which INSEAD is famous. There is a remarkable mix of discipline and hard work, along with a realization that having time for reflection requires a retreat-like formula. This must be one in which informal learning, chatting, getting to know fellow participants, and developing contacts for the future become an integral part of this executive work.

8. Faculty

"Great Minds don't Think Alike". INSEAD's professors represent many cultures, many disciplines, many perspectives. At the same time, they are acknowledged world experts in their own particular fields, and outstanding teachers. With strong track records in research and teaching, the INSEAD faculty also remain intimately close to business. Most are engaged in cross-disciplinary research.

9. International Factors and Diversity

The recent strategic alliance with the Wharton School, which has campuses in France and Singapore, and offers a depth of managerial research and experience in delivering intensely global program content to a diverse client base, combine to give INSEAD a truly international flavour. There were, for instance, 126 nationalities represented in executive programs 2007/08.

10. Relevance (to Executive Learning)

"There wasn't a single discussion or class which wasn't relevant to the challenges we face" (Marvin Romanow, Executive Vice President & CFO, Nexen Inc. commenting on his experience at the Advanced Management Program).

11. Connections to the Outside World (partnerships, alliances)

INSEAD is linked to the Wharton business school through a global strategic alliance. Through custom programs and consulting engagements, INSEAD enjoys a closeness to the international business community.

12. Testimonials

"As far as directors' education goes, this is probably the most senior, pragmatic, and international programme on the market" (Former Chairman, Aegon & Dutch Corporate Governance Commission).

"The first steps of an exploratory journey into yourself accompanied by 20 observers/commentators. A safari into one's soul. A chance to make new friendships, with a substantial kick-start, with people who share some common factors" (Vice President Sales & Logistics, TNK-BP Management, Russia).

13. Website Quote and Website(s)

"Welcome to the Business School for the World"

http://www.insead.edu/home/ (INSEAD homepage). A very good website, fairly similar to Harvard's; all there at the researcher's fingertips.

http://executive.education.insead.edu/ (executive education home)

http://en.wikipedia.org/wiki/INSEAD

Featured Programs

(1) The Advanced Management Program (AMP) for top executives is a four week program (plus a five day follow-up one year after the program), which runs three times per year, with a tuition fee of €32,000 (not including accommodation, which is estimated at around €6,400).

http://executive.education.insead.edu/advanced_management/videos/how.cfm (This short video describes how the AMP changes its participants).

The AMP is essentially a high-level international forum. It is not about techniques and tools for the general manager, because participants are already considered to be, and are selected for this program as, experienced general managers. It is more about refreshing existing management skills and understandings, and there is a respectful acknowledgement that attendees are there as practising experts – the same acknowledgement we saw at Harvard.

The AMP is quite specific about entry requirements: Participants must be CEOs or Managing Directors of firms with a €30 million turnover, or members of the executive leadership team for firms with turnover exceeding €100 million, or two levels down from the CEO for firms with turnover exceeding €100 million.

Typically the AMP comprises 120 people from 30 countries who work in sections of 40 people, because they feel that work in smaller groups amplifies the learning. The first week opens with session on what is going on in the world. Values are discussed in the second week; for instance, which values serve to make the organization and the world better places to work and live. The third week deals with innovation and change – leading organizations to become better at what they do and at what they are. In the fourth week, it is the participants who more or less take over in order to prepare and reflect upon their re-entry into changed professional and personal lives.

The program content includes four major segments: (1) Understanding an Evolving Context, comprising sub topics such as the geo-political scene, the global economy, and communicating across cultures; (2) Creating, Delivering, Measuring Value, comprising sub topics such as value innovation, ethical issues in global organizations, and value chain analysis; (3) Orchestrating and Leading Change, comprising sub topics such as organizational diagnosis, inspirational leadership, and fair process; (4) Formulating, Validating and Committing to a personal Leadership Agenda, comprising sub topics such as understanding oneself in relationship to others, setting a breakthrough agenda for the business, and coalition building and network management.

Creating a network one can tap into is a valuable benefit of attendance in the AMP, but the emphasis is on creating a tight bond with three or four individuals who might even become friends, and with whom participants can consult: that is the real treasure. The curriculum is not too tightly packed, in order to allow participants time to explore new things, and try them out among themselves.

There is the implication that there will be a transfer of knowledge and tools from INSEAD via program participants back to their whole organization.

(2) AVIRA: (Awareness, Vision, Imagination, Responsibility, Action) is a program for top management (€15,000 tuition, not including accommodation). This unique, five-day program for top executives is offered in both Fontainebleau and Singapore. "**AVIRA** is a unique opportunity for business leaders from around the world to put aside the urgent in order to consider the important. It gives them a forum for exploring and debating the current issues most prominent on their agenda".

More concretely, **AVIRA** is designed to explore the five critical dimensions of the CEO's role: Awareness (for instance, the path from the outside world of the corporation to the inner world of the top executive); Vision (for example, alternative models of the business-society interface, and the global corporation and its critics: coping with critics from outside), Imagination (for instance, the role of imagination in strategic thinking, and beyond confrontation: learning from our contradictions, managing "dualities"); Responsibility (for example, developing organisational capital and executive talent, and the corporation and the common good: implications for corporate leaders; and Action (for instance, re-invention and the relevance of 'practical' theories for action).

As one participant dramatically stated about AVIRA: "Five days out of the mainstream, coming back to work with a wealth of images. At some time; Much later, or at a different moment, images will resurface and help you make the right decision. If AVIRA doesn't help you, you should retire." (Chairman, Sithe Pacific Development, Thailand).

Appreciation

The INSEAD Mission is stated as follows on their website:

> To promote a non-dogmatic
> learning environment that brings
> together people, cultures and ideas
> from around the world, changing lives,

and helping transform organizations through management education; to develop responsible, thoughtful leaders and entrepreneurs who create value for their organisations and their communities and through research, to expand the frontiers of academic thought and influence business practice.

INSEAD at Fontainebleau is the international school for executives, *par excellence*. The diversity of its students and faculty is outstanding. INSEAD offers a vast array of 52 open enrolment programs, as well as three flagship lengthy programs for senior executives. This school could probably be considered as Europe's Harvard in scope, reputation and flair, and as diverse and international, or even more so.

Although the names of courses, and program outlines deal with some quite standard, "hard" skill subject matter, the teaching and learning approaches appear to be fairly "soft" in their appreciation of time for reflection, and for activities such as keeping a journal. As mentioned, the curriculum is not too tightly packed, so as to allow participants time to explore new things and try them out among themselves. Including AVIRA as one of the featured programs for senior executives emphasizes INSEAD's interests in the "softer" side of management. Building a network one can tap into is a valuable benefit of attendance, but the emphasis is on creating tight bonds with a few individuals with whom participants can consult long after the program is over.

Clients of customized programs that require expertise in learning about international topics such as cultural diversity, or global subjects like doing business in foreign countries (especially in Europe) might want to consider INSEAD. Custom programs here have an admirable follow-up mechanism called Measuring Organizational Impact (MOI). Interestingly, this acronym, "moi", is the French word for ME or I, and may emphasize the personalizing of custom programs.

INSEAD Online (IOL) is an initiative that creates an online community of learners during and after the major in-residence programs. INSEAD InterAct is the platform that provides course materials, as well as collaborative forums to enhance learning.

Case I - IESE Business School (Instituto de Estudios Superiores de la Empresa), University of Navarra, Barcelona, Spain

1.Scope of Executive Offerings

There is a total of 20 open enrolment programs offered in English and Spanish at IESE. Some of these are offered in several locations. For instance, the Advanced Management Program (AMP) is offered in Barcelona, Sao Paulo, Munich, Warsaw and the Middle East; The Global CEO Program is offered in Latin America and Chile. Nine Open Enrolment Executive Programs offered in English, of which three are major formats, and six are short, four day, focused programs (such as Leading Your Company to Global Growth and Getting Things Done). Many other programs are delivered in Spanish, and there is an emphasis on clients in Latin America and China. The three major programs in English for senior executives include: The Advanced Management Program, The Program for Management Development, and The Global CEO. Most of these programs are delivered in Barcelona, but several are held at international locations, including a few in the USA (for instance, Leading Your Company to Global Growth takes place at Radio City Music Hall in New York).

IESE Business School is also well-known for its fully customized programs.

2. Customized/Open Program Objective, Design and Style

The major open enrolment programs, such as the Advanced management Program, carry tuition fees of €33,000, inclusive of meals and accommodation and all course materials. The shorter four-day programs cost €4,500, also inclusive of accommodation, meals and materials.

The objective of customized programs is to transform boldly the mindset and behaviour of attendees through a collaborative approach, in a cooperative culture, among faculty, staff and client. The program design compromises academic analysis with experiential activities, which take attendees out of their comfort zones; emphasis is on impacting the individual as well as the organization.

3. Curriculum Elements (soft/hard skills)

There is a good blend of "hard/soft" skills in all programs, but with an emphasis on the "hard" side. For instance, of the 22 subjects listed for the AMP, 13 of them appear to be "hard" topics such as Corporate Finance, and nine seem to be "soft" topics such as Self-Management. Of the 18 subjects listed for the Global CEO Program for Latin America, nine topics are arguably "hard" such as Strategic Operations Management; six are convincingly "soft" such as Entrepreneurial Spirit. Of the 11 academic departments of the Business School, eight have "hard" sounding nametags such as Accounting and Control; and three have "soft" sounding nametags such as People in Organizations.

4. Face-to-face /Online Delivery

Most programs use a blended combination of face-to-face modules with online, distance learning.

5. Individual/Group Learning

Participants are encouraged to keep a "learning log" on a daily basis, and work mostly individually when they are not in residence. When participants are face-to-face in residence, most of the work is in groups.

6. Philosophy

In residence, interactive use of Case Studies is key, along with discussions, simulations, presentations, small group learning activities, and breakout sessions. Between residential modules, individual work in online discussion groups prepares participants for the next residential module.

7. Specialty or Differentiation

Encouragement of Lifelong Learning is apparent in one of the services provided by the Alumni Association (boasting one of the highest alumni membership rates in the world): after they graduate, alumni are given ongoing library access!

8. Faculty

The IESE Business School has a total of 175 full, part-time, emeritus and visiting faculty members. IESE professors lead 14 research centres located in Barcelona and Madrid, and the school has 16 academic business chairs.

Full-time professors come from 27 countries, and many of them gain global understanding and insight by teaching in the international executive programs. IESE is one of the largest producers of business cases in the world. The faculty's teaching and research efforts are global in outlook and content.

9. International Factors and Diversity

For the Open Enrolment Executive Programs, participants are selected to ensure a good diversity in companies, sectors and cultural backgrounds. They come from around the world, with the majority from Eastern and Western Europe. There are over 32,000 alumni representative of 109 nationalities.

Surprisingly however, the courses are not all that "global". For instance in the International AMP, only one of the 22 subjects listed among the four program modules is directly related to an international or global topic (Global Marketing). Of the 11 academic departments listed at IESE, none is specifically named as being 'global' or 'international'. Even so, there is in fact a completely separate offering called Global CEO, which is specifically offered for China and Latin America. Of the 18 courses offered in three modules, six of those courses seem to be related to global or international issues of concern for CEO level executives.

10. Relevance (to Executive Learning)

The IESE website does a good job, consistently underscoring the relevancy of their executive programs for participants. Most course content, as well program design and structure, seem utterly relevant to executive education.

11. Connections to the Outside World (partnerships, alliances)

(1) 'Company Relations': on this segment of the website, there are five ways mentioned on how to partner with IESE.

(2) The Harvard-IESE Committee, including faculty members from both schools, has met annually since the early 1960s to discuss global trends in management education, as well as joint research and teaching projects (frequently about international executive education).

(3) Joint Open Enrolment and Customized Executive Programs: these have been forged since 1993 with a growing number of top US business schools including Harvard Business School, Stanford Graduate School of Business, MIT Sloan School of Management, and University of Michigan Business School.

(4) Academic Alliances: these service an exchange program for 60 IESE MBA students per year; the school maintains a reciprocal arrangement with many of the world's leading business schools. For the 2009-2010 year, there are 23 such alliances – 15 of which are with business schools in the USA.

(5) Associated Business Schools: this is an international network of 17 business schools, which began in 1967. IESE, acting as a consultant, helped set up these schools, including eight in Central and South America, four in Africa, two each in Asia and North America, and one in Europe.

(6) International Faculty Development Program: this is geared toward business and management educators. Since its inception, 200 faculty members from diverse business schools have taken part. The program focuses on application of the Harvard-originated case writing and curriculum design.

12. Testimonials

Videos of AMP participants from the USA and Ireland emphasized the following positive attributes: (1) The wisdom and excellence of the faculty and their clear, in-depth understanding of each individual's particular professional situation; and the understanding of what participants were there for; (2) The take-home benefit of the face-to-face residency sessions; (3) The flexibility and rhythm of doing the four one-week residency segments over six months as being absolutely necessary for busy executives, and the additional benefit of such a schedule in permitting reflection time among the four face-to-face modules.

13. Website Quote and Website(s)

"Every organization is different. Each has its own structure, culture and ambitions. And each faces unique opportunities, threats and challenges".

http://www.iese.edu/en/ExecutiveEducation/Executive Education.asp (executive education at IESE) Very good and easy to navigate website.

http://www.iese.edu/en/ExecutiveEducation/customprograms/ Welcome.asp (custom programs)

http://insight.iese.edu/ (IESE's *Insight Magazine*)

Featured Program

The AMP – International Advanced Management Program

This is an open enrolment general management program designed to help executives with at least 15 years of senior management experience to attain new levels of success in managing and leading their firms. The program fee is €35,000 inclusive of tuition, reading and classroom materials, meals and accommodation.

The program structure combines four one-week residential modules in Barcelona (Sansi Hotel), which all take place over a six month period. Participation generally comprises 25-30 top tier executives from around the world, who have a great deal of senior management experience under their belts. Participants are selected to ensure a good diversity of companies, economic sectors and cultural backgrounds. The class of 2008/2009, for example, consisted of participants, with an average age of 43 years, from 22 countries.

The four residential modules are linked with a web community to ensure ongoing contact. Participants are assigned a faculty coach who assesses progress and stimulates deeper reflection. Participants work on their own take-home agendas, and action plans for themselves as well as for their companies.

The four residential modules include: (1) Understanding the Business Landscape (for example, economics and decision analysis);

(2) Managing Value Creation (for example, service management and self leadership); (3) Leading Innovation and Change (for example, competitive strategy and entrepreneurship); (4) Getting Things Done (for example, negotiation and Mergers & Acquisitions).

The stated program objective is to "provide a forum for discussion which will enable managers to take a step back and reassess their views on the current business environment". Methods to achieve this include analysis of best practices, having participants work together in virtual teams during the distributed learning modules (between face-to-face modules), and having participants, when together in residence, challenge their old concepts.

The video testimonials on the following link gives an excellent view and feeling for the AMP Program: http://www.iese. edu/en/ExecutiveEducation/GeneralManagementPrograms/ AdvancedManagementProgram(AMP)/videos/Videos.asp

Appreciation

In 2008, *The Financial Times* ranking of Executive Education programs placed this school #2 in Europe and #5 in the world. It appears to be a focused and traditional school, but one possessing a high degree of flexibility and an understanding of the pressures at play in an executive's demanding and almost impossibly busy life.

There are only nine open enrolment programs in English, but they are major ones. There is considerable flexibility shown in program design: the format of the flagship Advanced Management Program, which has its four one-week modules spread over six months, is a better fit with busy corporate schedules. It makes for a better paced learning experience in which participants are able to reflect on those experiences, and actually implement them into their everyday working life. As one participant stated: "The modular structure strikes the right balance: it maximizes the time we spend together, while minimizing the time we spend out of the office. And as we all know, time is the one thing we're all short of". (Boris Santosi – Regional Managing Director, Alcan International)

Another aspect of IESE's flexibility is seen in the staging of several of their programs in different international venues – not just the long-duration flagship offerings in China or South America, but the short four-day courses which IESE holds in Miami.

The IESE choice will likely be of great interest for those executives seeking a European flavour and quality to their learning. For instance, executives about to be assigned to Europe, or dealing with European customers, or wanting to become involved with EU countries, might want to look at the AMP offered in Barcelona.

IESE boasts absolutely superb worldwide connections and partnerships which are outlined in the IESE data chart, but which merit repeating here, for they celebrate IESE's truly global outlook and their realization about the importance of diversity. They include the Harvard-IESE Committee, comprising faculty members from both schools, which meets annually to discuss global trends in management education; Joint Open Enrolment and Customized Executive Programs with Harvard Business School, Stanford Graduate School of Business, MIT Sloan School of Management, and University of Michigan Business School; Academic Alliances involving international exchange programs for 60 IESE MBA students every year; Associated Business School network of 17 schools, which IESE helped set up in five continents; and an International Faculty Development Program geared toward business and management educators.

Although there are several ways that are explained about how organizations and groups can partner with IESE, it seems to be portrayed as rather a one-way street. There is no mention *per se* of the school's own outreach programs to connect with business, or to learn from business. There is a list of services, all of which concern offering research activities, advice or coaching to companies – but not the other way around in recognizing what business could possibly "teach" IESE – the kind of symbiotic relationship so respected, for example, at Harvard, Ivey and INSEAD.

Unlike several of the schools presented here, IESE makes full use of online learning as a vibrant tool of collaboration. As stated on the IESE website, globalization is causing on-line teamwork to be a must for business success. Therefore, residential modules are linked with a web community which keeps the participants in close contact throughout a program's duration. As deftly stated in the AMP brochure: "During the distributed learning modules the participants will confront the challenge of connecting not only across cultural barriers, but across time and space to work with their teams".

The Quintain of University Findings

Introduction

I become encouraged when I look over the details presented about these nine universities, for they are all excellent in different ways: in their points of view, specialties offered, degree of sophistication, style and reputation. The findings about them encourage one to think that valuable executive learning is indeed available from these institutions. It is up to individual firms to discover which kind of collaboration about executive education would result in the best fit. Based on its culture, a firm needs to decide upon its specific objectives and its budget, as to whether a customized program or one of the open enrolment programs is the better way to go. In fact, several universities have a third option which is to customize an open enrolment program to the specific needs of an organization. I have presented data on nine universities, but many more should be scrutinized by any organization considering new or reconsidering old executive learning initiatives.

The individual universities were each considered separately in the previous pages. Now the analysis is a collective one, and they will be looked at as a Quintain, just as was done for the interviews. The following chart shows a series of data about the nine institutions, and the more important narrative analysis occurs following that.

The First Chart: Some Preliminary Grouped Data and Personal Rankings of Excellence

The chart that follows on the next page provides general data about the relative importance of open and custom executive programs, the number of programs, the researcher's perspective about the degree of international content and diversity, and a word or two about the different brands, I have added a subjective opinion here regarding the quality of each institution's website.

Table#4: Grouped Data and Subjective Rankings of Excellence

Please notice use of lower case, upper case, and underlining to indicate the relative significance, high significance and very high significance of (O)pen Enrolment and (C)ustom programs.

Case A – McGill
Significance of Open Enrolment cf. Custom Programs:	<u>O</u> & C
Number of Major Executive Programs:	6
Number of Open Enrolment Programs:	26
Level of International Content & Diversity:	Very High

Subjective views of brand "personality" and website quality:
Home to Professor Mintzberg; Best in Action Learning initiatives; Website needs work; it seems incomplete and hard to navigate.

Case B - Ivey
Significance of Open Enrolment cf. Custom Programs:	<u>C</u> & o
Number of Major Executive Programs:	3
Number of Open Enrolment Programs:	7
Level of International Content & Diversity:	Medium

Subjective views of brand "personality" and website quality:
Case study powerhouse; closest in Canada to the business community; Website needs more consistency between it and related printed brochures.

Case C – Queen's
Significance of Open Enrolment cf. Custom Programs:	O & c
Number of Major Executive Programs:	3
Number of Open Enrolment Programs:	17
Level of International Content & Diversity:	Low

Subjective views of brand "personality" and website quality:
Current reputation as "Best in Canada"; Good website – logical and very navigable.

Case D - Rotman

Significance of Open Enrolment cf. Custom Programs:	O & c
Number of Major Executive Programs:	2 or 3
Number of Open Enrolment Programs:	25
Level of International Content & Diversity:	Low

Subjective views of brand "personality" and website quality:
Itegrative Thinking™; Use of case study; Good website – easy to navigate.

Case E - Schulich

Significance of Open Enrolment cf. Custom Programs:	O & c
Number of Major Executive Programs:	3
Number of Open Enrolment Programs:	83
Level of International Content & Diversity:	Low

Subjective views of brand "personality" and website quality:
Vast choice among open enrolment courses – perhaps too vast, but they are selling it. Fairly good website, but with a huge volume of information, making navigation challenging.

Case F - Harvard

Significance of Open Enrolment cf. Custom Programs:	O & c
Number of Major Executive Programs:	3
Number of Open Enrolment Programs:	71
Level of International Content & Diversity:	Very High

Subjective views of brand "personality" and website quality:
The inventor of the case study; excellent venue for North American and worldwide networking; Famous faculty; Excellent website – everything is there and conveniently so.

Case G – Duke Corporate Education (DCE)

Significance of Open Enrolment cf. Custom Programs:	All Custom Programs
Number of Major Executive Programs:	N/A

Number of Open Enrolment Programs: N/A
Level of International Content & Diversity: Variable

Subjective views of brand "personality" and website quality:
Custom programs offer the tightest connection to worldwide realities of particular businesses; Metaphoric Experience™; Website is excellent, fun and easily navigated.

Case H – INSEAD (Fontainebleau, France)

Significance of Open Enrolment cf. Custom Programs: <u>O</u> & c
Number of Major Executive Programs: 3
Number of Open Enrolment Programs: 52
Level of International Content & Diversity: Very High

Subjective views of brand "personality" and website quality:
Reputation for being *the* international venue; superb worldwide networking potential for participants; Use of the case study; Good website.

Case I – IESE (Barcelona, Spain)

Significance of Open Enrolment cf. Custom Programs: O & c
Number of Major Executive Programs: 3
Number of Open Enrolment Programs: 6
Level of International Content & Diversity: Medium

Subjective views of brand "personality" and website quality:
Emphasis on diversity; the venue for "European flavour" with participants coming mostly from EU countries.

Table #5: Comparative Costs (Canadian dollars)
Examples of Various Programs
(Revised February 2010)

Case A – McGill (excluding accommodation)
2 days:	$1595 - Effective Leadership
3 days:	$1995 - Strategic Planning & Execution
4 days:	$2595 - Essential Management Skills
5 days:	-
6 days:	-
3 weeks:	$150,000 for "table" of 5 or 6 participants - i.e. $25,000 per person- The Advanced Leadership Program at 3 international venues

Case B – Ivey
2 days:	-
3 days:	$4900 (excluding accommodation) - Ivey Influence and Persuasion Program
4 days:	-
5 days:	-
6 days:	$9100 (including accommodation) - Ivey Leadership Program
3 weeks:	$23,995 (including accommodation) - Ivey Executive Program

Case C – Queen's
2 days:	$2900 (excluding accommodation) - Developing Your Leadership Presence $1950 (excluding accommodation) - Planning for the Economic Recovery
3 days:	-
4 days:	$4100 (including accommodation) - Queen's Governance Program
5 days:	-

| 6 days: | $8900 (including accommodation) - Queen's Leadership Program |
| 3 weeks: | $23,900 (including accommodation) Queen's Executive Program |

Case D – Rotman

2 days:	-
3 days:	$3500 (excluding accommodation) - Evidence-Based Management
	$6500 (excluding accommodation) - Excellence in the Boardroom
4 days:	$6000 (excluding accommodation) - Emerging Leaders Program
5 days:	-
6 days:	$12,000 (including accommodation) - Leading Strategic Change
4 weeks:	$13,500 (excluding accommodation) - Advanced Program in Human Resources Management

Case E – Schulich (generally excluding accommodation)

2 days:	$1795 - Effective Goal Setting Skills
3 days:	$2395 - Developing Emotional Intelligence (EQ) in Your Workplace
4 days:	-
5 days:	$4950 - Management 3: The Leaders Program
6 days:	-
4 ½ weeks:	$10,950 - Masters Certificates in Innovation Management or in Marketing Communications Leadership

Case F – Harvard (including accommodation)

2 days:	-
3 days:	$5940 - Board Governance – Audit Committees
4 days:	$8525 - The Global Economy

5 days: -

6 days: $11,550 - Leadership for Senior Executives

$14,300 - Leading Change and Organizational Renewal

8 weeks: $66,000 - Advanced Management Program

Case G – Duke Corporate Education (DCE)

2 days: -

3 days: -

4 days: -

5 days: -

6 days: -

variable # weeks: Custom programs only: Cost for design is $54,000 - $216,000; and cost for delivery runs $430 - $2160 per person per day.

Case H – INSEAD (Fontainebleau, France – excluding accommodation)

2 days: -

3 days: $6100 - Leading Successful Change

$9,000 - Negotiation Dynamics

4 days: $10,300 - INSEAD Blue Ocean Strategy

5 days: $12,200 - Leading for Results

6 days: -

5 weeks: $47,400 (4 weeks plus 5 day follow-up module) The Advanced Management Program

Case I - IESE (Barcelona, Spain)

2 days: $2750 (excluding accommodation) - Creating Breakthrough Companies

3 days: $4600 (excluding accommodation) - Branding in Media and Entertainment

4 days: $6700 (including accommodation) - Getting Things Done

5 days:	-
6 days:	-
4 weeks:	$53,000 (including accommodation) - Advanced Management Program

Relevancy

After looking closely at executive programs at these nine excellent universities, and at many others not shown here, I am becoming convinced that the relevancy battle cry is losing its own relevance. It has been the easiest and most obvious item to criticize, when academically and traditionally focused learning, grounded in theory, is pitted against an urgent need for practically oriented educational programs for experienced and successful practitioners. However, the evidence about program irrelevancy is not convincing.

The sense of urgency about the material might be lacking in some cases, and the emphasis on some subjects may be misplaced, because the assumptions have been incorrect about exactly what executives are needing or missing about fairly well-known topics. Admittedly, on the few occasions where executive offerings mirror too closely what is being taught in the degree programs, a slight disconnection occurs in relation to what is really going on in the lives of practising executives. For, those degree programs often have to delve into topics, which the non-practising manager has to learn about, but the experienced executive does not.

All of the schools featured here manage their executive programs separately from their academic degree programs, with regard to curricula, day-to-day administration, development and delivery. The connection between them is mostly a positive one, in which the academic side is enriched by business relevancy: this happens, for instance, by having some professors of degree programs teach in the executive programs, thereby permitting them to witness what practising business leaders are saying and thinking. It can happen by providing fora, in which leaders build networks and discuss urgent matters on campus with their colleagues, and often seek advice of professors who act as coaches.

The potential bite of this relevancy issue is diminished even further when we see the relative growth of custom programs over open enrolment programs. Clearly, when a firm customizes its executive education, there can be no issue of relevancy. The argument about relevancy really boils down to whether a program is fairly relevant or very relevant; and to just how much relevance is required. For example, at issue is whether a firm wants the degree of relevancy available, for example, in case studies such as those used at Harvard or INSEAD; or whether they prefer action-oriented relevance such as provided by McGill's International Masters in Practicing Management.

Style and Approach

About half of the interviewees were against, or were luke-warm about, dealing with universities for their executive education requirements. The other half had some criticisms, but in most cases these had little to do with relevancy, and much more to do with the style of the relationship between the firm and the institution. These criticisms concerned control over curriculum and its development; flexibility in changing curriculum as needed and on the fly; and a sense of urgency about getting it all done: the preparation, design, and delivery. These impatient behaviours about getting the learning done are quite descriptive of corporate life generally, but they are not descriptive of academic life. They are behaviours which display a sense of urgency, and they are often what the client expects; it is unreasonable to think that this *modus operandi* can be appreciably altered during the course of a relatively short learning program.

Several of the universities outlined in this chapter seem to have understood these things: all offer customized programs, and go out of their way to promote working together with firms to develop and design custom curricula, and to be flexible while maintaining a sense of urgency; some boast using the client's executives themselves as "professors" in the programs alongside academic teachers. Some even mentioned that the client maintains control over the curriculum.

By any measure, Duke CE, because they provide only customized programs, is likely to be everyone's first choice when it comes to being relevant and most business-like when it comes to working *with* firms to develop curricula. It is of course easier to do this for customized programs than for open enrolment programs in which, by their very nature, a few sizes have to fit all participants. However, even for open enrolment programs, McGill (and others to a lesser degree), bridges this gap by having teams of executives attend from the same firm, and has them work together on the material in real-time at different locations around the world.

Curriculum

Custom and Open Enrolment Programs: It is interesting to compare the quantity of open enrolment executive programs provided, for instance, by Ivey with seven offerings, to the number provided by Schulich, with 90 offerings. One institution focuses on the few where it concentrates its resources, and the other focuses on the many where is spreads its resources. Their market positioning strategies suggest either spending more resources on a few costly programs, or fewer resources on many less expensive programs. This might explain Schulich's strategy of offering so many short two to five- day programs to middle managers, steering away from the very costly, long duration (four to 17 weeks) programs targeted at C-suite and other senior executives. From another angle, it could be that, as so many of the interviewed executives stated, nobody has time to spend more than a couple of days away from the office – a reality that may spell the end of the long, flagship offerings for very senior people.

The type of curriculum, custom or open, is key to creating an executive learning plan that properly fits an organization's culture. Every one of the institutions presented here, except Duke Corporate Education, provides both of these options. Duke CE only provides the customized program, and they do so in a manner which is convincingly flexible and engaging. Being a carve-out and not a reporting subsidiary of a university (Duke in North Carolina), they are willing to share with clients the control, design and even the delivery of their customized programs. They do not suffer, as the other institutions might, from any delusions about who owns the curriculum, or about the need to be able to change it with lightning speed as circumstances dictate.

As reported by Charlton and Osterweil (2005), the number of customized programs run by the world's top 40 business schools had grown by 36% in two years. Das Narayandas (2007) reported that a "recent" study (but they do not provide the date) of 45 business schools showed a year over year increased growth in open enrolment programs of 10.5 percent, but an increased growth in custom programs of over 20 percent. The same article reported a similar trend by the international University Consortium for Executive Education (UNICORN), in which 29 of 37 top-tier schools studied indicated that their custom programs were growing "significantly faster than their open enrolment programs" (p. 25). However, we should note that both are growing significantly.

Although open enrolment programs attract more resources, and have been around in business schools for a very long time, most players are scrambling to add more capability for customized programs to their rosters. Although the growth of customized education solutions will likely continue to outpace the growth of open enrolment programs, they are certainly not mutually exclusive. For the company that wishes an immediate, custom-tailored, flexible and confidential learning solution, in which they want to play a direct part in the development, "customized" is the way to go. However, for firms wishing to have their senior people networking with other executives, because they learn in a much more diverse educational environment, then flagship open enrolment programs for senior executives may still be the answer. This might be especially *à propos* in cases where a leader is about to make a significant job change, and therefore might have the time to punctuate this transition with such a longer learning experience.

"Hard" and "Soft" Skills: Among the nine universities presented here, examples of teaching the "hard" *and* "soft" skills was apparent in: McGill's Action Learning credo; Ivey's cross-enterprise perspective which, like Systems Thinking, sees the whole instead of the parts; Queen's traditional "hard" skill predominance, but with "soft" skill additions such as their PRESence model for leadership; Rotman's featuring of Integrative Thinking; Schulich's virtual encyclopaedia of "hard" skill courses; Harvard's hard-core case study method and global perspective; Duke CE's sole focus on giving the client the right mix of "soft" or "hard" skill learning: the mix they want and need; INSEAD's generally "hard" curriculum and internationalism – Europe's Harvard, and yet offering the "soft-skilled" AVIRA program (awareness, vision, imagination, responsibility, action); IESE's similarly "hard" traditional skills, but in a flexible format, combined with their considerable international outreach.

Teaching Methods

Online Web-based Learning: During the last seven years, my own graduate learning experiences at Royal Roads University at the Master's level, and at the University of Calgary at the doctoral level, have been blended models of face-to-face learning in residence with distance online learning. It has demonstrated to me the power of online learning as a collaborative forum, where vibrant discussions and sharing of ideas can occur, with the surprising benefit of hearing the voices of all participants – be they extroverts or introverts. Of the nine universities featured here, arguably only two of them (INSEAD and Duke) really grasp and make extensive use of the collaborative impact that online learning can exert on executive education; two use it to a certain extent (Harvard and IESE). The others, at least for their executive programs, seem only to want to use or want to advertise using the web for the delivery of information, pre or post program exercises, or disseminating webinars. The collaborative, team work, discussion group potential learning benefits of online work seem to be absent. The stand-out exception here is INSEAD, which clearly states an ability to supply total learning programs online, and devotes a section of the executive website to what is called IOL or INSEAD-on-line. Duke CE also mentions that they can provide programs that are virtual or face-to-face. The flexibility, inclusiveness, richness and scope of learning that can be provided online is something that either many universities do not realize, or are leery about visiting upon organizational clients. Perhaps this is an effort to distance themselves from the total online delivery orientation of some aggressive and growingly successful universities with which they are in competition, such as The University of Phoenix, Royal Roads University, The Fielding Institute or Athabasca University.

The Highly Heralded Case Study: Büchel and Antunes (2007) quoted Nick Schreiber from Tetra Pak as favouring individual professors as much as a specific institutions (as in Interview case No. 4 of this research) to deliver courses with creativity in delivery methods, an awareness of different learning styles, and connection to the world of business through consulting contracts. Schreiber specifically noted that, "We really try to move away from faculty members that just use case studies" (p. 404).

Several of the universities featured here boast the use of case study: Harvard almost exclusively; Ivey and INSEAD both use case studies extensively in teaching executive programs, and both claim to be the second most prolific producers of case studies in the world after Harvard. Queen's and IESE also make considerable use of the case study. McGill argues on their website that they prefer to work through "the current organizational challenges of participating firms rather than with case studies, which are simulations of other people's problems, and as such have a varying degree of relevance to participants". Duke CE maintains that their custom programs are ones in which the actual is the case, and therefore that the use of case studies is irrelevant. The other two players use case studies among various other teaching tools.

In my view, the effectiveness of the case study as a viable teaching method depends on who is facilitating it, and who is participating in it. For the famous professors at Harvard, it is something like "show time", and looking at some of their videos about case studies underway is quite exciting; one would want to be there. Added to this is the fact that participants could easily be CEOs or Presidents of large, Fortune 500 corporations. As a result, the learning atmosphere becomes electric and pregnant with promise. For lesser venues, I am not so sure, although INSEAD and IVEY could probably rise to the challenge, for the same Harvardian reasons just mentioned.

Some of the More Creative Teaching Methods: McGill's use of action learning where participants travel to three or five different countries to learn onsite and in real-time with fellow executives, is worthy of honourable mention as a creative and different teaching method. It is, of course, both costly and time-consuming to do this sort of thing, but participants have raved about these learning experiences ever since they were created by Henry Mintzberg in the early 1990s.

Rotman's Integrative Thinking™ model deserves recognition for its current and extensive usage in degree and executive programs.

Designing programs around this model, which involves holding more than one option in mind without having to choose among them, and then coming up with a new, better, blended option certainly holds a great deal of merit.

Duke CE's Metaphoric Experience™, where one appreciates a solution thanks to the metaphoric influence from another realm of excellence (dance, art, medicine, literature) is compelling, fun and apparently works to cause learning breakthroughs. More of these creative tools are necessary to enhance executive learning: to make it more engaging, and to be memorable, and therefore longer lasting.

Other worthy teaching models include:

- Ivey's Cross Enterprise Perspective, so reminiscent of the Systems Thinking model;

- Queen's Consultants in Residence™ in which executives interview potential coaches before selecting which one they want to engage with; and Schulich's similar offering in their Management 3 Program, after which participants are provided with monthly 15 minute coaching sessions for three consecutive months;

- Harvard's fame as the most exciting place to be whether as a professor, executive participant, guest speaker or donor;

- INSEAD's world-famous global perspective and diversity of participants and professors.

- IESE's gift to alumni of ongoing library privileges following major executive programs; and its international connections and ongoing activities with so many other institutions around the world.

International or Global Issues and Diversity

These days, any firm that has foreign operations, or that has clients or other interests such as partnerships in foreign lands, needs to acquire invaluable learning about such topics as cultural diversity, international and country-specific business regulations, customs, and behaviours. In this research, it seems that to several universities, being global and international only means conducting programs in various international locations, or having sales offices in those places. In some cases, global reach means having programs that were delivered in various cities around the world, or being able to launch custom programs internationally wherever a firm might be operating.

A major exception was McGill, where the student and faculty bodies were extremely diverse, and where there were executive education topics which dealt specifically with diversity, inclusion, global issues and concerns. Another that appears to be truly international is Harvard, where executive programs attract participants from many countries, and where learning diversity, in every sense of that word, is key. Also, INSEAD's global viewpoint, and insistence on diversity regarding faculty and participants makes it free from any dominant culture or prevalent dogma, and IESE boasts full-time professors who come from 27 countries. It should be noted, however, that a diverse faculty and student body does not necessarily mean that curricula is international in scope and content. One can assume that Duke CE would provide whatever international or global curriculum aspects the clients wanted to experience in their customized programs. Other universities, however, seem to lack international content in their executive courses and programs, and seem much less diverse in participants and professors than for the exceptions just mentioned.

If it is true that senior leaders who attend high level executive programs are generally those who govern large international and multinational organizations, then it makes sense for providers of executive education to be more vigilant about including global issues in the curriculum, and in the diverse makeup of those programs.

Educational Philosophy and Partnerships

There follows a compendium of quotes from or about each of the nine universities reviewed in this chapter. The quotes all come from the websites or brochures, and they provide a flavour of the different philosophies of each school, more fully developed in earlier pages featuring each school. All of the nine universities discussed in this chapter have significant relationships between their Business Schools and other institutions around the world, for the sharing of knowledge about management education. Those major and ongoing partnerships are mentioned in the brackets following the quotes:

McGill: Dr. Henry Mintzberg stated that, "You can't create a leader in a classroom. Management is not a science, nor a profession. It is a practice – it has to be appreciated through experience, in context".

"Case studies are simulations of other people's problems".

(Partnerships with Lancaster University, UK; The Indian Institute of Management, in Bangalore, India; Korea Development Institute School of Public Policy and Management in Seoul, Korea; and with INSEAD in Fontainebleau, France).

Ivey: "A propensity for action is considered an ingredient for executive success".

"The Ivey Experience: Changing the way you think and act".

(First Canadian Business School to have set up a permanent facility in Asia; Ivey professors are regular guests lecturing at two universities in China).

Queen's: "Programs for individuals and custom programs for companies".

"You set the agenda".

"Often just getting out of the way and letting the students take over".

(Joint MBA with Cornell; Centres for Corporate Social Responsibility; Governance; Business Venturing).

Rotman: "Developing the thinker of the future".

"Forming a learning partnership".

"Providing a thinking environment".

(Seven other Canadian business schools are learning partners, five of which are in Western Canada; Rotman has also forged partnerships with universities in France, Germany, Scandinavia, South America and Japan).

Schulich: "If you need to use it now, learn it now".

"SEEC and ye shall find".

"All programs are backed by a 100% Satisfaction Guarantee. Period."
(Relationships with 50 business schools around the world).

Harvard: "They live, dine, and work in an enclave devoted to executive development".

"Case studies open the window to actual business dilemmas in some of the world's most admired companies".

"Custom programs are virtual windows into the rich resources of the Harvard University Community".

(Relations with alumni around the world are paramount and are religiously maintained; there is a partnership with IESE in Barcelona, Spain; and consulting relationships between Harvard professors and clients on every continent).

Duke CE: "Because we employ few faculty, we have unlimited faculty. Academics and practicing professionals have been chosen from around the world to help design and facilitate DCE's custom programs".

"We design to outcome using any kind of learning method or technology that is appropriate to do that".

(Partnerships with parent Duke University in NC, and with the London School of Economics, and the Indian Institute of Management in Ahmedabad).

INSEAD: "Welcome to the Business School for the World!"

"It is not what you discover but what you **do** with your discovery that is important". "Great Minds don't Think Alike".

(Recent partnership forged with The Wharton School).

IESE:

"Every organization is different. Each has its own structure, culture and ambitions. And each faces unique opportunities, threats and challenges".

(Major partnership with Harvard, and ties with Stanford, MIT, the University of Michigan; participant in the International Faculty Development Program. IESE is also a consultant to17 business schools which they helped to create on five continents).

Chapter Seven – Presentation Of Findings And Analysis (Part 3)

Personal Experience of Executive Education Programs – Third Unit of Analysis

Introduction

This third and final unit of analysis for this collective case study is a short one, and it pertains to my own experience of managerial and executive education during a long career in the pulp and paper industry. The programs and learning events that I will feature here took place for me between 1975 and 2001. As such, they might normally be considered out of date. Although many aspects are indeed out of date, the flavour of what I experienced in executive education is still prevalent today in many large firms. This is evidenced by comments in the interviews, and by the research just reported, about executive programs at some of the world's top universities and in some large Canadian corporations.

In this segment, I will outline details about major learning programs and minor learning events in which I participated, along with a commentary about their effectiveness and their alignment with some of the themes of importance used so far in the analyses of the interviews and the nine universities. I will also discuss some of the differences between what I experienced and what appears to be happening right now in executive education.

Short Programs: MacMillan Bloedel/Island Paper Mills (1971-1993)

There were many short courses I attended at various times during my career, all of which I did because I asked to participate in them. Never was I invited, encouraged, asked or directed to attend any of these sessions. This in itself reflects an interesting mixture of corporate management styles as they applied to a learning philosophy: a mixture of *laissez-faire* with one of "ask and ye shall receive" (or, perhaps more accurately: "the squeaky wheel gets the grease").

These programs, about which I will not go into detail, and for which the dates are approximate because I cannot recall them precisely, included the following:

Interpersonal Skills Workshop (one week – internal course in 1975 in the middle of the Human Potential Movement) comprising courses that dealt with "soft" management issues and self awareness; Financial Skills for non Financial Managers (internal course of two days in 1980) dealing with "hard" skills regarding finance and accounting issues, The Finning Tractor Management Styles Seminar (two days in 1984) dealing mostly with the "soft" issues of leadership style and influencing people, The Program for Future Executives at the University of British Columbia (one week in 1986) which, surprisingly, involved a great number of small group discussions and encounters on "soft" management issues; The McKinsey facilitated *Operation Road Map*, which was a Strategic Planning Exercise looking at the future direction of MacMillan Bloedel (one to two days at a time over several months in 1987); and Total Quality Management (TQM) in Silicone Valley (three days in 1990) explaining and practising the hard statistical elements of the Dr. Edwards Deming quality model.

Major Learning Programs: MacMillan Bloedel/Island Paper Mills
(1971-1993)

Marketing Management Course: University of Western Ontario (MMC '85 – three weeks)

It was as a marketing manager that I attended this program at the Ivey School of Business, University of Western Ontario. The main teaching method, just as it is today, was the case study. As I recall it, the curriculum was "hard", with no "soft" skill subjects included other than the informal ones that occur naturally as a result of the networking process and getting to know a new group of people. Case studies were widely used, and students had to read them ahead of time, discuss them in small groups the night before, and finally deal with them in class all together with the professor.

The formal topics covered were technical business skills related to the marketing function. This was mostly a theoretical relationship with other companies' problems, and how we thought they should be resolved; and that was the extent of the program's relevancy. There was a fair amount of healthy competition in the preparation of small team final presentations to the entire group. In typical school cramming fashion, this preparation kept us up until the wee hours of the mornings leading up to that final day. This course does not appear to be offered any longer, probably because that material is now more appropriately part of the degree programs, including the Executive MBA.

Attending this course felt exactly like being an undergraduate again, except that the participants were older and had some work experience in management roles. Everyone seemed honoured to be there because, in those days, being sent on such costly and lengthy programs meant that you were being noticed for possible advancement. Even so, most of us felt like young students again, and still seemed to be hanging on the professors' every word. Just as Mintzberg (2004a) criticized the MBA for having a short shelf-life as far as students remembering the material was concerned, I suspect that I forgot most of the detailed learning in this program within six months. However, it was a valuable experience, thanks to the networking benefit of meeting new people, and to the prestigious shot-in-the-arm that it gave to my career.

The Senior Managers' Program at McGill (SMP '88 – three weeks)

As Director of Marketing, I attended this program at McGill University in Montreal. The "hard" aspect of the curriculum this time focused on general management rather than on marketing. It was very similar to the program I had completed at Ivey three years earlier, although it was for a more senior group of participants. The case study was rarely used; professors used a lecture format, but encouraged regular group discussion. Visiting lecturers from the business world gave brief talks followed by lengthy question periods. Once again, small group presentations were made at the end of the program, but the preparation for these was significantly more relaxed than it had been at Ivey. I attributed this to the fact that the group was more senior, and therefore a little more pragmatic about the importance of working on issues that were important as simulations but not as actual burning issues that had to be resolved on the job – that is, theoretical rather than practical. Since then, the Executive Institute at McGill has adopted a much more action learning approach for all of their management programs.

Major Learning Programs: Domtar/Island Paper Mills (1997-2000)

Introducing Domtar

In 2002, aged 55 years, I took early retirement. At that time, Domtar Inc. was a Canadian forestry company headquartered in Montreal, with pulp, paper and lumber operating plants and offices throughout North America. Domtar's annual net sales in that year were $5.5 billion with net earnings of $140 million. The lion's share of the business was in paper (65%), and employees numbered 12,000. Domtar produced some 2.8 million tons of paper per year, and was the largest paper company in Canada in terms of sales, and the third largest manufacturer of uncoated free sheet in North America. It produced three categories of paper: business papers (copy paper), commercial printing papers (used in brochures or books) and technical/specialty papers (candy wrappers or surgical gowns). Recently, in March 2007,

Domtar Inc. merged with Weyerhaeuser Paper, making it the largest uncoated free sheet producer (4.9 million tons) in North America. Back in 2002, the company spoke of three pillars of the company: employees, customers and shareholders.

The Firm's Learning Philosophy

All of Domtar's principal professional development initiatives were the result of a top-down emphasis on an action learning philosophy, in which teams learn to solve problems together. Very little development work at Domtar was done externally, which is based on the strong and respectful belief that the firm itself is a goldmine of professional expertise and experience. Thus, Domtar employees were clearly the firm's resource-of-choice to be tapped in respect to developing its people.

Domtar's employee development initiatives and practices demonstrated a steely-eyed focus on continuous improvement. Those initiatives were few in number, but crystal clear in their relationship to the company's values and strategic expectations. These professional development initiatives were not voluntary or negotiable. They were relentless in their repetitive continuity, and were marked by the persistent expectation that all employees would be on side about participating in them, with a view to building an understanding of how these initiatives related to the company's values and strategies.

Looking back at the learning experiences, initiatives and behaviours described below, I consider them to have been indicative of a corporation which took learning very seriously. I might not go so far as to term it a "learning organization"; however, there is no doubt that, in these programs, the combination of urgency, relevancy, and the action learning process which blended individual and group, as well as online learning added up to an admirably focused and up-to-date corporate education plan. There was a fierce insistence that these programs should be custom designed, and that they should be facilitated internally by practising managers. All programs and learning initiatives had buy-in from the CEO, and his entire natural reporting team. Managers lower down in the organization often resisted these learning incursions, and they were either persuaded to support them forthwith, or were eventually let go.

There were some delivery problems in the cases of Phil Training and Kaïzen (programs which are described below), because not all the facilitators knew how to facilitate. Furthermore, participants often resisted the kind of time commitment required for the two-week Kaïzen programs, which often occurred several times per year in the same operation. Nevertheless, over time, everyone realized that these programs were conditions of employment and not isolated, "get them over with" events. As a result, they became valuable learning experiences for all employees.

Admittedly each one of these programs or events represented learning "hard" skills, but they also required "soft" skill practice to make them work. In other words (and it was often very rough going for the first few days), it was necessary for people to work together, and to communicate properly, for these events to bear fruit. Otherwise the whole process, whether the Kaïzen, or the strategic sessions, would simply grind to a halt.

After the descriptions of the formal training programs, there follows a description about executive initiatives in coaching, mentoring, reflective practices and online learning.

Phil Training (1997 – two days computer simulation)

While Vice President Western Region Marketing & Sales, I attended the two-day Phil Training event, which all employees, from the vice-presidents and line managers to the union workers on the shop-room floor, had to complete. It occurred as cross-functionally as was practically possible: That is, groups of around 15 participants from a wide variety of locations and functions, comprising various management and worker levels, gathered for these two day sessions in various cities throughout North America. On "graduation", each person was awarded a company keychain, on which were etched the eight principal traits that the firm values the most: Innovation, Commitment, Initiative, Discipline, Perseverance, Integrity, Respect for others, and Leadership.

Phil Training was an action learning process that included an inter-active computer game featuring an imaginary bicycle company. Various scenarios were presented that required decisions to be made about human resources, financing, production, marketing, customers, inventory control, distribution flow-through, and expansion plans. Each decision choice produced results that had to be dealt with by each player. In this playful manner, employees became aware of Domtar's values and expectations. For example, a decision to cut staff would result in too negative an outcome, which underscored the company's belief in redeploying staff rather than downsizing. Other teamwork exercises involved production and inventory games, with hands-on production models that demonstrated and confirmed company beliefs and principles concerning workflow. Any lack of a cohesive, co-operative work plan caused bottlenecks which, if not quickly resolved, shut down the entire production line. Some participants remarked excitedly how similar these outcomes were to actual situations in the workplace.

The Kaïzen (1998 & 1999 – two weeks each time)

The centerpiece of the Domtar professional development plan was the two-week Kaïzen process of continuous improvement, which I attended on two occasions for a total time commitment of four weeks, while Vice President Western Region Marketing & Sales. This was a practical educational program that taught problem-solving techniques, and which also produced measurable benefits in the form of financial return for the company. As stated on the company website, it is a process that encourages employees to contribute to the organization "by applying their creativity, skills and commitment towards achieving our sustainable growth objectives".

The backbone of this approach is the Kaïzen continuous improvement methodology, through which employees take part in workshops to find practical solutions to specific issues. The company stated that "Over a thousand Quality and Productivity Kaïzen workshops have taken place since the program was launched in 1997, generating nearly $120 million in savings for Domtar" (Domtar, Sustainable Growth Report, 2006, p. 23). The Director of Quality and Productivity Improvement, stated: "It's about all of us doing a better teaching job when we host a Kaïzen. Continuous improvement is about sharing information and implementing best practices" (Domtar Website, Training Programs). In addition to twice attending these programs as a regular participant, I presented the learning piece about Sales and Marketing, just as other functional leaders within the firm acted as facilitators for the program.

The Kaïzen is a process originally developed, and still deeply practised, by the Toyota company worldwide. At Domtar, this process is a relentless but holistic one that involves all levels of employees at every division of the company, in continuous interdisciplinary teamwork, to resolve specific challenges in their particular workplaces. They do this by discovering and eliminating the root causes of problems. In doing so, they save the company millions of dollars annually. It is a learning process that is aligned with what Dall'Alba and Sandberg (2006) stated: "Professionals cannot meaningfully be separated…from their activities and the situations in which they practice", and that "practice is not a fixed or static container but, rather, a dynamic flow produced and reproduced by professionals" (p. 385).

The Kaïzen learning process is in sync with A. N. Whitehead's theory concerning *the rhythm of education*, discussed in such depth in Chapter Three and as revisited in Chapter Eight: For, the Kaïzen firstly encompasses a Romance Phase, in which excitement over the discovery of the proper burning issue to adopt engages all participants, and the novelty of having many supervisory levels working shoulder to shoulder as equals, adds to the enthusiasm. Secondly, fully four whole days are spent in what could aptly be called the Precision Phase, creating a tool box of analytical and communication skills that will be used during the hands-on time in the workplace to gather data. Finally, in the Generalization Phase, the data is put together from all sources; it is analyzed and recommendations are made towards immediate resolution of the problem. These data are then generalized, where possible, to benefit other groups within the company.

Domtar has done a remarkable job in inculcating this problem-based learning (PBL) process into the very fabric of the firm's culture, such that it has become a way of being, and a way of learning. Furthermore, using this has become second nature, even at the micro departmental level, for approaching everyday problems with cross-functional teams in a kind of continual 'mini Kaïzen' manner. The one concern about this process is whether the company manages completely and beneficially to capture the learning from these very good habits, acquired through all the major and minor PBL events, so that, as Dewey said, as quoted by Dall'Alba and Sandberg (2006): "every experience both takes up something from those which have gone before, and modifies in some way the quality of those which come after" (p. 393).

Annual Senior Management Rallies

I attended three of these events while a vice president with Domtar. This type of event was a gathering of the firm's 150 senior people for an annual two day meeting in Montreal. It is best described as a rally that celebrated the accomplishments of the previous year, and communicated the strategies that were on the horizon, and already firmly on the radar screen of the CEO. The CEO himself, along with the seven members of the executive team, portrayed the corporate vision for the next year and beyond in a surprisingly transparent way, not holding any cards too close to the chest. All plenary meetings were simultaneously translated into French or English, and smaller specialty items were discussed at break-out seminars that took place between plenary sessions. There were also panel discussions about current issues, such as *the paperless office* or *forest sustainability*. There was a gala dinner and other events that promoted networking and bonding among managers. It was tacitly understood that highlights of these meetings would be taken back by the managers, to be diffused within their own local operations.

The Senior Task Force: Redesigning the Sales and Marketing Functions (2000 – two days per month over four months)

As Vice President Western Region Marketing & Sales, I was appointed as a member of the senior management task force, which was facilitated by a local consulting firm in Montreal. It was an emotional time for me, because essentially it was a foregone conclusion that one of the recommendations that would come out of this process would be the dissolution, or at least the reassigning, of my Sales and Marketing group of 65 people in Vancouver. Domtar had purchased our company (E. B. Eddy) in mid 1997, and now, three years later, quite reasonably felt that it was time to consolidate the sales and marketing functions under one roof, and that this one roof was very unlikely to be in Vancouver. Hence, in some ways, I became an architect of my own demise. One learns a great deal at such a cross-roads.

I still refer to this as part of the company's overall learning plan for senior managers, because, although it was a traditional strategic task force that had been struck, it was in existence for all members to learn from a process that had brought together 20 senior people from all over the organization. The purpose was to get to know each other, and to come up with a logical solution to a real problem, and to do it by consensus. The outcome was not the main goal, because it was fairly clear from the outset what that would be. After all, the company could simply have decreed that such a change should take place, but it opted to make a learning process out of it. Good for them!

In retrospect, during the unfolding of this task force work, I was visited in Vancouver by a senior Domtar person responsible for various aspects of learning, especially for the Kaïzen. He personally took me aside and gently suggested that it might be time for me to "re-invent" myself. I remember at that moment feeling offended, and a little worried. In retrospect, I wish I had been aware, at that time, of the program offered by INSEAD, as described by Manfred Kets de Vries (2007), professor of leadership at INSEAD: "Once a year we run an open-enrollment [sic] leadership workshop that is aimed at creating reflective leaders capable of reinventing themselves and their organizations" (p. 382). Had I known about this, I would have requested to attend.

Coaching: The Special Consultant Sessions (2000 – one day plus a three hour follow-up)

It was as Vice President Business Development that I went through this process. As stated previously, Domtar did not often deal with consultants, feeling that there was ample expertise within the company to foster and develop workplace-based learning for all employees. An exception in this regard was the specialized activity of a psychological 'guru' who spent the better part of an entire day, one-on-one with each senior manager (that is, with approximately half of the 150 managers who attend the annual rally described earlier). Usually, the venue for this encounter was the local Tim Horton's. The purpose of this "learning event" was to analyze managers' reactions to various scenarios as portrayed by this consultant, and then to advise participants as to their 'performance' a few weeks later. My reaction to these scenarios was invariably to rely on my experience of similar situations, in order to discover the best response to them. As Bolman and Deal (1997) stated "In deciding what to do next, managers operate mostly on the basis of intuition – hunches and judgements derived from prior experience" (p. 266). But that *modus operandi* was insufficient for Domtar; I was complimented for my experience, but criticized for my lack of creativity in finding novel ways to respond – something beyond merely relying on what I had done previously.

At the subsequent meeting, the consultant, the senior manager, his/her supervisor, and the divisional VP Human Resources were all in attendance. This encounter can be threatening to some personalities, but to others it can be a frank, coaching-style exchange resulting in substantial professional growth, and a performance 'touch-up' for senior people – one that might not otherwise occur. The consultant handling these sessions was a street-wise, no nonsense confidant of the CEO; they had worked together for years.

Mentoring

Domtar did not promote or encourage, in any explicit manner, the powerful development tool of mentoring. There was, however, an implicit acceptance of mentoring in cases where certain managers may have wanted to use that process in the formation of their people. The time-honoured and venerable process of mentoring was perhaps discouraged (or at least not encouraged) because, in some hands, it can result in preferential treatment, or develop into a form of favouritism or cronyism. Nevertheless, the likely benefits that can accrue from mentoring often outweigh the potential drawbacks. Earlier in my career, I had wanted to implement a formal mentoring procedure for the group I managed, and I was given a free hand to do so if I really thought it worthwhile. In the end, I decided not to proceed for the reasons just mentioned.

Online Learning Components

As of 2002, Domtar had not provided online learning support for any of its learning initiatives. As already pointed out, the real-time action learning initiatives that Domtar provides to employees (Kaïzen and Phil Training are examples) are stellar in their immediacy, potent relevancy, and in their ability to foster personal networking connections and community. However, in order to ingrain the learning, these experiences need to be reflected upon and discussed. A vehicle for that to happen is blended learning. Vaughan and Garrison (2005) stated that face-to-face sessions may be better suited "to allow personal relationships and a sense of community to develop, which in turn creates a climate for sharing of ideas and experiences amongst participants....An online component could then build on this community to extend the exploration, integration and testing of ideas" (p. 4).

Personal Coaching Initiative

On my own recognizance, when I first became a vice president in 1990, I decided to engage the services of a personal consultant, with a view to having him witness me in action from time to time, to advise me on my management style, and to warn me about any blind spots that he perceived I had *vis à vis* dealing with people. He occasionally attended sales meetings with the group, at which he participated as a colleague. He always respected individual confidences and never divulged to me anything that was someone else's opinion, only reflecting on what he saw and experienced about my behaviour and *modus operandi*. I probably saw him in his role of personal coach (long before that function became fashionable) once or twice a quarter, during the last twelve years of my career. It was a friendly, professional, very frank, and most useful and helpful note of balance in keeping my performance as a leader on an even keel.

Summary Comments

The principal difference between what I experienced then and what is happening now in executive education is how formalized managerial and executive programs have become. Generally, if a firm is dedicated to learning, it will have a carefully staged plan for the education of its employees, and that plan will span all employees, not just the top tiers. Even at the forest industry giant, MacMillan Bloedel, that operated a full Corporate Training Department in the early 1970s, whether individuals made use of any, or many, of the programs offered very much depended on their supervisors. In my own case, my bosses were very much oriented towards the philosophy of what I called "radical experiential learning", in which all that counted was learning by doing and what you could glean from it. It was kind of a "sink-or-swim" attitude from which you might acquire some valuable learning experiences; perhaps with a little help from some leaders who took a mentoring interest in your abilities.

Another difference lies in the "hard/soft" aspects of the curricula, which have become over time less oriented towards "hard" topics, with the notable exception of Developing Interpersonal Skills. That was a course that I attended for a week in the mid 1970s, and it was the "softest" management subject I have ever encountered - complete with meditation, and visualization exercises within a group encounter framework, so typical of what was called The Human Potential Movement. This evolution from "hard" to "soft" subjects has been very gradual, however, and in some of the interviews conducted with executives from very large and traditional corporations I could hardly see much change in this regard.

The proportion of learning that happens individually, compared to group work or work in teams, has not appreciably changed. Ever since I have been attending learning programs, corporations have considered a balance between these two as almost second nature, mirroring exactly what is supposed to happen on-the-job. Learning to work effectively with others always has been *de rigeur* in the corporate world. Managers and executives on the outskirts of that required behaviour (bullies, lone wolves, or those with anti social habits) are sent away to be "fixed" or are let go. It has always been thus.

My learning experiences were different during my MacMillan Bloedel (MB) years from the final five years of my career as a vice president with Domtar. These differences had something to do with my being at a more senior level in the latter case, but a great deal more to do with the learning philosophies of those firms. With MacMillan Bloedel (and related companies), I was never overly encouraged to attend courses, as my various supervisors seemed to feel that the best training was what I was learning while doing my job, and I certainly also espoused that theory. I notice with surprise and interest that I stated in a performance review from early 1984, when I was a regional sales manager aged 38 years and wholly devoted to market development, and to the professional development, of the three sales people reporting to me: "This is the excellent on-the-job training I am acquiring at present. I have no extra time for other kinds of training at this stage of my career". Nevertheless, I did in fact attend many training and learning programs and events during my MB years. I had to ask, and sometimes nag, supervisors to let me do so, but they always permitted it, perhaps more as a reward for doing what they perceived as a good job than for the benefits I might get from such learning.

At Domtar, there was a very specific learning plan in place that was not negotiable, and was company-wide in scope. The formal learning programs, which included the Phil Training and the Kaïzen, were created in concert with consultants, and everyone in the company participated. It is worth repeating here what Domtar says on their own website under "The Phil and Kaizen Era": (http://www.domtar.com/en/corporate/overview/399.asp):

> A management philosophy is all well and good, but how to communicate the changes to the front lines? Two innovative programs exemplify the "new" Domtar in action.

> "Phil" is an imaginative two-day multimedia training module that enables employees to see and understand their vital role in relation to customers and shareholders in a new light. This is the first step toward taking ownership of their jobs and building accountability at every level.

Kaizen, from the Japanese word for "improvement", has had an equally profound effect on Domtar operations. The Kaizen workshops, in which twelve employees participate over a two-week period, are based on a bold assumption — that employees are the best authorities on how to improve production, health, and safety.

Over 5,000 Domtar employees have already taken part in the Kaizen workshops, for a contribution of some $230 million in production cost savings since the program's launching in 1997.

In summary, I believe that in different ways, I enjoyed some good learning experiences in both phases of my business career. Sometimes I had to fight for them, but I can safely say, and I do so with pride and gratitude, that the firms I worked for were certainly "pro" learning.

Conclusion

The data and its analyses from the interviews, and from reading about what university programs exist for senior management, demonstrated many positive aspects about current executive learning initiatives. In executive education today, there seems to be more attention being focused upon themes of cultural diversity, inclusiveness, learning as an integral and never-ending requirement for any conscientious individual, and broadening horizons to deal with and understand the rest of the world more fully. Furthermore, there is the profoundly shattering, but positive, impact which the internet and the worldwide web has brought, and will continue to bring: It expands everyone's world, and makes for greater transparency in all interactions. This in turn affords everyone the opportunity to know more, and to be able to research anything at any time. Not to be a learning organization in this kind of environment will surely spell utter failure.

Chapter Eight – Conclusions, Recommendations And Ideas For Future Study

Introduction

Eight major and general conclusions, and 19 related and precise recommendations will be presented in this chapter under most of the same categories as the data was presented and analyzed in the previous chapter. These conclusions and recommendations are based entirely on those findings and analyses. However those units of analysis are also affected and embellished by the theoretical framework of Alfred North Whitehead's philosophy of education in Chapter Three. To recap: the units of analysis, from which all conclusions and recommendations emanate, are the following:

1. Unit of Analysis #1: The interviews with senior executives at 10 Canadian firms.

2. Unit of Analysis #2: The review of executive programs at nine universities (five in Canada, two in the United States, and two in Europe).

3. Unit of Analysis #3: The review of my experience of executive education during my business career.

Prior to presenting the conclusions and recommendations of my research, I have included a section on Dr. Whitehead's influence. However, readers should not expect a full-blown Whiteheadian critique of the research revelations. For example, the interview guideline questions had nothing to do with whether participants agreed or disagreed with any particular educational philosophy. The one hour time limit on those interviews did not permit presentation of Whiteheadian views for subsequent discussion; that would have been irrelevant to those executives. The purpose of the interviews was to hear what leaders had to say about their own experiences of and ideas about executive education.

The Whitehead Influence

Whitehead's educational views were described in detail in Chapter Three. Those views inspired my thoughts about what an excellent executive learning program could look like. It was not possible from a time or interest perspective to "lecture" interviewees about Dr. Whitehead's educational thought, and then to question them on their opinions about it. However, it may be useful in this final chapter to overview what I believe are the most pertinent tenets of that Whitehead philosophy that might be applied to executive education. In the several ways described below, the ideas expressed in the interviews, discovered on the university websites and experienced in my own career learning can be made to jibe with Whitehead's educational thought. A careful review of Chapter Three will provide readers with a host of additional material to inspire their own thoughts about executive program development along Whiteheadian lines.

Alfred North Whitehead's connection to Harvard University as a professor and as a staunch supporter of the then new business school led him to describe that institution (1932/1959) as being "on a scale amounting to magnificence" (p. 137). This reverence is an invitation for us who are interested in business learning to draw nigh and listen carefully to what he has to say about education and its potential for excellence. Perhaps if we can understand and discuss the magnificence he once saw at the newly minted Harvard Business School, we can apply it effectively and beneficially to executive learning in our modern day organizations.

Executive Learning along Whiteheadian Lines

In my view, corporations would be impressed with the cohesive, logical model for management education apparent in ANW's *rhythm of education* process. This would be a breath of fresh air compared to the bombardment they have had to endure about executive education in what is so often an un-orchestrated, and helter-skelter fashion, involving the latest fads hitting the market, such as the human potential movement and its offspring: developing interpersonal skills, self-expression, flattening of organizations, right sizing, and more recent "must-have" sessions, such as emotional intelligence, and endless variations on the leadership theme.

Whitehead's model, which calls for a carefully orchestrated, properly sequenced and cyclical rhythm can, I believe, be applied to developing management and executive curriculum. In choosing the actual elements of an executive curriculum, designers must attempt to follow Whitehead's oft-repeated advice: to teach a few things well, rather than to cover a great deal of material. Curriculum designers should also consult a firm's senior management members to understand properly the direction in which they want the learning to go.

One might hope that not only could Whitehead's *rhythm of education* be a potential teaching/learning process to be used for executive curriculum, but also that the curriculum content itself could boast an equally holistic and organic flavour.

As Dunkel (1965) pointed out, Whitehead's pedagogical method contains a "constant emphasis on movement from the particular to the general, from the concrete to the abstract, and then the reverse" (p. 117). This demonstration of flexibility in thinking and of tolerance for ambiguity is exactly the kind of mental gymnastics required in the decision making, and overall vision-making life of a senior executive. As Whitehead himself said, "The essential course of reasoning is to generalise what is particular, and then to particularise what is general. Without generality there is no reasoning, without concreteness there is no importance" (1932/1959, p. 83). Corporations should be quite impressed with this measured and logical pedagogical approach to their organizational learning, especially for their senior managers. It mirrors a most respected ability in the executive of being able to see a general relatedness from afar and then to zoom into the details in order to make an effective intervention.

Relevancy

Every executive interviewed and all university websites visited for this dissertation highlighted the importance, in educational programs, of creating a tight connection between learning and business activity in the so-called "real world". As we saw earlier, Whitehead insisted on a continuous intermingling of theory and practice. He complained that the tendency to segregate universities from the world of practical affairs was a recent development, and cited that "the great medieval universities did not make that mistake, nor did the Greeks" (Whitehead, 1932/1959, p.45). He believed that despite their vocational flavour, business schools belonged within the hallowed halls of a university where they could more easily enjoy a symbiotic relationship with academia – one in which there could be a dramatic sharing of theory and practice. Whitehead was quite aware of the "aloofness of the university from practical life" (Price, 1954, p. 56). As reported by Hendley (1986), Whitehead insisted that "a certain ruthless definiteness is essential in education", and that the secret is to adopt the right pace: "Get your knowledge quickly, and then use it. If you can use it, you will retain it" (p.97).

The Case 6 executive interview dealt at length with the company-wide creation of Communities of Practice as its principal action learning device, and it was an excellent example of an intermingling of theory with practice. The International Masters in Practicing Management (IMPM) and the Advanced Leadership Program (University Case A – McGill), fully described in the last chapter, are perhaps the best examples of institutional action learning within executive open enrolment programs, where theory mingles with practice.

The Rhythm of Education

Whitehead's concept of the *Rhythm of Education* represents his principal advice on curriculum design: namely that, to be effective and long lasting, it should contain the progressive stages of romance, precision and generalization. In the context of executive education, this might mean:

- Introducing and getting the course underway with enthusiasm, and stirring up interest about it; perhaps beforehand in some pre-course work or reflection, and at the beginning of the face-to-face sessions with an expert or famous guest speaker;

- Dealing fully with the technical aspects needed to understand the content, including practising these tools and concepts in real time;

- Allowing opportunities to relate excitement about and practice of this learning to the executives' on-the-job experience, perhaps in the form of small and plenary group discussions in which participants would share how the course or program would relate to his/her job upon return to their firms.

Many of the learning programs and initiatives described in the executive interviews and also in many of the university programs do a very good job with the precision stage, into which they are so quick to jump. That leap emphasizes the relevancy of getting immediately to the point and developing the skill, but this approach often misses out on creating the excitement and providing the background (the romance stage), as well as making the connections (generalization stage) which are so necessary in preventing learning from becoming, as Whitehead would say, "inert" because it does not become useful. Whitehead believed that education is much more than merely packing articles into a trunk.

A notable exception concerning the exclusion of the useful romance stage among the programs offered by universities appeared in Case G (Duke Corporate Education), in which playfulness and imagination were encouraged as catalysts to learning. For instance, that institution featured Metaphoric Experience™, which is designed to take participants out of familiar environments and force them to experiment with new behaviours, skills and perspectives (for example, auditors at a public accountancy firm have "become" doctors engaged in medical diagnosis).

My own executive learning experience, as described earlier in the Kaizen initiative at Domtar was quite similar in process to Whitehead's rhythm of education, complete with:

(1) The initial romance stage when participants formed into teams to solve real problems; the teams were endowed with an uncharacteristically vast authority to actually and immediately change the way things were done at the mills. The power had moved to the people.

(2) The precision stage in which participants learned the skills to do the work, including process and workflow management, tutorials about sales and marketing, interview techniques, analytical tools.

(3) The generalization stage in which the teams worked together to present an action plan, through which the information they had gathered and analyzed from the workplace could be used to resolve problems.

Interplay between the precise and the general

Whitehead's (1929/1957) belief that "organized thought is the basis of organized action" (p.103), and his conclusion that "education should give equal weight to facility with abstractions and to appreciation of [the] concrete" (as reported by Brumbaugh, 1982, pp. 16 & 85) underscore the necessary, but often difficult, marriage between learning conceptually and practically. Difficult as this may be to implement, it should be one of the burning aims of excellent program design in executive education. The much touted and prized "gut feel" ability in successful executive decision making would likely be even more fruitful if it were preceded by some thoughtfulness and succeeded by some reflection. Perhaps we would then have to coin another phrase along the lines of "gut knowledge".

In the executive interviews, there was little mention about the conceptual and the practical, except the odd reference to that hackneyed business expression, "thinking outside the box", or a preference at the higher executive levels for a certain degree of flexibility in realizing that every learning situation and every learner are different (for example, in Interview Case No. 5).

Several of the university programs did address this issue about interplay between the precise and the general. The best example of this was perhaps in University Case D (The Rotman School of Business at the University of Toronto), where so many of the programs rely on Integrative Thinking™. That process calls for an ability to hold more than one option in abeyance while creating an alternative third approach, rather than choosing between the two. As mentioned in the analysis of this case, this approach is remarkably similar to Whitehead's criticism about professionals and vocational trainees tending to see this or that set of circumstances, but not both sets together.

One can also see some aspects of this precise/general interplay in all of the executive interviews and in each of the university programs in terms of a desire for and availability of learning programs that contained both "soft" and hard" curricular aspects.

Dr. Whitehead's theory concerning the *Rhythm of Education* is clear in its encompassing of "hard skills" in the precision stage, and of the "soft" content in the romance stage, and of the "soft" skills in the generalization phase. Thus, as Jones (2007) stated in an article about Whitehead's educational thought, "learning outcomes are enhanced through the oscillating influence of freedom and discipline" (p.1).

Interconnectedness and Mastering Complexity

A consistent theme in Dr. Whitehead's work is interconnectedness, most likely born out of his process theory in which, for example, seemingly unrelated physical particles still maintain a relationship. This concept is strongly related to the topic of Systems Thinking mentioned in several leadership programs (Ivey's "Cross Enterprise Perspectives", in seeing the whole organization beyond its parts), and referenced in the executive interviews (for instance, in Interview No.5). Another aspect of interconnectedness is the overall requirement for cohesiveness and continuity that needs to be in play within an organizational learning plan. There cannot be a separate plan for executives, for middle managers, for staff, and for contract employees. This point was made in several interviews: most notably in Case No.1 (stratified apprenticeship model), Case No.3 (multi-tiered educational program), in Case No. 6 (Communities of Practice), and in Case No. 10 (total inclusiveness of organizational learning). It was also featured by most of the universities in terms of the requirement for an integrated learning approach when creating custom executive programs. In my own experience at Domtar, all levels of the organization participated in the Kaïzen problem solving events and every employee did the Phil Training, both described in the last chapter. Several firms, however, lacked cohesion in their programs, by concentrating on leadership development for high potential candidates without integration with a company-wide education effort.

Whitehead and the Worldwide Web – Luddite or Fan?

Given the huge significance of the internet as a worldwide communication and information system and its ever-growing use in organizations, it has become and will become even more of an indispensable partner in organizational learning. It is one, which I believe has been underutilized as a learning vehicle for executive education, and I have made this point among the specific conclusions and recommendations that follow. While completing this dissertation, I have wondered what Dr. Whitehead would have thought about the web of learning connectivity, which the internet and intranet can provide. Would he have embraced it because of its influence and potential usefulness for communication; or would he have rejected it because of its potential to minimize learning by diluting the basic process of thinking?

Conclusions and Recommendations about Executive Learning

Conclusion A: Teaching and Learning Relevance

There has been too much facile criticism about the relevancy of executive programs to the real world of business. That criticism has come both from competing providers and from the students. It is time that the clients themselves take more responsibility for ensuring that programs they take or develop are exactly as relevant as they want them to be. The "market" is quite capable of self-regulating in this respect. In other words, if sufficient relevancy is not present in an executive program, then enrolment will diminish, and the program will either be changed or cancelled. Degree of relevancy comes down to questions of teaching and learning preferences, the subject matter being taught, or the type of program desired to fill learning gaps or shortfalls. A university's longstanding, successful, and preferred teaching method may be primarily the case study, as it is at Harvard, INSEAD and Ivey; an executive's preferred learning style could be more introverted and intellectual, or else more extroverted and "hands-on". A course on research methodology or economics for executives could appropriately be more theoretical than practical; a program about how to deal with board members could be quite different in degree of urgent practical relevancy than a program on the art of dialogue to deepen an ability to think holistically.

By their very nature, custom tailored programs will necessarily be more relevant and directly applicable to the job than can be the open enrolment programs. Given that these custom programs, which exactly mirror on-the-job activities, or else actually *are* those activities, are growing significantly faster (some say twice as fast) as open enrolment programs, this issue of relevancy could become relatively less important. Nevertheless, these formats (open enrolment and custom) are not mutually exclusive. Each has a valued status in educating executives: In my view, open enrolment programs are particularly good at educating participants, where custom programs are perhaps better at showing them how to learn. Although custom programs may be growing much faster in popularity, both designs are in fact growing.

Much of the criticism regarding relevancy has been levelled at degree programs, and particularly at the MBA. The typical MBA student is now somewhat older and possibly in mid-career compared to a few decades ago, when that same student would not yet be in a career. Both are very different from seasoned corporate executives. The MBA student requires the basic "hard" skills in preparation for a management career, whereas the executive presumably has already mastered those. The style of teaching, the sizes of classes, the urgency of issues facing these "students" are all quite different.

It should be remembered that there is more to relevancy than simply whether or not a program or course relates directly to an executive's job. Relevancy also has a personal meaning, concerning whether an executive's learning needs were met. To exaggerate this point: It could be that what executives really need when they are about to take a huge promotions is something not at all relevant to the actual job they are doing, or even the ones they are about to do. In any case, executives and the organizations in which they work need to take responsibility for their own learning endeavours, and then decide to go with the provider that makes the most sense, given those corporate and individual learning goals.

Recommendation #1: Clarity and responsibility regarding relevancy

Program providers must be very clear on this relevancy issue, and not simply imply or state that everything they do is absolutely relevant. They could spell out which programs lean to the theoretical side and why; and which go to the practical side and why. Client organizations should take full responsibility for decisions about whether they want to take an existing program off the shelf (open enrolment), or whether they need something more urgently and directly related to their own challenges in the form of a custom program. Some universities will customize an existing program to the special requirements of clients.

Recommendation #2: Planning for and monitoring relevance

To monitor relevance and ensure how it is happening in all senses of the word (on the job and personally for the learner in his/her life), it is imperative that proper planning be done prior to, and following, every learning program. There are several facets to this recommendation and they are as follows:

1. The selection process for any executive program should become arduous both on the part of the providers and the clients. To borrow Jim Collin's (2001) expression in this new

context of learning: "you need to have the right people on the bus" for learning to flourish. Some universities like INSEAD and Harvard are very meticulous about this, but others are not, accepting virtually all applicants into their programs. On the client side, participants should explain to their own firms why they want to attend a particular program, and they need to be convincing about it, or should not be permitted to go. Senior executives especially want to be able to network with other worthy, interesting, successful people, partly for the fun and intellectual stimulation of it, but also in order to make new and valuable contacts.

2. Providers and clients should solicit thoughtful feedback about the learning experience from all participants, and should immediately use that feedback to make positive changes to the program. Perhaps it would be possible here to have provider and client agree upon and share feedback. The relevancy issue in all its meanings should be part of this feedback. Feedback is not about how much participants enjoyed the program; it needs to be about what learning took place or did not take place in a personal as well as an organizational sense.

3. There should be some pre and post reflective activities for all executive programs; they should not be overly time consuming, but rather should be focused and very clear. These could be done online, which would have the added advantage of getting executives familiar with, for example, creating an online community and discussion groups. Another strategy might be to have participants agreeing to put a few "small tasks" into practice when they return to the office. For instance, if participants have learned during the program that they are not very good listeners, they might create a few small listening behaviours that they agree to try out at least a few times per day when they return to the office. If executives do not have time to do a few hours prep and post work relating to the program, then perhaps they should not be attending.

Recommendation #3: Teaching relevance

Where possible, have operating senior leaders facilitate some parts of courses or certain segments of the longer open enrolment programs, but only if they are "good teachers". Although having illustrious or famous guest speakers taking an hour or two out of their busy lives to address a class is an added advantage in some programs, this recommendation refers to having operating executives actually facilitate open enrolment sessions.

For custom programs, it is imperative that executives within the client firm take an active role in "teaching" the program. Once again, this does not simply mean turning up for an hour at the beginning or the end, but actually facilitating a discernable segment of the learning. The choice of only those senior people who can actually teach is once again crucial. While properly respecting a firm's most senior people, it is important to choose as instructors only those who really enjoy being at the front of the class as teachers, or being at the back of it as facilitating catalysts to the learning that will take place. As Kliner (2003) stated, "the biggest single factor... in improving student performance is... the quality of the teachers" (p. 180), and one cannot compromise on this issue.

Recommendation #4: Learning relevance

Action Learning is an excellent and highly recommended way to infuse relevancy into an educational context. In action learning, participants actually make an intervention in real-time operational events. A good example of this would be the continuous, on-the-job improvement process, called The Kaïzen, or executive learning pods from the same firm who work together in an academic setting to solve their real organizational dilemmas.

Recommendation #5: Uncoupling degree programs from executive programs

Given the profound differences between the requirements and objectives of degree and executive programs regarding program design, participants' experience, curricula content, teaching and learning styles, it might be advisable to uncouple the administrative connection between those programs. It might make sense to Business School degree programs to operate and to be managed completely separately from the executive programs, along the lines of how Duke University's Fuqua School of Business has become a completely separate entity from Duke Corporate Education.

Conclusion B: Program Accountability and Return on Investment (ROI)

Concerning executive education and learning, Return on Investment (ROI) cannot be measured along the same financial lines as other organizational expenditures. The benefits of executive education are both tangible and intangible, and they relate to personal as well as organizational development. This does not forgive the need for accountability; it just makes the details of that accountability different from the norm.

Recommendation #6: Return on Learning (ROL)

Organizations should invent a system of accountability regarding their executive education programs. These should include pre and post assessments by the organization and individuals about the purpose and goals of attending particular developmental events prior to that attendance; and by the attendees after the programs about their perceived learning benefits. These measurements can be as quantitative or qualitative as best fits the overall culture of the firm, and the individual personalities of its executives. Borrowing the term from the Caterpillar University: the concept of Return on Learning (ROL) should replace the idea of the search for Return on Investment (ROI) regarding the measurement of value in executive education.

Conclusion C: Curriculum Design

Curriculum design needs to emulate the kinds of priorities with which executives live every business day: That design should include a similar sense of urgency, efficiency and flexibility in managing time, clarity of purpose, enjoyment of challenge, tolerance for ambiguity, mixture of "soft" and "hard" management styles, networking with like-minded individuals, and working cohesively in teams toward common goals. Curriculum content needs to encompass relevant topics that are directly useful as tools for executives to accomplish their tasks better or more efficiently, or which are indirectly useful as reflective *agents provocateurs* in encouraging executive creativity and innovation. The teaching style and atmosphere in play during executive programs, while being fun and challenging should not in any sense be casual, or even all that "emergent". These busy people have come to learn, to gain insights that they perhaps did not have time to entertain during their frenetically paced days at the office. They want a professional atmosphere in which challenging objectives are clearly set out and then can be steadily worked through.

As for the "sense of urgency", it could be reflected in the institutional ability, for custom programs, to change curricula at a moment's notice in concert with precisely what is happening at any particular time within the client organization. Such an ability to change course content quickly in line with client needs, such as in managing major alterations in strategic direction, is actually an argument for custom over open enrolment programs. Changing any curriculum in the regular academic context (for open enrolment programs, for instance) is generally fraught with delays, difficulties and impossibly complicated levels of approval that nimble corporations simply cannot afford to wait for.

There are some famous examples of lengthy flagship programs whose design has stood the test of time, and these continue to attract large enrolment. Most universities have a few of these on their roster, and some examples in this study have included the International Masters in Practicing Management and the Advanced Leadership Program at McGill, the Advanced Management Program at Harvard, and the Advanced Management Program at INSEAD in France. The value of these programs for networking is undeniable, and the opportunity to learn with senior people from diverse cultures and different industries over fairly long periods of several weeks or months could be invaluable. Such programs may be of considerable impact and interest at dramatic moments of executive career transition when, for instance, a divisional vice president is about to become a member of the senior executive team (as was described in Interview Case No. 6). Thus, these programs serve to give the newly promoted leader a rewarding time-out for reflection before returning to increased responsibilities. However, I question the future of such programs in the fast paced world we now live in – one of "permanent white water", to use Vaill's (1996) expression. Not one of the executives I interviewed would have time to attend this type of program, even though two of them had done so earlier in their careers.

Of course, universities are not the only providers of executive education. This research does not delve into programs offered by other providers such as consultants, or internally managed programs such as the creation of Communities of Practice (CoP), around which an entire organizational learning plan can be built. We heard a description of CoPs in Interview Case No. 6, in which that firm not only was building these CoPs, but that they were also becoming the foundation for the creation of a corporate university. Worthy of mention here, therefore, is a firm's possible consideration of building the organizational education plan around a particular learning model that makes sense in the culture of that company. Five models were described in Chapter Three, which principally featured Whitehead's *Rhythm of Education*.

Recommendation #7: Time management and flexibility

Whether open enrolment or custom design, programs should generally be of short duration and repeated several times with relatively long periods between each segment. For instance, a program could be designed around quarterly sessions of two or three days each, over a two year time span. In addition to properly permitting executives to do their regular and demanding jobs, this would invite assimilation and practice of learned concepts between the intense periods of face-to-face learning.

In case the flagship programs, which last several weeks or months, become much less attractive for senior level executives to attend in the current era, it behooves all providers to widen the scope of their shorter offerings, and/or to redesign the longer programs so that they can take place in, say, five or more segments of three to five days over a year.

There are many creative ways to infuse program flexibility: One example is to stage several offerings of the same program, in offset sync with each other, such that executives who may have to miss one segment could still pick it up with another cohort before moving on to the next segment. Another example of added flexibility is to blend periods of face-to-face with online learning. The online sessions, which can be practised and learned on campus can then be flexibly used at times convenient to participants when they are back at the office between campus sessions.

Recommendation #8: A question of STYLE

Through the actual set-up of physical venues, the energetic teaching approach, the carefully thought-out program organization, and the reputation of professors and facilitators, the design of courses and programs should contain the same kind of wonderful sense of excitement, expectancy and urgency that executives experience on the job. The more challenging the material and the conversations become, the better it will be, as this ilk of student is not looking for the easy road. Varying learning styles among participants suggests that, just as on the job, a variety of approaches in accomplishing this excitement about the program is what is needed: intellectual stimulation and conceptualization, learning by doing, learning through relational activities, visualization and imagination.

Recommendation #9: Ability to make quick changes to curriculum of custom programs

This recommendation can only effectively apply to custom programs, as open enrolment courses are subject to all the design and approval delays prevalent in academic course creation and alteration. Providers of executive custom programs are already very good at turning around quickly in redesigning courses, as required by client firms. They also realize how important it is to have the client involved at every step of the design process and even for the actual delivery or facilitation of these programs. This recommendation then, is simply a reminder that they are doing a good job in this respect, according to what executives have reported, and what these providers themselves have advertised; and that the more nimble they become, the better will be the results. That said, the university which discovers the key to also bringing this kind of flexibility to being able to alter open enrolment programs quickly, as the market requires, and with the minimum of bureaucratic fuss, will surely become a frontrunner in executive education.

Recommendation #10: Alternative learning plan designs

In addition to forging learning relationships with universities, there is also the possibility of internally creating alternative designs for executive and company-wide learning plans:

1. A total learning plan that can be created using Communities of Practice, such as the process described in Case Interview #6.

2. Learning Programs can be built around theories such as Alfred North Whitehead's Rhythm of Education, and his other educational philosophies explained in considerable detail in Chapter Three.

3. They can be constructed around such practices as the Scenario Planning sessions at Royal Dutch Shell, described as an alternative theoretical framework for this dissertation in Chapter Three.

4. They can be organized with reference to Peter Senge's Five Disciplines, also described as an alternative theoretical framework in Chapter Three.

5. There is also the possibility of using models like the one Domtar used, as described in my personal unit of analysis in Chapter Seven, namely the Kaïzen Process.

If a firm has a predilection for models such as these, they have the option of seeking help from universities, favourite professors, or consultants in order to build them; and I would highly recommend such outside help if that were the objective.

Conclusion D – Curriculum Content

To be able to design curriculum around topics and issues that really matter, especially if one has adopted the earlier recommendation for a series of shorter learning sessions, it will be necessary to target exactly those areas that can do the most to develop needed executive abilities quickly. Therefore, providers should assume, more than they seem to have done, that "hard" skills, for the most part, but not entirely, have already been learned by executive participants. What is needed in executive curricula content is a good proportion (more than we saw in the nine profiled universities) of the so-called "soft" material, but with hard edges as far as delivery and applicability is concerned; let us call this *reflection and thoughtfulness with an action orientation.*

Content should be engaging for executives, and this can sometimes be accomplished, or at least enhanced, by introducing new teaching perspectives such as Rotman's Integrative Thinking™, and Duke CE's Metaphoric Experience™ (both mentioned in some detail in Chapter Five), or such ideas as Gareth Morgan's use of metaphor described in the Literature Review.

Almost every program looked at from those universities providing executive programs featured a predominance of working in teams: small discussion groups, mid-sized project teams, or large plenary session groups. This is appropriately similar to on-the-job realities of executives working together in teams and of distributed leadership. However, too few program designs included the importance of individual work and time for reflection as also being necessary in an executive's work.

There is the issue of management fads and fashions that do not stand the test of time. Most dangerous are the colourful, attractive looking management books, which catch the eyes of high level executives in airports, and which one of the executives I interviewed (case No.1B) referred to as "the Heathrow Horror" (or syndrome): The executives might read the book on an overseas flight, and bring it back to their unsuspecting corporations with instructions to implement what they have just discovered within those pages. The current smorgasbord of management writing, even some of its excellent contributions (usually in the form of an edited book about such topics as the learning organization), do not seem to possess the basic type of cohesive, relevant and immediately applicable material that businesses require.

One of the questions I asked all executives interviewed for this research was whether a corporation should be involved in teaching busy executives how better to balance their personal and working lives. The general consensus was that this was a personal matter; that for some people, working 12 hour days *was* balanced (Interview Case No. 1B); that if help were requested, it would be provided (Interview Case No. 4); but otherwise, it was none of the organization's business to delve into such matters (Interview Case Nos. 5 and 7). As a result of those responses, I have changed my mind on this issue: I do not think it should be part of an executive program.

Mentoring and individual coaching met with mixed reviews from those executives I interviewed: Helping junior people to advance in their careers, and the more obvious requirement of an organization's succession planning, meant that all executives were expected to devote part of their time to these important developmental issues (Interview Case No. 7). However, instituting a formalized mentoring system, in which specific junior people were assigned to individual executives was not at all a popular idea (interview Case No. 2). That was mostly because not all executives were good at mentoring, and not all junior managers were good at being mentored. There could also be a feeling of jealousy about who was and who was not singled out for such a program, and about who got which mentor. As for coaching: Despite a consensus that having a coach seemed to have evolved from being a stigma for weaklings to an honour for high potential managers, its best use was still mentioned as being a remedial one.

Recommendation #11: Mix of "soft" and "hard" skill enhancements

Even though most of the "hard" skills should already have been acquired by most seasoned executives, some "hard" topics are still useful and should be rightfully and effectively included in executive programs. Included should be those that deal directly with executive tasks, such as developing abilities in public speaking, dealing with media, handling board meetings, using senior level networking tools, understanding cultural diversity, working with electronic communications and social platforms, and perhaps the mechanics of setting up and operating internal Communities of Practice.

Executive programs should however concentrate more on the understanding and practice of "soft" skills. Some examples of these include: the art of dialogue and conversation; discussions about motivation, innovation and imagination; creative networking; concepts of diversity and inclusion; and something Royal Dutch Shell used to refer to in executive performance reviews as "helicopter" sensibility – "the ability to focus on minute details one moment, and then zoom up to the big picture" (Kleiner, 2003, p. 24). This helicopter sensitivity is remarkably similar to Whitehead's prescriptions about developing the valuable learning ability to move back and forth fluently between views of the general and the precise. Borrowing the subtitle of David Whyte's (1994) book, we might even dare to include among "soft" skill enhancements something about *Poetry and the Preservation of the Soul in Corporate America*.

Recommendation #12: Mix of individual with group learning

Although learning in groups should take precedence, because that is the principal working framework for the practising executive, individual work should not be overlooked, and it needs to be included meaningfully in executive programs and courses. This could occur in various ways including, but not limited to: periods of reflection, the practise of keeping a journal, reading widely, writing letters (not e-mails) to friends or loved-ones, whether or not these are ever sent, meditation and contemplation.

Recommendation #13: On management fads and fashions

There is an awesome amount of relatively useless literature available that proposes adopting the latest, greatest management fads; or slightly less aggravating, but terribly time-consuming, is the incidence of large tomes on business and management subjects whose principal messages could be delivered in five or six pages. Readers must be as vigilant in separating the sheep from the goats in this respect as they are about discerning which websites to trust on the internet. I have found that one of the best gate-keepers in this respect is "word of mouth". Read only those management books that are recommended by trusted peers. Providers of executive education would do well to choose carefully any texts they expect executive participants to read. Of course, very popular are the condensed notes about important topics that certain professors are wont to provide.

Recommendation #14: Mentoring and coaching

There does not seem to be a crying need for including a formal mentoring activity within an organizational learning plan. If it is felt that one would be useful, I would suggest having it outsourced to an impartial consultant or an institution, so as to minimize any internal debates about favouritism and mentoring expertise. Alternatively, it could be partially outsourced as suggested in Interview Case No. 1, where board members served as mentors to high potential leaders.

On the coaching front, I found it very useful in my own career to have engaged a fairly hard-nosed consultant as a personal advisor/ coach during my last 12 years as a vice president. He became very familiar with our marketing and sales group, and would attend many of our meetings. He would whisper in my ear, sometimes rather forcefully, if he thought I was wandering off track in my management style, relational abilities, or in my priority setting.

Conclusion E: Electronic Communication, Social Platforms and Online Learning

It is curious that universities, and particularly some business schools, which make substantial use of the internet and intranet in the delivery of their degree programs, do not seem to do so to any worthwhile extent in their executive programs. The longer programs that comprise several segments might require some online work that takes place back home between the face-to-face periods. However, in a world that is so highly connected electronically, and as the most highly electronically connected generations ever seen are beginning to move into senior leadership positions, executives at all organizational levels need to become more fluent with the internet. It is no longer acceptable to have senior people acting as though they are too old to get involved. If they have any legitimate reasons (for instance, time management) not to become "hands-on" practitioners in electronic communication, then at least they should know a great deal more about it than many of them apparently currently do. It would appear that perhaps the current program providers, aware of senior executives' aversion to things electronic, prefer to steer clear of including such unpopular material in their curricula. It could also be that to offer this kind of training is counter-productive in that individual executives tend to be at such varying levels of competency concerning these matters: some can hardly do their own e-mail, while others are creating websites and responding to blogs.

Recommendation #15: Electronic communications in open enrolment and custom programs

Short courses should be offered for executive level participants to learn about electronic communication, including Facebook, Twitter, LinkedIn, blogging, common workspaces, handling e-mail, online collaboration, and the creation of online communities. Other courses could feature use of the intranet in enhancing internal communications and fostering innovation, as well as information about greater use of the internet to develop and manage external relationships more effectively; generally to learn to use the internet for much more than simply sending out information in one direction; in essence, to use it for a conversation with the rest of the world.

For the longer open enrolment programs (several weeks), possibly one whole day could be spent on these subjects, preferably early on, so that the learning can be put into practice and to good use in the form of a fully operational online Community of Practice, during, and perhaps following, the program.

For custom programs, providers should offer to include sessions on these important topics. For both the open enrolment and the custom programs, it might be a good idea to have some of the degree program students (B.Com and MBA) acting as coaches to the executives for these topics, especially because executives will be at radically different levels of expertise on computer matters, and will require different coaching expertise from these "visiting" students. This approach is inspired by Jack Welch's initiative to do similarly for his senior people at General Electric, where junior computer technicians helped executives better understand the use of computers. This reverse mentoring process would have the obvious added advantage of providing those degree students with opportunities to link up with practising executives.

Conclusion F: Internationalism and Global Concerns

Too many universities providing executive programs indicate that they are internationally diverse and global in their nature, when what they really mean is that they can offer programs at various locations around the world, or that they have offices in several major international cities. Having a global point of view and being internationally diverse means a great deal more than that. It means providing courses or programs that are global in scope and content, wherever they may be offered to students who represent a good mix of nationalities, facilitated by professors who hail from many different countries, and who have personally experienced those different cultures first-hand.

Recommendation #16: Rendering programs more international and global

For those institutions, which are many, that really do provide global and international understanding and global reach in their degree programs, this expertise should be easily transferrable into the executive courses and programs. That transfer needs to occur, and it needs to be advertised as having occurred on business school websites and in program brochures.

Conclusion G: Forging and Deepening the Two-Way Relationships between Providers and Participants in Executive Education

Valuable liaisons can be created between firms and providers of executive education in many ways: These can be forged with consultants, with universities or other institutions or think-tanks, such as the Aspen Institute. These relationships can be the positive result of reconnecting with one's alma mater, with a university at which one has been invited to act as a regular guest speaker during MBA programs, with an institution where one may have attended a particularly useful program, or with a consultant who helped in launching an effective strategic or learning initiative.

Related to the deepening of relationships, Harvard and INSEAD stand out for the respect they demonstrate for the professional expertise of the participants in their executive programs. At those schools, everyone is a teacher and everyone is a learner, and I have heard that professors there compete with each other for the excitement of facilitating programs with practising executives, because to do so enhances their teaching abilities in other (degree) programs, as well as in their research endeavours.

Recommendation #17: Alliances with institutions, individual professors, or other advisors

It matters not with whom these relationships are forged. What does matter is that one or more of these occur with the specific aim of having an advisor, or advising group, which becomes familiar over time with individual executives in a firm, and with the general operating culture of that firm. The advising can happen on many fronts, but the one I am highlighting here pertains to executive education and its relationship to the overall learning plan of an organization. For example, two of the executives interviewed for this research stated that they favoured such a connection with individual professors, whose work they admired and respected, over a relationship with a university. They in fact had several such professorial connections at several universities.

Recommendation #18: The issue of mutual respect

It is meet, right and useful for institutions and their professors to graciously acknowledge the professional expertise of practising executives who attend their programs. The river of learning flows in both directions between facilitators and participants. On a related issue, and borrowing from the Queen's University teaching philosophy: Often just getting out of the way and letting the students take over is where the best learning takes place.

Conclusion H: Website Quality of University Executive Program Sites

Whether it is logical or not, there is a perceived connection between the quality of an organization's website and the quality of the organization itself. If the website is difficult to navigate and to understand, or if it is frustrating in other ways, it often follows that its "owner" is also confusing, frustrating, difficult to navigate, or understand. It was surprising to have discovered so many excellent universities supplying superb executive education courses and programs, only to find that even the best of the best often had websites that were not that attractive or easy to follow. In other cases, it was a pleasure to look for the information, because one did not have to dig very deeply for it: It was all right there for the taking; it made the research job much easier and more fun, not to mention how it might also affect the enrolment choices of potential executive participants. If they become frustrated by the website experience, they will almost inevitably avoid signing up for programs. Websites are often the first moment of contact firms or individuals make with educational providers.

Recommendation #19: Websites

Providers of executive education should be utterly vigilant regarding the quality of their websites. Website quality encompasses:

- Beauty of the presentation in terms of colour, scope of information available, and interesting options to read articles or testimonials, listen to audio bytes, or watch video clips;

- Continuity between what is on the website and in the program brochures;

- Ease of navigation, which means its inherent logic and flow;

- Easy use of options, such as printability for pages that might not be printer-friendly;

- Transparency in divulging the truth about programs and courses. For instance, viewers should not have to dig too deeply to find out how much a course or program costs; and fees should be presented in a consistent format – not some programs including and others excluding accommodation;

- Overall completeness of the website. For example, if claims are made about the teaching and research excellence of faculty, then faculty bios should obviously be included. They probably should be included anyway;

- Useful, related and erudite links;

- Frequent website updates to keep them constantly current and "refreshed";

- An interactive component to enhance website feedback and to encourage contact with potential students.

Ideas for Future Study in Executive Education and Learning

Obvious Extrapolations of this Research

The most obvious continuation for this current research on executive education and learning would be to expand it to include:

- Interviews with a larger group of private sector executives in Canada, in more segments of the economy, and in more regions of the land. Related to this, if a researcher wanted to follow a similar presentation to this one, would be the addition of data about many more universities in Canada and elsewhere.

- Similar research on public sectors of the economy, including non-profits, government departments, and NGOs (non-governmental organizations).

- Similar research in the USA and Europe, and a comparison between the two.

New Endeavours Related to this Research

Other ideas for future research, which I am personally interested in pursuing, are related to executive education and learning, but they are in new areas. These could include:

- Looking into executive education provided by major consulting firms in North America and Europe.

- Looking into the kinds of executive education currently available at major corporate universities in North America, and interviewing administrators and participants as to how successful the learning there has been.

- Researching the progress and success accomplished in building Communities of Practice at the firm represented by Interview Case #6 of this present research.

- Research featuring the executive learning stories of the executive interviewed in Interview Case #5. This individual's vast experience at the highest levels of corporations, government and board governance in Canada represents a goldmine of experience about the opportunities and pitfalls of executive learning and performance. Furthermore, the stories are fascinating, instructive and fun.

- Research featuring the progress of the remarkable learning philosophy at the firm overviewed in Interview Case No.10: *The Building of a Learning Organization.*

Final Words

In concluding this dissertation, I would like to say that I have been pleasantly surprised by the overall sturdiness of the learning plans in place at the firms whose executives I have interviewed for this research. As I have admitted earlier, these people were likely well disposed to the importance and the existence of organizational learning plans within their firms, otherwise they would not have agreed to the interviews. Furthermore, the open enrolment and custom executive programs offered at the nine excellent universities reported on here are really quite remarkable in their ability to adapt to the ever-changing requirements of organizational learning. I sincerely hope that some of my recommendations will serve to improve their offerings even further.

The question still remaining for me is whether the real purpose of executive education should be to help leaders think better, or to help them perform better. Of course, it is very likely that these two objectives are inextricably linked.

References

Allan, G. (2005). Whitehead's modes of experience and the stages of education. In F. G. Riffert (Ed.), *Alfred North Whitehead on Learning and education: Theory and application* (pp. 59-88). Newcastle, UK: Cambridge Scholars Press.

Alsop, R. (2002, September 9). The top business schools (a special report) -Playing well with others: Recruiters say the 'soft skills' are just as important as the hard stuff; and a lot harder to teach. *The Wall Street Journal*, p. R11.

Argyris, C. (1990). *Overcoming organizational defenses: Facilitating organizational learning.* Upper Saddle River, NJ: Prentice Hall.

Bailey, D. M. (1997). *Research for the health professional: A practical guide* (2nd ed.). Philadelphia, PA: F.A. Davis.

Bakan, J. (2004). *The corporation: The pathological pursuit of profit and power.* Toronto, ON: Viking Canada.

Bennis, W. G., & O'Toole, J. (2005). How business schools lost their way. *Harvard Business Review, 83*(5), 96-104.

Bettis, P. J., & Mills, M. R. (2006). Liminality and the study of a changing academic landscape. In V. A. Anfara & N. T. Mertz (Eds.), *Theoretical frameworks in qualitative research* (pp. 59-72). Thousand Oaks, CA: Sage.

Bishop, P. (2008). Multi-site case study: Conceptual overview and discussion. Manuscript submitted for publication.

Bleak, J. L., & Fulmer, R. M. (2009). Strategically developing strategic leaders. In Linkage Inc's (Ed.), *Best practices in leadership development handbook* (2nd ed.). San Francisco, CA: Pfeiffer.

Bohm, D. (1996). *On dialogue.* London, UK: Routledge.

Bolman, L. G., & Deal, T. E. (1997). *Reframing organizations: Artistry, choice and leadership* (2nd ed.). San Francisco, CA: Jossey-Bass.

Brumbaugh, R. S. (1982). *Whitehead, process philosophy, and education.* Albany, NY: State University of New York Press.

Büchel, B., & Antunes, D. (2007). Reflections on executive education: The user and provider's perspectives. *Academy of Management Learning & Education, 6,* 401-411.

Burns, T., & Stalker, G.M. (1961). Mechanistic and organic systems. In J.M. Shafritz, J.S. Ott, & Y.S. Jang (Eds.), *Classics of organizational management* (pp. 198-202). Belmont, CA: Thomson Wadsworth.

Charlton, K., & Osterweil, C. (2005, Autumn). Measuring return on investment in executive education: A quest to meet client needs or pursuit of the Holy Grail? *The Ashridge Journal,* 6-13.

Cleveland, H. (2002). *Nobody in charge: Essays on the future of leadership.* San Francisco, CA: Jossey- Bass.

Clinebell, S. K., & Clinebell, J. M. (2008). The tension between academic rigor and real-world relevance: The role of executive professors. *Academy of Management Learning & Education, 7,* 99-107.

Collins, J. (2001). *Good to great: Why some companies make the leap... and others don't:* New York: Harper.

Cousin, G. (2005). Case study research. *Journal of Geography in Higher Education, 29,* 421-427.

Creswell, J. W., & Plano Clark, V. L. (2007). *Designing and conducting mixed methods research.* Thousand Oaks, CA: Sage.

Dall'Alba, G., & Sandberg, J. (2006). Unveiling professional development: A critical review of stage models. *Review of Educational Research, 76,* 383-412.

Das Narayandas (2007). Trends in executive education in business marketing. *Journal of Business-to-Business Marketing, 14,* 23-41.

De Geus, A. (1997). *The living company: Habits for survival in a turbulent business environment.* New York: Long View.

Doh, J. P., & Stumpf, S. A. (2007). Executive education: A view from the top. *Academy of Management Learning & Education, 6,* 388-400.

Doll, W. E. (2003). Modes of thought. *Complexity Science and Educational Research Conference,* 1-10. Edmonton, Canada: University of Alberta. Retrieved September 5, 2009, from http://74.125.155.132/search?q=cache:K7c6GLkTNmcJ:www.complexityandeducation.ualberta.ca/conferences/2003/Documents/CSER_Doll.pdf+Modes+of+Thought+Doll&cd=2&hl=en&ct=clnk&client=safari

Domtar Inc. (2006). *Sustainable Growth Report.* Retrieved July 10, 2007, from http://www.domtar.com/files/Sustainable-Report-final.pdf

Domtar Inc.Website. (n.d.). *Training Programs.* Retrieved July 10, 2007, from http://www.domtar.com/en/careers/glance/2245.asp

Donham, B. (1931). *Business adrift.* New York: McGraw-Hill.

Dulworth, M., & Bordonaro, F. (2005). *Corporate learning: Proven and practical guidelines for building a sustainable learning strategy.* San Francisco, CA: John Wiley.

Dunkel, H. B. (1965). *Whitehead on education.* Columbus, OH: Ohio State University.

Dye, D., Kletter, D., & McFarland, W. (2006-2008). The case of the passive-aggressive culture: Transform the organizational DNA. *The Linkage Leader.* Retrieved August 18, 2009, from http://www.linkageinc.com/thinking/linkageleader/Pages/Linkage%20eNewsletter.aspx

Egan, K. (2002). *Getting it wrong from the beginning: Our progressivist inheritance from Herbert Spencer, John Dewey, and John Piaget.* New Haven, CT: Yale University Press.

Environics Research Group (2006). Report on executive education in Canada. *Environics Executive Survey 2006.* Retrieved August 3, 2009, from http://www.business.queensu.ca/about_us/docs/Environics_Report.pdf or from http://business.queensu.ca/about_us/index.php (side bar).

Ferguson, K. (1984). *The feminist case against bureaucracy: Women in the political economy.* Philadelphia, PA: Temple University Press.

Frank, T. (1999). Management guru Henry Mintzberg. *Frank Communications.* Retrieved September 6, 2009, from http://temafrank.tripod.com/id31.htm

Fulmer, R., & Vicere, A. A. (1996). Executive development: An analysis of competitive forces. *Planning Review, 24,* 31-36.

Gates, W., Myhrvold, N., & Rinearson, P. (1995). *The road ahead.* New York: Viking Penguin.

Goldsmith, B. (2009, June 26). CEOs stay old-school; most shun social media. The Globe and Mail, p. L2.

Goleman, D., & Boyatzis, R. (2008). Social intelligence and the biology of leadership. *Harvard Business Review, 86*(9), 74-81.

Griffin, D. R. (1995). The future of process thought. *Newsletter of the Center for Process Studies,* 18 (3), 1-5.

Harris, G. (1993). Networking: Men's superficial ties don't work for women. *Harvard Business Review, 71*(1), 8-9.

Hartshorne, C. (1954). Whitehead's philosophy of reality as socially structured process. *Chicago Review, 8,* 60-77.

Heifetz, R., Grashow, A., & Linsky, M. (2009). Leadership in a (permanent) crisis. *Harvard Business Review, 87*(7/8), 62-69.

Hendley, B. P. (1976). The philosopher as teacher: A Whiteheadian model for teaching introductory philosophy. *Metaphilosophy, 7,* 307-315.

Hendley, B. P. (1986). *Dewey, Russell, Whitehead: Philosophers as educators.* Carbondale, IL: Southern Illinois University Press.

Howe, S. N. (2005). *Leaning organization disciplines and their impact on a high-technology company's adaptive capacity.* Master's thesis, Royal Roads University, Victoria, British Columbia, Canada.

Jones, C. (2007). Contemplating Whitehead's freedom and discipline. *Journal of University Teaching & Learning Practice, 4*(1), 1-13.

Kearney, K. S., & Hyle, A. E. (2006). A look through the Kubler-Ross Theoretical Lense. In V. A. Anfara & N. T. Mertz (Eds.), *Theoretical frameworks in qualitative research* (pp. 109-128). Thousand Oaks, CA: Sage.

Kelly, M. (2001). *The divine right of capital: Dethroning the corporate aristocracy.* San Francisco, CA: Berrett-Koehler.

Kets de Vries, M. F. R. (2007). Creating transformational executive education programs. *Academy of Management Learning and Education, 6,* 375-387.

Kingwell, M. (2000). *The world we want: Virtue, vice and the good citizen.* Toronto, ON: Penguin.

Kleiner, A. (2003). *Who really matters: The core group theory of power, privilege, and success.* New York: Currency Doubleday.

Kotter, J. P. (1999). *What leaders really do.* Boston, MA: Harvard Business.

Kumar, R., & Usunier, J-C. (2004). Management education in a globalizing world: Lessons from the French experience. In C. Grey & E. Antonacopoulou (Eds.), *Essential readings in management learning* (pp. 291-320). Thousand Oaks, CA: Sage.

Leonard-Barton, D. (1995). *Wellsprings of knowledge: Building and sustaining the sources of innovation.* Boston, MA: Harvard Business School Press.

Levine, R., Locke, C., Searls, D., & Weinberger, D. (2000). *The cluetrain manifesto: The end of business as usual.* New York: Perseus.

March, J. G. (2009, June). *Wear sunscreen.* Convocation address presented at the University of Alberta School of Business, Edmonton, AB, Canada.

March, J. G. (2003). A scholar's quest. *Journal of Management Inquiry, 12,* 205-207.

Megginson, D. (2003). Planned and emergent learning: Consequences for development. In C. Grey & E. Antonacopoulou (Eds.), *Essential readings in management learning* (pp. 91-106). Thousand Oaks, CA: Sage.

Micklethwaite, J., & Wooldridge, A. (1996). *The witch doctors: Making sense of the management gurus.* New York: Random House.

Mintzberg, H. (1983). The power game and the players. In J.M. Shafritz, J.S. Ott, & Y.S. Jang (Eds.), *Classics of organizational management* (pp. 334-341). Belmont, CA: Thomson Wadsworth.

Mintzberg, H. (1999, spring). Managing quietly. *Leader to Leader, 12,* 24-30.

Mintzberg, H. (2004a). *Managers not MBAs: A hard look at the soft practice of managing and management development*. San Francisco, CA: Berrett Koehler.

Mintzberg, H. (2004b). Managerial correctness. *Across The Board, 41* (4), 19-24.

Mitroff, I. I., Mason, R. O., & Pearson, C. M. (1994). *Frame break: The radical redesign of American business*. San Francisco, CA: Jossey-Bass.

Morgan, G. (2006). *Images of organizations*. Thousand Oaks, CA: Sage.

Murphy, K. (1995). Generative coaching: A surprising learning odyssey. In Sarita Chawla & John Renesch (Eds.), *Learning organizations: Developing cultures for tomorrow's workplace*. Portland, OR: Productivity Press.

Nunn, P. (1945). *Education: Its data and first principles* (3rd ed.). London: Edward Arnold.

O'Connor, J., & McDermott, I. (1997). *The art of systems thinking: Essential skills for creativity and problem solving*. San Francisco, CA: Thorsons.

Olsen, W. (2004). Triangulation in social research: Qualitative and quantitative methods can really be mixed. In M. Holborn (Ed.), *Developments in sociology*. Ormskirk, Lancashire, UK: Causeway Press. Retrieved August 3, 2009, from http://scholar.google.com/scholar?hl=en&client=safari&rls=en&q=author:%22Olsen%22+intitle:%22Triangulation+in+social+research:+qualitative+and+...%22+&um=1&ie=UTF-8&oi=scholarr

Oshry, B. (1995). *Seeing systems: Unlocking the mysteries of organizational life*. San Francisco, CA: Berrett-Koehler.

Palloff, R. M., & Pratt, K. (1999). *Building learning communities in cyberspace: Effective strategies for the online classroom*. San Francisco, CA: Jossey-Bass.

Peters, T.J., & Waterman Jr., R.H. (1982). In search of excellence: Simultaneous loose-tight properties. In J.M. Shafritz, J.S. Ott, & Y.S. Jang (Eds.), *Classics of organizational management* (pp. 436-440). Belmont, CA: Thomson Wadsworth.

Pfeffer, J., & Fong, C. T. (2002). The end of business schools? Less success than meets the eye. *Academy of Management Learning and Education, 1* (1), 78-95.

Prasad, A., & Prasad, P. (2002). The coming of age of interpretive organizational research. *Organizational Research Methods, 5*(1), 4-12.

Price, L. (1954). *Dialogues of Alfred North Whitehead.* New York: Mentor.

Priestley, J. G. (2000). The essence of education: Whitehead and the spiritual dimension. *Interchange, 31,* 117-133.

Regnier, R. (1995). Bridging Western and First Nations thought: Balanced education in Whitehead's philosophy of organism and the sacred circle. *Interchange, 26,* 383-415.

Rosenblum, J. (2009, July). What will it take to shape a new class of professionals? Retrieved from the Duke CE website (media), August 1, 2009 from http://www.dukece.com/news-media/news-and-stories.php

Russell, B. (1956). *Portraits from memory and other essays.* Sydney, Australia: Allen & Unwin.

Schwartz, P. (1991). *The art of the long view: Planning for the future in an uncertain world.* New York: Currency/Doubleday.

Scott, J. & Marshall, G. (Eds.). (2005). *Oxford dictionary of sociology* (3rd ed.). Oxford, UK: Oxford University Press.

Senge, P. (1999). *The dance of change: The challenge to sustaining momentum in learning organizations.* New York: Doubleday.

Senge, P., Kleiner, A., Roberts, C., Ross, R., & Smith, B. (1994). *The fifth discipline fieldbook – Strategies and tools for building a learning organization.* London, England: Nicholas Brealey.

Senge, P.M. (1990). The fifth discipline: The art and practice of the learning organization. In J.M. Shafritz, J.S. Ott, & Y.S. Jang (Eds.), *Classics of organizational management* (pp. 441-449). Belmont, CA: Thomson Wadsworth.

Shepard, M. (2003, January/February). Women experience changes at the top. Women in Business, *55*(1), 24.

Stake, R. E. (1995). *The art of case study research.* Thousand Oaks, CA: Sage.

Stake, R. E. (2006). *Multiple case study analysis*. New York: Guilford.

Starkey, K., & Tempest, S. (2008). A clear sense of purpose? The evolving role of the business school. *Journal of Management Development, 27*, 379-390.

Stevenson, R. B. (2004). Constructing knowledge of educational practices from case studies. *Environmental Education Research, 10*(1), 39-51.

Tapscott, D., & Williams, A. D. (2008). *Wikinomics: How mass collaboration changes everything*. New York: Portfolio-Penguin.

Terry, R. (2005). The 6Ds™: A new paradigm for executive education. *Industrial and Commercial Training, 37*, 232-239.

Tichy, N., & Cardwell, N. (2002). *The cycle of leadership: How great leaders teach their companies to win*. New York: Harper Business.

Tushman, M. L., O'Reilly, C. A., Fenollosa, A., Kleinbaum, A. M., & McGrath, D. (2007). Relevance and rigor: Executive education as a lever in shaping practice and research. *Academy of Management Learning & Education, 6*, 345-362.

Usher, R., Bryant, I., & Johnston, R. (1997). *Adult education and the postmodern challenge: Learning beyond the limits*. London: Routledge.

Vaill, P. B. (1996). *Learning as a way of being: Strategies for survival in a world of permanent white water*. San Francisco, CA: Jossey-Bass.

Van Der Heijden, K. (1996). *Scenarios: The art of strategic conversation*. Chichester, West Sussex, UK: Wiley.

Vaughan, N., & Garrison, D. R. (2005). Creating cognitive presence in a blended faculty development community. *The Internet and Higher Education, 8*(1), 123-140.

Vicere, A. A., & Fulmer, R. M. (1996). *Leadership by design: How benchmark companies sustain success through investment in continuous learning*. Boston, MA: Harvard Business School Press.

Weiss, P. (1980). Recollections of Alfred North Whitehead. *Process Studies, 10*, 44-56.

Welch, J. (2001). *Straight from the gut*. New York: Warner.

Wenger, E. (2003). Communities of practice and social learning systems. In D. Nicolini, S. Gherardi, & D. Yanow (Eds.), *Knowing* in organizations: *A practice-based approach* (pp. 76-99). Armonk, NY: M. E. Sharpe.

Wheatley, M. J, & Kellner-Rogers, M. (1996). *A simpler way.* San Francisco, CA: Berrett-Koehler.

Winchester, I. (1986). Introduction – Illuminating education. *Interchange, (17),* 3-8.

Winchester, I. (1988). Varieties of university reforms. *Interchange, 19,* 177-187.

Winchester, I. (2005). Who was Whitehead? *Interchange, 36,* 1-3.

Whitehead, A. N. (1925/1967). *Science and the modern world.* (The Lowell lectures). New York: The Free Press.

Whitehead, A.N. (1929/1957). *The aims of education and other essays.* New York: The Free Press/Macmillan

Whitehead, A. N. (1929/1978). *Process and reality* (Corrected Edition). New York: The Free Press. (Original work as the Gifford Lectures 1927/28 and published 1929)

Whitehead, A. N. (1932/1959). *The aims of education and other essays.* London: Ernest Benn.

Whitehead, A. N. (1933/1956). *Adventures of ideas.* New York: The Macmillan Company.

Whitehead, A. N. (1947/1968). *Essays in science and philosophy.* New York: Greenwood Press.

Whitney, J.O. & Packer, T. (2000). *Power plays: Shakespeare's lessons in leadership and management.* New York: Touchstone.

Whyte, D. (1994). *The heart aroused: Poetry and the preservation of the soul in corporate America.* New York: Currency Doubleday.

Winters, M-F. (2009). CEO's [sic] who get it!: Diversity leadership from the heart and soul. *The Linkage Leader.* Retrieved August 20, 2009, from http://www.linkageinc.com/thinking/linkageleader/Pages/Linkage%20eNewsletter.aspx

Wood, J. H. (1995). Restructuring education: Designing tomorrow's workplace. In S. Chawla & J. Renesch (Eds.), *Learning Organizations: Developing cultures for tomorrow's workplace.* (pp. 402-415). Portland, OR: Productivity Press.

Woodhouse, H. (1995). Why Whitehead? Introduction to a symposium on process philosophy of education. *Interchange, 26,* 341-345.

Woodhouse, H. (1999). The rhythm of the university: Part one –
Teaching, learning and administering in the Whiteheadian vein.
Interchange, 30, 191-211.

Woodhouse, H. (2000). The seduction of the market: Whitehead,
Hutchins, and the Harvard Business School. *Interchange, 31*,
135-157.

Yin, R. K. (2003). *Case study research: Design and methods.* Thousand
Oaks, CA: Sage.

About the Author

Bruce Fowler's professional career spanned 31 years in the pulp and paper industry, including the last 12 of those years as Vice President (Sales and Marketing) of a fine paper company that produced coated and uncoated printing papers for the North American market. After taking early retirement in 2002, Bruce went back to school, completing a Master of Arts in Leadership and Training at Royal Roads University, and graduating in 2005 with the Chancellor's award for highest academic achievement in his class. He then embarked on a Doctoral Program in Higher Education Leadership through the University of Calgary, completing all the requirements for that degree (course work, written and oral candidacy, field research, written dissertation and its defence) in December 2009.

Bruce decided to publish his dissertation, "Executive Education in Canadian Firms", in order to share his reserach findings with those he interviewed, the institutions he featured in the data, and more widely with all other interested executives and scholars.

Dr. Fowler lives in Surrey, British Columbia, Canada. Beyond his interest in executive learning, his passion is horseback riding, and his specialty is dressage. Bruce spent two years in the mid 1960s at the French Cavalry School of Saumur where he received instruction during that period from various officers of the famed Cadre Noir, earning the full instructor designation from the Fédération Française des Sports Equestres. His other interests are opera and poetry, visiting children and grandchildren in Ottawa, Montreal, Williams Lake and Port Moody.